Praise for

The COMPLETE INFIDEL'S GUIDE to the KORAN

"Robert Spencer incarnates intellectual courage when, all over the world, governments, intellectuals, churches, universities and media crawl under a hegemonic Universal Caliphate's New Order. His achievement in the battle for the survival of free speech and dignity of man will remain as a fundamental monument to the love of, and the self-sacrifice for, liberty. In our epoch of intellectual jihadism, this honest book is essential to understand the challenges of the 21st century."

—**Bat Ye'or**, author of *Eurabia; The Decline of Eastern Christianity Under Islam*; and *Islam and Dhimmitude*

"Tony Blair calls the Koran "progressive [and] humanitarian" but Robert Spencer has actually read the scripture and begs to differ. In an informed, sardonic antidote to the usual soft-peddling of the Koran, he concludes that its actual contents should alarm infidels and prompt them to defend their "freedom of speech, freedom of conscience, and the legal equality of all people.""

—**Daniel Pipes**, director, Middle East Forum

"For 1,400 years Muslim leadership spread misinformation and covered up what is in the Koran, even criminalizing exposing the truth or asking questions. The truth is too scary for many, both Muslims and non-Muslims. I thank Robert Spencer for bringing the truth of what is in the Koran to non-Muslims."

—**Nonie Darwish**, ex-Muslim and author of *Now They Call Me Infidel*

"This book is an incisive analysis of how Islamic jihadists read the Koran and understand it to be commanding them to wage war against non-Muslims. Military and intelligence analysts, as well as all Americans interested in protecting our freedoms, will find *The Complete Infidel's Guide to the Koran* to be a valuable guide to the thought processes and core beliefs of Muslim terrorists."

—**Steven Emerson**, author of *American Jihad*

"Meticulous, comprehensive, indispensable. 'I read the Koran so you don't have to,' Spencer writes—but even for those of us who have read the Koran, this is a richly illuminating work."

> —**Bruce Bawer**, author of *Surrender: Appeasing Islam, Sacrificing Freedom* and *While Europe Slept.*

"Governing officials and media spokesmen may ignore Spencer's warnings, but they do so at their own risk, because Islamic jihadists are not ignoring what's in the Koran, and are working to destroy our freedoms in obedience to Koranic dictates. In illuminating for Westerners exactly what the Koran teaches, Spencer has performed a valuable service in the defense of Western civilization against the Islamic jihad."

> —**Geert Wilders**, Member of Parliament and Chairman of the Party for Freedom (PVV), the Netherlands

"Unlike most of today's self-styled experts, Robert Spencer won't tell you that 'slay the idolaters wherever you find them' really means 'love your enemies and pray for those who persecute you.' In *The Complete Infidel's Guide to the Koran*, Spencer shows once again that he is America's most informed, fearless, and compelling voice on modern jihadism, insisting that we come to grips with the words behind the ideology that fuels international terror."

> —**Andrew C. McCarthy**, senior fellow at the National Review Institute and author of *Willful Blindness: A Memoir of the Jihad.*

The
COMPLETE
INFIDEL'S GUIDE
— to the —
KORAN

The

COMPLETE
INFIDEL'S GUIDE

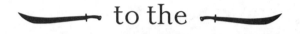 to the

KORAN

ROBERT SPENCER

Since 1947
REGNERY
PUBLISHING, INC.
An Eagle Publishing Company • Washington, DC

Cataloging-in-Publication data on file with the Library of Congress

ISBN 978-1-59698-104-1

Published in the United States by
Regnery Publishing, Inc.
One Massachusetts Avenue, NW
Washington, DC 20001
www.regnery.com

Manufactured in the United States of America

10 9 8 7 6 5 4 3 2 1

Books are available in quantity for promotional or premium use. Write to Director of Special Sales, Regnery Publishing, Inc., One Massachusetts Avenue NW, Washington, DC 20001, for information on discounts and terms or call (202) 216-0600.

Distributed to the trade by:
Perseus Distribution
387 Park Avenue South
New York, NY 10016

Dedication

For Lorenzo, who knew

CONTENTS

Notes
Page 235

Index
Page 255

Chapter One

WHY EVERY AMERICAN NEEDS TO KNOW WHAT'S IN THE KORAN

I T IS THE MOST REVERED and reviled of books. It is the primary religious text of one of the world's most prominent and influential religions—one that attracts a steady stream of converts in non-Muslim countries today.

For more than a billion Muslims, the Koran is the unadulterated, pure word of Allah, eternal and perfect, delivered through the angel Gabriel to the prophet Muhammad.[1] In many Muslim countries, boys memorize large sections of it before they can even read.

The book is to be treated with the deepest reverence. Muslims consider it so holy that they are not to touch a Koran unless they are in a state of ritual purity; non-Muslims, according to Islamic law, are not supposed to touch it at all except under strictly defined circumstances.[2] And the failure to show proper respect for a Koran, anywhere in the world, can be fatal—a false report in *Newsweek* magazine in 2005 that U.S. military interrogators at Guantanamo Bay had flushed a Koran down a toilet sparked rioting in Muslim countries, resulting in at least fifteen deaths.[3]

This reverence for the Koran is even expressed by non-Muslims. Michael Potemra, deputy managing editor of *National Review* magazine, asserts, "The Koran is one of the loveliest books ever written, a distillation of monotheism that is full of spiritual wisdom, and I never fail to profit from my reading of it."[4] And at Guantanamo Bay, contrary to *Newsweek*'s false account, U.S. military procedures require guards to don gloves before touching a prisoner's Koran, which must be handled "as if it were a fragile piece of delicate art."[5]

So what exactly does the Koran say? The U.S.-based Council on American-Islamic Relations (CAIR) claims that the book reveals the true, peaceful nature of Islam and promotes interfaith harmony. As CAIR's "Explore the Quran" campaign urges, "In today's climate of heightened religious sensitivities and apparent cultural clashes, now is the time for people of all faiths to better acquaint themselves with Islam's sacred text, the Holy Quran." CAIR indicates that this campaign is a response to those who dare to claim that Islam has something to do with terrorism:

> This campaign, titled Explore the Qur'an, serves as a response to those who would defame and desecrate the holy book of Muslims without full knowledge of its teachings. False and uninformed accusations have been leveled against the Qur'an for some time. But now, this initiative places the sacred text directly in the hands of people of other faiths in the American public and encourages people of conscience to discover the truth about Islam. Explore the Qur'an allows the holy book to speak for itself and educate people of other faith traditions about the universal teachings of Islam.[6]

Muslims often insist vociferously that the Koran teaches peace. Adil Salahi, the Muslim author of a biography of Muhammad, maintains, "You only need to open the Koran and read to realize that what it calls for is peace, not war."[7] Likewise, Spc. David Burgos, a Muslim operations clerk for the 492nd Harbormaster Detachment, Fort Eustis, Virginia, has said, "I have read the Koran several times....Islam teaches its followers to be peaceful. Islam is all about giving life, not taking it."[8]

Not only is the Koran's message ostensibly peaceful, but the book also seems to contain timeless wisdom that is hailed by leaders across the world. Former British prime minister Tony Blair insists that "the authentic basis of Islam, as laid down in the Koran, is progressive, humanitarian, [and] sees knowledge and scientific advance as a duty, which is why for centuries Islam was the fount of so much invention and innovation. Fundamental Islam is actually the opposite of what the extremists preach."[9]

Blair's genuflection was perhaps exceeded by former U.S. president George W. Bush's second Inaugural Address, which classed the Koran with the formative texts of Western civilization: "Self-government relies, in the end, on the governing of the self. That edifice of character is built in families, supported by communities with standards, and sustained in our national life by the truths of Sinai, the Sermon on the Mount, the words of the Koran, and the varied faiths of our people."[10]

On the other hand. . .

Yet many non-Muslims, believing the Koran preaches intolerance and warfare, regard the book as about as holy as *Mein Kampf*. In fact, the direct comparison has been made more than once. Speaking of the Koran, Dutch parliamentarian Geert Wilders called upon the Netherlands to "ban this wretched book like *Mein Kampf* is banned!"[11] Wilders' view was shared by the late, world-renowned Italian journalist Oriana Fallaci, who said in 2005 that "the Koran is the *Mein Kampf* of a religion which has always aimed to eliminate the others.'"[12] Even the great Winston Churchill, in denigrating *Mein Kampf,* called it "the new Koran of faith and war: turgid, verbose, shapeless, but pregnant with its message."[13] And it's not only Westerners who discern hateful messages in the Koran; Hindus in Calcutta petitioned the government to ban the book as hate speech.[14]

What exactly do these critics find in the Koran that is so objectionable? Wilders asserts that the Muslim holy book "calls on Muslims to oppress, persecute or kill Christians, Jews, dissidents and non-believers, to beat and rape women and to establish an Islamic state by force."[15] Fallaci likewise found the roots of Islamic violence in the book Muslims venerate most of all: "Read it over, that *Mein Kampf,*" she declared. "Whatever the version, you will find that all the evil which the sons of Allah commit against us and against themselves comes from that book."[16]

Does the Koran really incite people to commit violence? Most Western analysts dogmatically deny it, characterizing jihadists as an infinitesimally small group of extremists who misunderstand the Koran's peaceful message. In fact, for contradicting these assumptions, Wilders is denounced as a hatemonger by much of the European political establishment. Although he's become one of the most popular political leaders in the Netherlands, Wilders has paid the price for contravening conventional wisdom about the Koran: he was recently denied entry to Britain, he faces prosecution for "incitement" by Dutch courts, and constant death threats have forced him to

How's that again?

Allah's words don't change: "The word of thy Lord doth find its fulfilment in truth and in justice: None can change His words: for He is the one who heareth and knoweth all" (6:115).

But then again, maybe they do: "Whatever communications We abrogate or cause to be forgotten, We bring one better than it or like it. Do you not know that Allah has power over all things?" (2:106)

adopt a permanent security detail. Fallaci faced something similar; shortly before her death, she was put on trial in absentia in Italy in 2006 on the charge of "defaming Islam."[17]

Of course, what is more consequential than the views of Wilders and Fallaci is that many Muslims themselves find calls to warfare in the Koran. And this group of "misunderstanders" is not as insignificant as Western analysts contend. To the contrary, they comprise a global movement, active from Indonesia to Nigeria and extending into Europe and North America, that is dedicated to waging war against "unbelievers"—that is, non-Muslims—and subjugating them as inferiors under the rule of Islamic law. This movement sees in the Koran its divine mandate to wage that war.

For example, in March 2009, five Muslims accused of helping plot the September 11 attacks, including the notorious Khalid Sheikh Mohammed, wrote an "Islamic Response to the Government's Nine Accusations." In it they quote the Koran to justify their jihad war against the American Infidels. "In God's book," asserts the letter, "he ordered us to fight you everywhere we find you, even if you were inside the holiest of all holy cities, The Mosque in Mecca, and the holy city of Mecca, and even during sacred months. In God's book, verse 9 [actually verse 5], Al-Tawbah [the Koran's ninth chapter]: *Then fight and slay the pagans wherever you find them, and seize them, and besiege them and lie in wait for them in each and every ambush.*"[18]

Osama bin Laden's communiqués have also quoted the Koran copiously. In his 1996 "Declaration of War against the Americans Occupying the Land of the Two Holy Places," he quotes seven Koran verses: 3:145; 47:4–6; 2:154; 9:14; 47:19; 8:72; and the notorious "Verse of the Sword," 9:5.[19] Bin Laden began his October 6, 2002, letter to the American people with two Koran quotations, both of a martial bent: "Permission to fight (against disbelievers) is given to those (believers) who are fought against, because they have been wronged and surely, Allah is Able to give them (believers) victory" (22:39); and "Those who believe, fight in the Cause of Allah, and those who disbelieve, fight in the cause of Taghut (anything worshipped other than Allah, e.g. Satan). So fight you against the friends of Satan; ever feeble is indeed the plot of Satan" (4:76).[20]

In a sermon broadcast in 2003, bin Laden rejoiced in a Koranic exhortation to violence as being a means to establish the truth: "Praise be to Allah who revealed the verse of the Sword to his servant and messenger [the Islamic Prophet Muhammad], in order to establish truth and abolish falsehood."[21] The "Verse of the Sword" is Koran 9:5: "Then, when the sacred months have passed, slay the idolaters wherever ye find them, and take them (captive), and besiege them, and prepare for them each ambush. But if they repent and establish worship and pay the poor-due, then leave their way free. Lo! Allah is Forgiving, Merciful."

The idea that the Koran commands them to do violence to unbelievers runs from the very top of the international jihadist movement—Osama bin Laden—down to the rank and file. In January 2004, Reem Raiyishi, a Gazan mother of two children aged one and three, blew herself up at an Israeli checkpoint, murdering four Israelis. Before she did that, she posed for pictures holding a rifle in one hand and the Koran in the other. In a videotaped recording she declared, "It was always my wish to turn my body into deadly shrapnel against the Zionists and to knock on the doors of heaven with the skulls of Zionists."[22]

Apparently nothing she read in her holy Koran dissuaded her from pursuing that wish.

Nor was Raiyishi by any means the only jihad terrorist, or even the only suicide bomber, to invoke the Koran as justification for violence against non-Muslims. In January 2006, a gang of Muslims in Paris kidnapped Ilan Halimi, a 23-year-old Jew, who was tortured, mutilated, and ultimately murdered. During Halimi's weeks-long ordeal, his captors called his family, demanding half a million euros in ransom money and reciting verses of the Koran.[23]

On March 3, 2006, 22-year-old Iranian student Mohammed Reza Taheri-azar drove an SUV into a crowd of students on the campus of the University of North Carolina at Chapel Hill, injuring nine. In a letter written soon afterward, Taheri-azar declared that "in the Koran, Allah states that the believing men and women have permission to murder anyone responsible for the killing of other believing men and women." In another letter he asserted,

> I live with the holy Koran as my constitution for right and wrong and definition of justice.... Allah gives permission in the Koran for the followers of Allah to attack those who have raged [sic] war against them, with the expectation of eternal paradise in case of martyrdom and/or living one's life in obedience of all of Allah's commandments found throughout the Koran's 114 chapters. I've read all 114 chapters approximately 15 times since June of 2003 when I started reading the Koran.... I live only to serve Allah, by obeying all of Allah's commandments of which I am aware by reading and learning the contents of the Koran.[24]

Later he sent a detailed exposition of the Koran's teachings on warfare to the Carolina campus newspaper.[25] The campus chapter of the Muslim Students Association disavowed Taheri-azar's interpretation of the Koran, but did not offer an alternative understanding of the verses he cited.

Overall, it is extremely rare—if not impossible—to find a jihadist who does not cite the Koran to justify his actions. Britain-based jihadist preacher, Abu Yahya, asserts simply, "It says in the Koran that we must try as much as we can to terrorise the enemy."[26] And Pakistani jihad leader Beitullah Mehsud claims that "Allah on 480 occasions in the Holy Koran extols Muslims to wage jihad. We only fulfill God's orders. Only jihad can bring peace to the world." He specified that his jihad—*struggle* in Arabic—is an offensive military operation: "We will continue our struggle until foreign troops are thrown out. Then we will attack them in the US and Britain until they either accept Islam or agree to pay jazia."[27] The "jazia," or jizya, is a tax that the Koran (9:29) specifies must be levied on Jews, Christians, and some other non-Muslim faiths as a sign of their subjugation under the Islamic social order.

One pro-Osama website put it this way: "The truth is that a Muslim who reads the Koran with devotion is determined to reach the battlefield in order to attain the reality of Jihad. It is solely for this reason that the Kufaar [unbelievers] conspire to keep the Muslims far away from understanding the Koran, knowing that Muslims who understand the Koran will not distance themselves from Jihad."[28]

It is noteworthy that the leaders of the global jihad insist that they are scrupulously reading and interpreting the Koran correctly, and they are consistently unimpressed by Westerners who insist that the Koran is a book of peace. The Ayatollah Khomeini, who brought the rule of Islamic law to Iran, once thundered, "There are hundreds of other [Koranic] psalms and Hadiths [sayings of Muhammad] urging Muslims to value war and to fight. Does all this mean that Islam is a religion that prevents men from waging war? I spit upon those foolish souls who make such a claim."[29]

And indeed, there are scores of Koranic psalms and Hadiths commanding Muslims to engage in violent jihad. Yet even after the September 11 attacks, and the 2005 London bombings, and the 2008 Mumbai terror attacks, and countless other bloody jihadist operations all over the world, the media, academia, and even our government continue to insist that the Koran contains no such imperative.

Why read the Koran?

It's hard to imagine that Blair, Bush, and Potemra are reading the same book as that read by Wilders, Fallaci, and Khomeini. Can the Koran really preach peace and love if it encourages believers to knock on heaven's door with the skulls of the enemies of Allah?

It is imperative for Americans to read the Koran and discover the answer. A huge number of policy decisions are predicated upon the assumption that the Koran teaches peace, and that those who brandish Korans and commit violence are misunderstanding their own religion and perverting the teachings of their own holy book. These include U.S. government postures toward Pakistan and Egypt; immigration matters; airport security procedures; military strategies in Iraq and Afghanistan; domestic anti-terror policies; and our acquiescence to Saudi Arabia's Islamic proselytizing campaign in America and many other countries.

But most government and media analysts dare not even question the assumption that the Koran is peaceful, for they believe that any insinuation to the contrary is racist, bigoted, and effectively brands all Muslims as terrorists. In other words, they think the implications of the possibility that the Koran teaches warfare against unbelievers are too terrible even to contemplate. Thus, many policymakers simply assume the Koran teaches peace without bothering to study the text, an act which might raise some uncomfortable questions.

Others don't read the Koran because they believe its contents simply don't matter. Fourteen centuries have passed since it was written, the argument goes. The world has changed, and surely Islam has changed, too. And besides, anyone can see whatever he wants to see in a sacred text, right?

In fact, no. The contents of the Koran matter because, contrary to what many would have us believe, sacred texts are *not* entirely determined by what the faithful wish to see in them. The fashionable philosophy of deconstructionism teaches that written words have no meaning other than that given to them by the reader, but in reality, the words of sacred texts are not infinitely malleable; "slay the idolaters wherever you find them" cannot easily be transformed into "love your enemies and pray for those who persecute you." For the believer, the actual words of the Koran are generally not difficult to understand, as hard as they may be to put into practice.

Miracles of the Koran

TAKE THE KORANIC CHALLENGE!

The Koran in Arabic is renowned for the sublimity of its poetry—and presents that sublimity as miraculous evidence of its divine origin. When asked for a miracle, Muhammad pointed to the Koran itself, claiming that it confirmed earlier divine revelations: "And they say: If only he would bring us a miracle from his Lord! Hath there not come unto them the proof of what is in the former scriptures?" (20:133) Allah even addresses unbelievers and fence-sitters with a challenge: "And if ye are in doubt as to what We have revealed from time to time to Our servant, then produce a Sura [chapter] like thereunto; and call your witnesses or helpers (if there are any) besides Allah, if your (doubts) are true" (2:23).

This is a challenge many have taken up over the centuries, but of course it is based on wholly subjective criteria, and as such can never be successfully met in the eyes of those who issue it. Many have imitated the syntax and rhythm and language of the Koran, but no pious Muslim would ever acknowledge that any of these approximated the Koran itself, no matter how close they got: in short, the challenge can never be won. Allah himself acknowledges this, when elsewhere in the Koran he declares that those who take up the challenge will never succeed: "They could not produce the like thereof" (17:88).

Finally, there are those who argue that the Koran's violent commandments are largely meaningless since similar ones are found in the Bible. This lazy moral equivalency overlooks the glaring fact that there is hardly a single organization today that commits violent acts and justifies them by quoting the Bible and invoking Christianity. The media frequently warns us of the danger of "Christian terrorism," citing examples like Timothy McVeigh (who, in fact, was agnostic when he committed the 1995 Oklahoma City bombing)[30] and Scott Roeder, the alleged killer of late-term abortionist George Tiller. Such examples, of course, are extremely rare, especially compared to the daily attacks by Islamic fundamentalists throughout the world, which are so common that the mainstream press only bothers to report the biggest outrages anymore. What's more, Tiller's killing was condemned by the Catholic Church and every major pro-life group. This is unsurprising, since there is no school of Christian thought that cites the Bible as justification for committing terrorism. In contrast, Islamic jihadists around the world point to the Koran to explain what they are doing and why—and heap contempt upon those Muslims who deny the Koran's martial contents.

The Koran's presidential whitewashing

For a lesson in the hazards of not understanding the Koran, let's look at President Obama's June 4, 2009, Cairo address to the Muslim world. Filled with reverential references to the supposedly compassionate teachings of the "holy Koran," the speech serves as an abject lesson in the wishful thinking, self-delusion, and political correctness that pervades Western assumptions about Islamic scripture.

In praising the Koran's ostensibly peaceful teachings, Obama cited verse 5:32: "The Holy Koran," said the President, "teaches that whoever kills an innocent, it is as if he has killed all mankind; and whoever saves a person, it is as if he has saved all mankind."[31] This sounds peaceful enough, but Obama studiously ignored the next verse (5:33), which mandates punishment for those whom Muslims do not regard as "innocent"— punishments including crucifixion or amputation of a hand and a foot for those who fight against Allah and Muhammad. The axiom against killing innocents, as we will see in chapter three, came from the Jewish tradition; in the

Koranic passage, however, it becomes a warning of dire earthly punishment for those Jews who resist Muhammad and his religion.

Obama also quoted a Koranic verse (9:119) that supposedly supports his call for inter-religious tolerance:

> As the Holy Koran tells us, "Be conscious of God and speak always the truth." That is what I will try to do—to speak the truth as best I can, humbled by the task before us, and firm in my belief that the interests we share as human beings are far more powerful than the forces that drive us apart.[32]

Once again, this Koranic passage is actually about fighting unbelievers, and doesn't remotely advocate peaceful coexistence. One principal English translation, that of Mohammed Marmaduke Pickthall, renders the verse this way: "O ye who believe! Be careful of your duty to Allah, and be with the truthful." The passage continues:

> It is not for the townsfolk of Al-Madinah and for those around them of the wandering Arabs to stay behind the messenger of Allah and prefer their lives to his life. That is because neither thirst nor toil nor hunger afflicteth them in the way of Allah, nor step they any step that angereth the disbelievers, nor gain they from the enemy a gain, but a good deed is recorded for them therefor. Lo! Allah loseth not the wages of the good. Nor spend they any spending, small or great, nor do they cross a valley, but it is recorded for them, that Allah may repay them the best of what they used to do. And the believers should not all go out to fight. Of every troop of them, a party only should go forth, that they (who are left behind) may gain sound knowledge in religion, and that they may warn their folk when they

return to them, so that they may beware. O ye who believe!
Fight those of the disbelievers who are near to you, and let them
find harshness in you, and know that Allah is with those who
keep their duty (unto Him). (9:120–23)

In this passage, the Koran is scolding Muslims who refused to accompany Muhammad on his expedition to Tabouk in northern Arabia, where he wanted to fight a Byzantine garrison. The Byzantines weren't there when he arrived, and so there was no battle, but he was considerably angered that some Muslims in Medina and among the Bedouins had refused to make the trip—they "prefer[red] their lives to his life." The Koran promises that if they do anything that "angereth the disbelievers," they will be credited with having done a good deed, and Allah will repay them for such good deeds. The message here is simple and stark: Muslims should fight the unbelievers and be harsh with them.

Out of this command to wage jihad warfare against unbelievers, Obama cherry-picked one sentence that made it appear as if the Koran were simply counseling one to speak the truth, mindful of the divine presence. He took a passage about warfare and division and passed it off as a call for us all to come together and sing "Kumbaya."

This brings up an important question: if one doesn't even know what the Koran says, is it wise to make policy based upon what one assumes it says?

> ## Bible vs. Koran
>
> "We hurl the truth against falsehood, and it knocks out its brain, and behold, falsehood doth perish!"
> —Koran 21:18
>
> "Speaking the truth in love, we will in all things grow up into him who is the Head, that is, Christ."
> —Ephesians 4:15

Based on the erroneous assumption that jihad violence is a reaction to American actions, Obama has announced numerous new aid programs for the Islamic world. He doesn't seem to have considered that if the Koran mandates jihad against non-Muslims, displays of U.S. goodwill are unlikely to have much effect. As South African Mufti Ebrahim Desai said, "In simple the Kuffaar [unbelievers] can never be trusted for any possible good they do. They have their own interest at heart."[33]

One man's opinion? Sure. But it is an opinion with deep roots in Islamic tradition, and it would therefore be naïve to dismiss it as simply Desai's own mean-spiritedness. Why? Because the Koran contains a warning against those who turn "in friendship to the Unbelievers. . . . If only they had believed in Allah, in the Prophet, and in what hath been revealed to him, never would they have taken them for friends and protectors, but most of them are rebellious wrong-doers" (5:80–81). It also tells Muslims that "never will the Jews or the Christians be satisfied with thee unless thou follow their form of religion" (2:120).

These are words that Obama should consider carefully.

Why an Infidel's Guide?

Muslims, of course, know what's in their own holy book, and they know when someone like Obama gets it wrong. But these misinterpretations will slip right by most non-Muslims. That's why there's a need for this book, *The Complete Infidel's Guide to the Koran*.

What is an Infidel? Well, if you are reading this book, *you* are probably an Infidel—at least in the Koran's eyes.

An Infidel, as far as the Koran is concerned, is anyone who refuses to submit to Allah as the one true god and to recognize Muhammad as his prophet. While Islamic apologists commonly claim that the Koran does not refer to Jews or Christians as Infidels, in fact it asserts that "they indeed have disbelieved who say: Lo! Allah is the Messiah, son of Mary" (5:17)—

in other words, if you believe in the traditional Christian doctrine of the divinity of Christ, you're an Infidel. And the Koran asserts, oddly, that the Jews claim that the prophet Ezra is the Son of God—a claim which earns them Allah's curse (9:30). So they're Infidels, too.

Those whom the Koran asserts are Infidels need to know what the Koran is saying about them and what must be done about them, because Muslims around the world today are acting upon these teachings.

This can be hard to believe, especially when one is acquainted with Muslims who have anything but warfare against Infidels on their minds. Friendship with kind and loving Muslims can give non-Muslims the impression that the Koran cannot possibly teach warfare and hatred, and that anyone who says otherwise must harbor some kind of anti-Muslim animus.

Yet if the Koran does indeed, as Khomeini insisted, urge Muslims "to value war and to fight," then it is not an act of hatred toward Muslims to point that out. It is simply a fact. Different people will react to this fact in different ways: non-Muslims will of course look at it negatively, but Osama bin Ladon and others like him revel in this fact and promote it far and wide.

That's why it is imperative for Infidels to know what is in the Koran. It's a simple matter of knowing who those who have vowed to destroy us think they are, and what they think they're doing, and what they hope to accomplish. They themselves tell us the answers to these questions are found in the Koran.

And that's why an Infidel's guide to this strange and little-understood book is so urgently needed.

It's a question of self-protection.

Why is a guide to the Koran needed at all?

Why not just read the Koran on your own? Why does any self-respecting Infidel need a guide?

Primarily because reading the Islamic holy book isn't easy for non-Muslims. The book is hard to follow because it's not arranged chronologically or by subject matter, but by the length of the chapters, called "*suras.*" With the exception of the brief first chapter, its 114 suras are arranged more or less from the longest to the shortest. This organization was completed long after Muhammad's death. Chronologically (according to Islamic tradition), the first revelation that Muhammad received can be found in the Koran not as sura 1, but as sura 96. The last revelation Muhammad received, which came to him while he was on his deathbed, is sura 110, not sura 114 (the last chapter in the book).

The Koran is less a collection of historical narratives, as is much of the Bible, as it is a collection of sermons in which the historical material is not told for its own sake, but is used to illustrate various points. It makes no attempt at linear history, either as a whole or, generally, within the individual chapters. While the Bible contains historical books that are more or less in chronological order, and in broad outline follows a coherent historical trajectory, the focus of the Koran's suras often moves from subject to subject, with various historical incidents recounted only in fragments.

The chapter titles can cause further confusion to the novice Koran reader, as they generally bear no connection to the subject matter of the chapter itself. Most of the chapters—"The Cow" (sura 2), "The Spider" (sura 29), "Smoke" (sura 44)—take their name from an apparently randomly chosen element of the chapter itself, one that does not necessarily have any particular importance. Only a few chapters, such as "The Spoils of War" or "Booty" (sura 8), bear titles that actually summarize their contents.

In the longer suras, stories are told, laws are given, and warnings to unbelievers are issued with no evident regard for logical sequence. The shorter suras, meanwhile, particularly those that run only a few lines near the end of the book, are poetic and arresting warnings of the impending divine judgment. Although the Koran is shorter than the New Testament, in keeping with its character as a collection of sermons designed to inculcate various ideas and attitudes, a surprisingly large amount of what it says is said more than once.

In the original Arabic, the repetitions are accompanied by rhymes and rhythms that create a kind of incantatory effect; shorn of these musical effects, however, when translated, the printed Koran risks becoming "wrist-slittingly boring," in the words of John Derbyshire.[34] And Derbyshire isn't alone: the great eighteenth-century historian Edward Gibbon called the Koran an "endless incoherent rhapsody of fable and precept," and nineteenth-century writer Thomas Carlyle complained that it was "as toilsome reading as I ever undertook; a wearisome, confused jumble, crude, incondite."[35]

But never fear. I read the Koran so you don't have to.

This guide eliminates the repetitions and dry passages, and gives you the book's message without the long trudge through yet another denunciation of unbelievers, yet another description of the tortures of the damned, yet another retelling of Moses' confrontation with Pharaoh.

Critics of jihad violence and Islamic supremacism are often accused of taking quotes from the Koran "out of context." This is a bitterly ironic charge given that much of the Koran has no context in the first place. For long stretches there is little or no narrative unity. The text moves from topic to topic with scant regard for any conventional notion of continuity. Many verses appear as abstract maxims, related without regard to any particular situation; to demand that they be quoted "in context" is to demand something that was never possible in the first place.

To be sure, much of the Koran is perfectly clear, but there are numerous passages that refer to incidents in Muhammad's life or an event in early Islamic history without providing key elements of the story—as if taking for granted that everyone who hears the Koranic account will know the omitted details. That makes reading some passages of the Koran rather like listening in on a conversation between two people you don't know, who are discussing events in which you were not involved—and they are not bothering to stop and explain to you the details of what they are discussing. To fill in the gaps, Muslims turn to commentaries on the Koran and to Hadith (traditions of the words and deeds of Muhammad), and we will have recourse to the same material here in order to illustrate how Muslims themselves understand their holy book.

THE HADITH
ILLUMINATES THE KORAN

The Koran is not the mainstream Muslim's only guide. A Muslim scholar, Abu Abdir Rahmaan, says Satan has suggested "to the hearts of some of the Muslims that the Qur'an, as Glorious as it is, is sufficient enough alone as guidance for Mankind. Meaning that the Sunnah, or way of the Messenger of Allah...is something that can be left off, or abandoned. Without a doubt this is a growing disease that has no place in this wonderful way of life of ours."[36]

The Islamic scholar Mohammed Nasir-ul-Deen al-Albani declares, "There is no way to understand the Qur'an correctly except in association with the interpretation of the Sunnah."[37] Scholar Wael B. Hallaq concurs, observing "that the Sunna is binding on Muslims" and has been established "on the basis of the Quran which enjoins Muslims to obey the Prophet and not to swerve from his ranks."[38]

And the Sunnah, the words and deeds of Muhammad, is largely made up of the Hadith: voluminous collections of accounts of the Islamic prophet's sayings and activities, as recounted by his followers. There were many opportunistic forgeries

Which Koran?

There are numerous helpful translations of the Koran. N. J. Dawood's translation is the most smoothly readable English translation. However, it can be difficult to use for reference since most versions do not mark the verse numbers precisely. Also, some people—both Muslim and non-Muslim—dislike it because Dawood uses "God" for Allah—although since Arabic-speaking Christians use "Allah" for the God of the Bible, and have for over a millennium, this is not really a serious objection to anyone who

among the hadith, however, giving rise to a veritable science within Islam: the science of determining the authenticity of various traditions. Early in the history of Islam several Muslims assembled collections of accounts of Muhammad's words and deeds that were considered more or less definitive and free from fabricated stories. Six collections were almost universally recognized early on, and continue to be regarded today, as reliable—generally free of forgeries and inaccuracies—and two of these were deemed *sahih*: the most "sound" or "reliable."[39]

Nearly all the hadiths that will appear in boxes throughout this book are taken from the sahih.[40] They range from ludicrous to alarming, and are included so that Infidels may be fully informed as to the nature of the belief system from which has sprung today's comprehensive threat to the West—including the superstition and bellicosity that runs through it.

Are these merely long-forgotten rulings dug up for the purpose of ridicule out of dusty books that no Muslim reads anymore? Hardly. These are selections from the most authoritative hadith collections. In fact, Muslim schools in Britain forbid music and chess in accord with hadiths quoted in this book[41]—indicating that these statements are taken very seriously in Muslim communities even in the West today.

knows both languages. Many Muslims dislike this translation simply because Dawood was not a Muslim, but Infidels may find it more helpful than translations produced by Muslims, since Dawood generally doesn't whitewash the Koran's more jarring passages.

Two translations by Muslims, those by Abdullah Yusuf Ali and Mohammed Marmaduke Pickthall, are generally reliable, although both write in a stilted, practically unreadable pseudo-King James Bible English. Of the two, Ali's contains more liberties with the text—such as adding "(lightly)" to sura 4:34 after the directive to husbands to beat their disobedient wives. The Arabic doesn't say to beat them lightly, it just says to beat them. Pickthall's version, while sharing the dense archaism of Ali's, is generally accurate.

Despite their infelicities, because they are two common translations, I have generally used these throughout this book. There are other good translations, and more are being produced all the time. It is best to have more than one on hand for comparison.

But wait: Isn't this book anti-Islam?

This is not a general guide to the Koran. You will find nothing in this book about Islamic ritual practices or prayers. This is an Infidel's guide, focusing on where the Koran came from and its specific portions that are—or should be—of concern to Infidels.

Many Muslims, however, would prefer Infidels remain in the dark about these elements of their holy book. Protesting against the FBI's use of informants to ferret out jihad terrorist activity in mosques in the United States, Hussam Ayloush, executive director of CAIR for greater Los Angeles, said to a Muslim audience at a mosque in April 2009, "We're here today to say our mosques are off limits. Our Koran is off limits."[42]

"Our Koran is off limits." Of course, Ayloush is not trying to dissuade Infidels from reading the Koran, which after all, is something that CAIR encourages. It's just that Ayloush doesn't want Infidel FBI agents to draw the "wrong" conclusions from their own readings—conclusions that might contradict CAIR's insistence that the Koran teaches peace.

Such an investigation is imperative for America's defense against the global jihad. Nevertheless, *The Complete Infidel's Guide to the Koran* will inevitably be branded as "anti-Islamic," as well as "bigoted," "hateful," and "Islamophobic."

But is it, really? Is the point of this book to spread hatred of the Koran, Islam, and Muslims?

Of course not.

Certainly this book is not written from the standpoint of Islamic faith. It is, in fact, a guide designed for those who do not believe in Islam, to help them understand why Islamic terrorism and supremacism continue to threaten the United States and so many other countries around the world today. But while it is not a believer's guide, it is a trustworthy guide. This book is designed to present a 100 percent accurate view of the Koran, so that Infidels can know what they should expect from a devout Muslim who reads his Koran and takes it seriously as the word of the one true God.

Whether the Koran really says what this guide claims it says can easily be verified. And if this guide reports its contents accurately, that couldn't possibly be an act of "hatred" or "bigotry." If the Koran really curses Jews and Christians (9:30) and calls for warfare against them in order to bring about their subjugation (9:29), it is not "Islamophobic" to forewarn Infidels by pointing this out. It is simply a fact. And it should go without saying that it is not a fact that should move any reader of this book to hate anyone. The fact that the Koran counsels warfare against unbelievers should move readers to act in defense of freedom of speech, freedom of conscience, and the legal equality of all people, before it is too late.

Jihadist activity will continue as long as there are Muslims who believe that the Koran commands it. And that's why Infidels have a responsibility to themselves and to their children to know exactly what is in the Koran, and to act accordingly.

It's not a matter of "hate." It's a matter of survival.

Behold, I bring you tidings of Great Joy, which shall be to all People.

For unto you is born this day in the city of David a Savior, which is Christ the Lord. And this shall be a sign unto you; Ye shall find the babe wrapped in swaddling clothes, lying in a manger.

LUKE 2:10

Chapter Two

WHAT IS THIS BOOK ANYWAY, AND WHAT'S IN IT?

What exactly is the Koran?

L IKE G. K. CHESTERTON, who wrote a book with an introduction entitled, "In Praise of This Book," the Koran is not shy about proclaiming its own virtues.

So let's begin by letting the Koran tell you what the Koran is.

The word *Koran* means "recitation" in Arabic—a title that refers to Muhammad's reciting of the eternal divine words that were delivered to him by the angel Gabriel beginning in 610 AD. The first divine command that Gabriel delivered to Muhammad was to "recite" (sura 96). Over the next twenty-three years, Muhammad received further revelations from Gabriel, who was transmitting the direct words of Allah. These revelations were compiled by Muhammad's followers, ultimately forming the Koran.

According to orthodox Islamic belief, the earthly Koran is a perfect copy of the *Umm al-Kitab*, the "Mother of the Book," which has resided forever with Allah (85:22). As the Koran says of itself, "And verily, it is in the Mother of the Book, in Our Presence, high (in dignity), full of wisdom" (43:4). It is "the wise book, a guide and mercy to the doers of good" (31:2–3).

The Koran calls itself a divine production: it is "not such as can be produced by other than Allah" (10:37). It is, among other things, "the criterion" or "standard" of judgment of what is right and what is wrong (3:3; 25:1). It offers "healing and mercy to those who believe," but "to the unjust it causes nothing but loss after loss" (17:82).

The Koran is, simply, "the Book." It provides "guidance sure, without doubt, to those who fear Allah" (2:1). It is "the indubitable truth" (69:51), "full of wisdom" (36:2). It is "honorable and pious and just" (80:16)—indeed, it is a "glorious Koran" (85:21), "a mighty scripture," so mighty that "falsehood cannot reach it from before or from behind" (41:41–42). It is "free from any flaw" (39:28). Allah, speaking in a royal plural that does not, according to Muslim theologians, compromise his absolute unity, proclaims that "it was We that revealed the Koran, and shall Ourself preserve it" (15:9). It is not, rest assured, "the word of an evil spirit accursed" (81:25).

There is only one speaker throughout: Allah himself (although there are a few exceptions that bedevil Koranic commentators to this day). Because it is without doubt, and because it is entirely Allah's word, without any human element whatsoever, and because he guarantees its preservation, it cannot be questioned. Historically this has made the words of the Koran—on wife-beating, the treatment of non-Muslims, and much more—a virtually insurmountable obstacle to reform within Islam. Reformers are immediately branded as heretics or apostates, and are frequently subject to persecution from authorities anxious to safeguard Islamic orthodoxy. To the pious Muslim, the Koran's word is eternally fresh and ever applicable, no matter what social conditions may prevail in any given society. Whatever is non-Koranic is inferior to the Koran's word and must give way.

The Koran is absolutely central to Muslim life and culture. An Islamic introduction to the study of the Koran calls the book a "protective haven and lasting gift of bliss, excellent argument and conclusive proof." Additionally, it "cures the heart's fear, and makes just determinations whenever there is doubt. It is lucid speech, and final word, not facetiousness; a lamp whose light never extinguishes . . . , an ocean whose depths will never be fathomed. Its oratory stuns reason . . . it combines concise succinctness and inimitable expression."[1]

Islamic scholar Seyyed Hossein Nasr of George Washington University says that the Koran "constitutes the alpha and omega of the Islamic religion in the sense that all that is Islamic, whether it be its laws, its thought, its spiritual and ethical teachings and even its artistic manifestations, have their roots in the explicit or implicit teachings of the Sacred Text."[2] Islamic scholar Caesar Farah asserts that the Koran "constitutes the Muslim's main reference not only for matters spiritual but also for the mundane requirements of day to day living."[3]

In fact, some Muslims insist the Koran offers a clearer picture of Islamic life than does actual experience in the Islamic world. For example, the Nobel Prize winning British writer V. S. Naipaul traveled in Muslim countries in 1979. A Pakistani official explained to a colleague that Naipaul wanted to see "Islam in action." The colleague's response was telling: "He should read the Koran."[4]

The uncreated Koran

Muslims believe the Koran is not only perfect, but that it's uncreated. What's that mean? The Koran says that Allah has in his possession the "Mother of the Book" (13:39). And Allah made the Koran "in Arabic, that ye may be able to understand" (43:3) and tells Muhammad that "it is in the

Mother of the Book, in Our Presence" (43:4). The "Mother of the Book" is, according to Islamic tradition, the Preserved Tablet, the copy of the Koran that has existed for all eternity with Allah (85:21–22). The Koran that the angel Gabriel provided to Muhammad throughout his career as a prophet is a perfect copy of this eternal book. Muslims point to the Koran's poetic character as proof of its divine origin, and evidence that it was not made up by Muhammad, whom they say was illiterate.

However, not all Muslims have always believed that the Koran is eternal and uncreated—a fact that has important implications for modern-day hopes for the emergence of a moderate brand of Islam. The reformist Mu'tazilite movement swept through the Islamic world in the ninth century, becoming the state religion of the Abbasid Caliphate (Islamic empire). The Mu'tazilites ("Separated Ones," or "Those Who Have Withdrawn") held that reason rather than simply blind faith in the Koran must play a role in a Muslim's encounter with Allah. Accordingly, Mu'tazilite theologians were uncomfortable with literal interpretations of some Koranic passages, and even declared that the book itself was created.

The debate over whether the sacred book was created or existed eternally had enormous practical implications. The Mu'tazilites developed a method

Bible vs. Koran

"O ye who believe! Ask not questions about things which, if made plain to you, may cause you trouble. But if ye ask about things when the Qur'an is being revealed, they will be made plain to you, Allah will forgive those: for Allah is Oft-forgiving, Most Forbearing. Some people before you did ask such questions, and on that account lost their faith."

—Koran 5:101–2

"Always be prepared to make a defense to any one who calls you to account for the hope that is in you, yet do it with gentleness and reverence."

—I Peter 3:15

of Koranic interpretation that was freer from the literal meaning of the text than most Muslim divines dared to venture. For example, they reinterpreted the injunction that Allah "leads the wrongdoers astray" (14:27) so as to reject predestination; they simply denied that Allah would lead people astray and condemn them to Hell.

The caliph (Islamic emperor) Ja'far al-Mutawakkil (847–861), however, crushed the Mu'tazilite movement and branded it a heresy. Asserting that the Koran was created became a crime punishable by death. And to this day, the marginalization and discrediting of the Mu'tazilites casts a long shadow over "moderate Islam." If today's moderates stray too far from a literal reading of the Koran (including its ferocity toward unbelievers), they risk being accused of advocating long-discredited heresies.

The Mu'tazilite experience provides ample historical precedent and a ready methodology that literalists use to cast suspicion on any reading of the Koran that doesn't take all its words at face value.

So what is this perfect, eternal book about?

The message of this book that Muslims revere as the perfect and immutable divine word is in many ways similar to the message of the Bible, and will be familiar to Jewish and Christian readers. At the same time, however, as we shall see, there are striking divergences—ones of particular concern to Infidels.

The Koran, again like the Bible, is about many things, but its primary message is that there is one God, in Arabic *Allah*—"the God." The worst of all sins in the sight of Allah is idolatry. One of the Koran's principal preoccupations is expressing fury and contempt for the "unbelievers," meaning non-Muslims, who refuse to acknowledge the manifest signs of Allah's presence and power, and who will be duly punished with the tortures of hell.

The oneness of Allah and the necessity to obey and worship him are the Koran's central themes. All other Koranic preoccupations can be subsumed under these headings. The text has in Islamic history allowed for nothing like the theological elaboration that characterized early Christianity. Islam began as a simple creed and has remained one—and most of the Koran's stories are designed to reinforce the same basic points.

The Koran—always unchanged?

The Council on American-Islamic Relations says the Koran "was memorized by Muhammad and then dictated to his companions. The text of the Quran was cross-checked during the life of the Prophet. The 114 chapters of the Quran have remained unchanged through the centuries."[5]

This is a point of great pride among many Muslims, who regard the absence of alternate versions of the Koran as evidence of its miraculous character and proof that Allah is, indeed, preserving the book, in contrast to the thousands of variations one finds in Biblical manuscripts. Osama bin Laden bragged in his 2002 letter to the American people that the Koran "will remain preserved and unchanged, after the other Divine books and messages have been changed. The Quran is the miracle until the Day of Judgment."[6]

As is so often the case, however, reality is not so simple. Muhammad received Koranic revelations from Gabriel piecemeal—or, as the Koran itself says, "in slow, well-arranged stages, gradually" (25:32)—for twenty-three years. But Muhammad himself was "unlettered" (7:157), and did not write down his revelations. Before he died rather suddenly in 632, he had a premonition of his death—a premonition that was connected to the text of the Koran: "Every year," he told his daughter Fatima, "Gabriel used to revise the Qur'an with me once only, but this year he has done so twice. I think this portends my death."[7]

Nevertheless, Muhammad didn't make any provisions to pass on the complete Koranic text to his followers. Some of the Koran had been written down; other portions were preserved only in the memories of various Muslims. Accordingly, some revelations were forgotten, as the Koran itself acknowledges: "None of Our revelations do We abrogate or cause to be forgotten, but We substitute something better or similar: Knowest thou not that Allah Hath power over all things?" (2:106)

Compiling the Koran

The impetus for collecting Muhammad's revelations into a single volume came after Muhammad and other important early Muslims started dying off. Late in the year Muhammad died, 632, a group of Arab tribes that Muhammad had conquered and brought into the Muslim fold revolted. The first caliph, Abu Bakr, led the Muslims into battle to subdue them. The two sides met in the Battle of Yamama, in which some of the Muslims who had memorized segments of the Koran were killed. One of the casualties was a freed slave named Salim whom Muhammad had listed as one of four men from whom Muslims should "learn the recitation of the Qur'an."[8] Salim was also said to be the first Muslim to collect all the Koranic revelations into a single volume. But now Salim was dead, and his collection of the Koran apparently lost.

And not only Salim's collection, but specific passages of the Koran were lost as well. One Islamic tradition notes that "many (of the passages) of the Qur'an that were sent down were known by those who died on the day of Yamama...but they were not known (by those who) survived them, nor were they written down, nor had [the first three caliphs] Abu Bakr, Umar or Uthman (by that time) collected the Qur'an, nor were they found with even one (person) after them."[9]

The entire Koran, the Islamic community's *raison d'etre*, was at risk. Abu Bakr accordingly sent for a Muslim named Zaid bin Thabit, who was said to be a *hafiz*—one who had memorized the entire Koran. Zaid found Abu Bakr with Umar, another powerful and influential early Muslim, and eventually Abu Bakr's successor as caliph. Abu Bakr told Zaid, "Umar has come to me and said: 'Casualties were heavy among the *Qurra'* of the Qur'an (i.e.

those who knew the Qur'an by heart) on the day of the battle of Yamama, and I am afraid that more heavy casualties may take place among the *Qurra'* on other battlefields, whereby a large part of the Qur'an may be lost. Therefore I suggest, you (Abu Bakr) order that the Qur'an be collected.'"

Abu Bakr told Zaid he was initially hesitant, since Muhammad himself had not undertaken such a project: "I said to 'Umar, 'How can you do something which Allah's Messenger did not do?'" But Umar stuck to his guns, insisting, "By Allah, that is a good thing to be done."

Finally Abu Bakr relented: "Umar kept on urging me to accept his proposal till Allah opened my chest for it and I began to realize the good in the idea which 'Umar had realized.'" Turning to Zaid, Abu Bakr told him, "You are a wise young man and we do not have any suspicion about you, and you used to write the Divine Revelation for Allah's Messenger. So you should search for (the fragmentary scripts of) the Qur'an and collect it (in one book)."

How's that again?

Allah is beyond human comprehension, and he cannot be seen: "No vision can grasp Him, but His grasp is over all vision: He is above all comprehension, yet is acquainted with all things" (6:103). For indeed, it would not be proper for human beings to behold Allah directly: "It is not fitting for a man that Allah should speak to him except by inspiration, or from behind a veil, or by the sending of a messenger to reveal, with Allah's permission, what Allah wills: for He is Most High, Most Wise" (42:51).

Yet Muhammad did see Allah: For the Islamic prophet "was taught by one mighty in power, endued with wisdom," who "appeared (in stately form) while he was in the highest part of the horizon" (53:5–7). Allah challenges the unbelievers who doubt the veracity of Muhammad's divine vision: "Will ye then dispute with him concerning what he saw? For indeed he saw him at a second descent, near the lote-tree beyond which none may pass" (53:12–13).

If he were really a hafiz, Zaid should have been able to complete this project simply by sitting down and writing out the Koran from memory. But instead, he received his new assignment as a crushing burden: "By Allah! If they had ordered me to shift one of the mountains, it would not have been heavier for me than this ordering me to collect the Qur'an." He asked Abu Bakr the same question the caliph had initially asked Umar: "How will you do something which Allah's Messenger did not do?" But Abu Bakr simply repeated Umar's answer to him: "By Allah, it is a good thing to be done."

So Zaid set to work interviewing various Muslims and recording verses they claimed had come from Muhammad. As Zaid recounted, "I started locating Quranic material and collecting it from parchments, scapula, leaf-stalks of date palms and from the memories of men (who knew it by heart). I found with Khuzaima two Verses of Surat-at-Tauba [sura 9] which I had not found with anybody else."[10]

Zaid's recollection testifies to the ad hoc nature of his work. For example, it was Khuzaima himself, Zaid's sole source for the last two verses of sura 9, who approached Zaid and informed him of the omission: "I see you have overlooked (two) verses and have not written them." When he had recited them, an influential companion of Muhammad and the future third caliph, Utman, declared, "I bear witness that these verses are from Allah."[11] And so they were included in the Koran (9:128–29).

Despite the sparse number of witnesses to the authenticity of verses such as these, Zaid completed his task, compiling what would become the canonical Koran.

Lost passages of the Koran

Other sections of the Koran, some mandating stringent punishments for unbelievers and other violators of Islamic law, failed to make it into Zaid's canon. One early Muslim declared, "Let none of you say, 'I have acquired the whole of the Qur'an.' How does he know what all of it is when much of the Qur'an has disappeared? Rather let him say 'I have acquired what has survived.'"[12]

Some passages did not survive because they were deliberately replaced—the Koran itself refers to this, depicting Allah saying, "When We substitute one revelation for another—and Allah knows best what He reveals (in stages)—they say, 'Thou art but a forger': but most of them understand not" (16:101). He is, of course, addressing Muhammad, whose detractors accused him of forging divine revelations when he would replace one with another.

Other Koranic verses disappeared without replacement. One of these stated, "The religion with Allah is al-Hanifiyyah (the Upright Way) rather than that of the Jews or the Christians, and those who do good will not go unrewarded." Al-Tirmidhi, the compiler of one of the six collections of Hadith, or Islamic traditions, that Muslims consider to be the most reliable, said that this verse was at one time part of sura 98.[13] It is not found there, however, in Zaid's version.

Another Islamic tradition reports that one elderly Muslim once said to three hundred men trained in the art of reciting the Koran, "We used to recite a surah which resembled in length and severity to (Surah) Bara'at." "Surah Bara'at" is the Koran's ninth sura, which contains its most extended exhortation to warfare against unbelievers, and the book's sole explicit exhortation to wage war against Jews and Christians and subjugate them under the rule of Islamic law (9:29). Yet this second martial sura was lost forever. The old man continued, "I have, however, forgotten it with the exception of this which I remember out of it: 'If there were two valleys full of riches, for the son of Adam, he would long for a third valley, and nothing would fill the stomach of the son of Adam but dust.'"

The old man added, "And we used to recite a surah which resembled one of the surahs of Musabbihat, and I have forgotten it, but remember (this much) out of it: 'Oh people who believe, why do you say that which you do not practise' (lxi 2.) and 'that is recorded in your necks as a witness (against you) and you would be asked about it on the Day of Resurrection' (xvii. 13)." This is a warning to the Hypocrites—supposedly insincere Muslim converts suspected of undermining Muhammad—to practice what they preach and not to pretend to believe in Islam.[14]

Most notoriously, a passage mandating death by stoning as the penalty for adultery was originally part of the Koran but was later omitted. The second caliph, Umar, worried about the omission:

> I am afraid that after a long time has passed, people may say, "We do not find the Verses of the Rajam (stoning to death) in the Holy Book," and consequently they may go astray by leaving an obligation that Allah has revealed. Lo! I confirm that the penalty of Rajam be inflicted on him who commits illegal sexual intercourse, if he is already married and the crime is proved by witnesses or pregnancy or confession.... Surely Allah's Apostle carried out the penalty of Rajam, and so did we after him.[15]

Ubayy ibn Ka'b, who is noted in early Islamic tradition as the compiler of one of the alternative texts of the Koran that Muslims now deny ever existed, explained that sura 33, which is seventy-three verses long, once had 213 additional verses, including this one: "The fornicators among the married men (ash-shaikh) and married women (ash-shaikhah), stone them as an exemplary punishment from Allah, and Allah is Mighty and Wise."[16]

Although women, accused adulterers, and Infidels in general can take some solace that these verses did not make the Koran's final cut, other injunctions in the same spirit as these found their way into the Muslim holy book, as we shall see.

The Koran under wraps

Oddly enough, even though the caliph himself had given him the job of collecting the Koran, once Zaid completed his work it was not widely distributed for many years. No copies were made, and Zaid's original text was kept in Abu Bakr's home until the caliph's death. Then it passed to Abu Bakr's successor, Umar, and then to Hafsa, Umar's daughter and one of Muhammad's widows.[17]

One indication that Zaid's Koran was relatively unknown for years after Muhammad's death was the fact that during Uthman's reign as caliph (644–656), Muslims from Syria and Iraq began to argue about the correct text of the Koran. A leading Muslim came to Uthman and asked him to save the situation: "O chief of the believers! Save this nation before they differ about the Book (the Qur'an) as Jews and the Christians did before them"—a statement that reflects the Islamic belief that the Jews and Christians corrupted the Scriptures they received from Allah, twisting their original Islamic message to create Judaism and Christianity.

Uthman heeded the request, asking Haifa to send him Zaid's Koran, and ordering Zaid and three other Muslims to start writing out copies. Uthman anticipated that Zaid's colleagues might disagree with his version of the Koran, and so told the three, "In case you disagree with Zaid bin Thabit on any point in the Qur'an, then write it in the dialect of Quraish [Muhammad's tribe], the Qur'an was revealed in their tongue."[18] This strange order may be a hint that some Koranic material originated outside of Mecca and Medina, and possibly even outside of Arabia itself, for if it was all transmitted to and through Muhammad, presumably it would all have been in the Quraish dialect in the first place.

Other Korans

Once these four had completed their task, Uthman sent a copy of Zaid's Koran to every Muslim land and ordered them to burn all other versions.

This provoked some resistance, most notably from one of Muhammad's former servants, Abdullah bin Masud. Muhammad himself had praised Abdullah's Koranic acumen, recommending him as one of four Muslims from whom the other believers should learn how to recite the Koran.[20] Muhammad did not include Zaid bin Thabit in this list.

Abdullah had compiled his own Koran, which differed from Zaid's version in several significant ways. Most conspicuously, it had only 111 chapters, instead of the 114 of the standard version, omitting suras 1, 113, and 114. Each of these are short prayers that don't alter the theological content of the Koran, but the omission of each was notable. The first chapter, the Fatiha, is the most common prayer in Islam, and Islamic tradition says that Muhammad recited suras 113 and 114, which are charms against evil spirits, on his deathbed. But Abdullah held that these prayers were not part of the Koran, and he was not about to discard his work in favor of Zaid's. For one thing, he had learned much of what he knew of the Koran straight from the prophet of Islam himself: "I acquired directly from the messenger of Allah seventy surahs when Zaid was still a childish youth," Abdullah thundered. "Must I now forsake what I acquired directly from the messenger of Allah?"[21]

> # THE HADITH ILLUMINATES THE KORAN
>
> . . . .
>
> ### Try nasal strips
>
> "The Prophet said, 'If anyone of you rouses from sleep and performs the ablution, he should wash his nose by putting water in it and then blowing it out thrice, because Satan has stayed in the upper part of his nose all the night.' "[19]

There was, meanwhile, as we have seen, yet another early compilation of the Koranic revelations—that of Ubayy bin Ka'b—yet another Muslim whose Koranic prowess won praise from Muhammad, who called him "the best reader (of the Qur'an) among my people."[22] Ubayy's Koran had not 111 chapters like Abdullah ibn Masud's, or 114 like the canonical version, but 116—Ubayy added in two additional brief prayers.

MIRACLES OF THE KORAN

THE MOON IS CLEFT ASUNDER—IN 1969!

The Islamic apologist Harun Yahya finds a miraculous prophecy in Koran 54:1, which he translates as, "The Hour has drawn near and the moon has split." Yahya explains, "The word 'split' used in this verse is the Arabic *shaqqa*, which in Arabic it [sic] has various meanings. In some commentaries on the Qur'an, the meaning 'split' is preferred. But *shaqqa* in Arabic can also mean 'ploughing' or 'digging' the earth." And that, you see, is what the astronauts did when they took samples from the lunar surface. Says Yahya,

> If we went back to the year 1969, we would see one of the great wonders of the Qur'an. The experiments carried out on the surface of the moon on July 20, 1969, may be hinting at the fulfilment of news given 1,400 years ago in Surat al-Qamar [sura 54]. On that date, American astronauts set foot on the moon. Digging at the lunar soil they carried out scientific experiments and collected samples of stones and soil. It is surely very interesting that these developments are in complete agreement with the statements in the verse.[23]

Very interesting, perhaps, but a bit forced. Did the astronauts "split" or even "plough" the moon? No, though they did indeed "dig" a little. No Muslim authority before 1969—or before Yahya, for that matter—ever read Koran 54:1 and saw in it a prophecy that someday men would walk on the moon.

Even after Uthman standardized Zaid's Koran, further corrections had to be made. At one point Muhammad's favorite wife, Aisha, now a revered widow known as the "Mother of the Believers," asked her servant to write out a copy of the Koran for her. But she directed him to depart from the standard version of Koran 2:238, telling him, "When you reach this ayat [verse], let me know, 'Guard the prayers carefully and the middle prayer and stand obedient to Allah.'" She told him to write instead, "Guard the prayers carefully and the middle prayer and the asr [afternoon] prayer and stand obedient to Allah." Her authority for this change? "I heard it from the Messenger of Allah, may Allah bless him and grant him peace."[24]

Uthman managed to destroy most of the alternative Koran variants, although records of some of them were preserved in Islamic traditions, and others have reemerged in recent times. In 1972, construction workers who were restoring the Great Mosque of Sana'a in Yemen chanced upon a cache of ancient manuscripts. These turned out to be pages of the Koran dating back to the seventh and eighth centuries, many of which contained passages that differed from the canonical and universally accepted Koran. Although most of these differences were minor, their very existence is enormously significant for the same reason as is knowledge of Aisha's Koranic modification: they challenge the Muslim assumption that the Koran is the perfect book of Allah, sent from Paradise in perfect form and preserved without any variants or modifications at all.

Chapter Three

THAT SOUNDS FAMILIAR

The Koran—Allah's exact words (with a little help from the Jews)

ACCORDING TO ISLAMIC TRADITION, Muhammad received his first revelation around 610 AD and continued to receive them until his death in 632. That would make Islam about 1,400 years old, right? Wrong. As far as Muslims are concerned, Islam is the oldest religion on earth, and the original religion of all the authentic prophets—including Abraham, Moses, and Jesus: "Lo! This, your religion, is one religion, and I am your Lord, so worship Me" (21:92). And these three are just some of the most noteworthy among the many prophets whom Allah sent to the world in order to guide erring human beings back to the straight path.

The Koran teaches that Allah sent a messenger to every people on earth (10:47), calling people back to the true God and true worship in their own language (14:4). No people has been without a prophet, and those prophets warned the people of the earth about the impending judgment of Allah (35:24). Muhammad is the seal of the prophets (33:40)—which is why mainstream Islam has always been inhospitable to those who claimed to be prophets after Muhammad.

Revealingly, with a few notable exceptions, the only prophets mentioned in the Koran are the Jewish prophets of the Hebrew Scriptures. The most important of these were Noah, Abraham, Jacob and, as one Koranic passage lists them, "David and Solomon, Job and Joseph and Moses and Aaron . . . Zacharias and John, Jesus and Elias . . . and Ishmael, Elisha, Jonah and Lot" (6:84–87). (As we will discuss later, Jesus is mentioned here merely as a human member of this roster of prophets, not as the Son of God.)

Jews and Christians are in for a tough time at the hands of their own prophets, according to the Koran. On the Day of Judgment the prophets will bear witness against those who rejected Islam, and "then will no excuse be accepted from unbelievers, nor will they receive any favours" (16:84). Of course, Infidels already have "no excuse," as the Koran insists they are ignoring manifest signs that Muhammad is a prophet. But after the Day of Judgment they will come face-to-face with their perversity, earning eternal torture for their rejection of Allah and Muhammad (33:64–68; 35:36–37; 40:47–50).

Although the Koran seethes with unrelenting hostility toward the Jews, it's clear from the Koran's many Biblically derived stories that Judaism

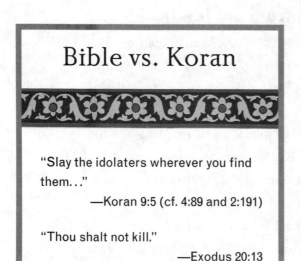

Bible vs. Koran

"Slay the idolaters wherever you find them . . ."

—Koran 9:5 (cf. 4:89 and 2:191)

"Thou shalt not kill."

—Exodus 20:13

greatly influenced Islamic theology. The story of Noah's ark appears in sura 10; Jonah and his whale in sura 37. The patriarch Abraham appears in many suras. And as we shall see, Moses figures prominently throughout the Koran, with his confrontation with Pharaoh retold numerous times.

The Fall of Adam

The Koran's borrowings from the Bible go all the way back to the story of Adam and Eve, although it does not appear at the beginning of the Koran as it does at the beginning of the Bible. Like many stories in the Koran, this one is told in whole or part several times, most fully at 2:30–39; 7:11–25; 15:28–42; 20:115–26; and 38:71–85.

The basic outlines of the Koran's Adam and Eve story will be familiar to Bible readers, but in the Koran it has many embellishments. The story, like so many other Bible stories recounted in the Koran, shows no dependence on the Biblical text, but is retold as if by someone who had heard it recited—and assumes that his own audience is already familiar with the outline of the story.

The story begins in the Koran with some material—uncredited, of course—from Jewish traditions that fill in lacunae in the Biblical text. Allah creates Adam from mud (15:26) or from dust, as another Koranic passage has it: "He created him from dust, then said to him: 'Be.' And he was" (3:59). Allah tells the angels to prostrate themselves before Adam (2:34; 7:11; 15:29; 18:50; 20:116)—a command that appears to depend upon the Biblical notion of mankind's having been created in the image of God, since otherwise it would make no sense for greater beings to bow before lesser ones.

It is noteworthy, however, that the Koran does not specify that mankind was created in the divine image (Genesis 1:26). Satan refuses to prostrate himself, thereby becoming an unbeliever (2:34). When Allah asks him why he refused his command, Satan answers out of his pride, "I am better than he: Thou didst create me from fire, and him from clay" (7:12; 38:76; cf. 15:33; 17:61).

The venerable Koran commentator Ibn Kathir explains that Satan was wrong—he was not actually better than Adam. Satan "lost hope in acquiring Allah's mercy," he says, adding that

> he committed this error, may Allah curse him, due to his false comparison. His claim that the fire is more honored than mud was also false, because mud has the qualities of wisdom, forbearance, patience and assurance, mud is where plants grow, flourish, increase, and provide good. To the contrary, fire has the qualities of burning, recklessness and hastiness. Therefore, the origin of creation directed Shaytan [Satan] to failure, while the origin of Adam led him to return to Allah with repentance, humbleness, obedience and submission to His command, admitting his error and seeking Allah's forgiveness and pardon for it.[1]

For Satan's disobedience, Allah curses him (38:77–78) and banishes him from Paradise (7:13; 15:34)—but then Satan asks for and receives a reprieve until the Day of Judgment (15:37; 38:79–81). His pride wounded, he boasts to Allah, "Seest Thou? This [Adam] is the one whom Thou hast honoured above me! If Thou wilt but respite me to the Day of Judgment, I will surely bring his descendants under my sway—all but a few!" (17:62) Satan says he will use this reprieve by spending his time tempting the Muslims away from the straight path of Islam (7:16–17; 15:39). He vows to lead astray all of mankind except Allah's "single-minded slaves" (38:83; 15:40), although Allah warns him that "over My servants no authority shalt thou have, except such as put themselves in the wrong and follow thee" (15:42).

Allah vows to fill Hell with Satan's followers (38:85). "Go thy way," he tells Satan. "If any of them follow thee,

How's that again?

In the Bible, of course, Satan is a fallen angel, cast out from Heaven for his overweening pride. But in the Koran, it is not entirely clear who Satan is. Most passages that describe him group him among the angels (2:34; 7:11; 15:28–31; 20:116; 38:71–74). However, another passage asserts that "he was one of the jinns" (a kind of invisible spirit) (18:50). And it is hard to square the idea that Satan, who is only known for his disobedience, was an angel with the Koranic affirmation that the angels "resist not Allah in that which He commandeth them, but do that which they are commanded" (66:6). If he were a jinn, his disobedience would be much more understandable, since many of the jinns "have hearts wherewith they understand not, eyes wherewith they see not, and ears wherewith they hear not. They are like cattle, nay more misguided: for they are heedless (of warning)" (7:179).

If Satan is a jinn, however, this creates another difficulty beyond the fact that he is repeatedly called an angel: why is he blamed in sura 7 and its cognate passages for disobeying a command Allah gave not to the jinns, but to the angels?

This has led to some ingenious explanations throughout Islamic history. One venerable and still widely respected commentary on the Koran, the *Tafsir Al-Jalalayn,* squares the circle with a vague assertion that Satan was "the father of the jinn, who was among the angels."[2] Similarly, a twentieth-century translator and interpreter of the Koran, the Jewish convert to Islam Muhammad Asad, identifies the jinns with the angels, though this contradicts the Koran's declaration that angels are not disobedient.[3]

The contemporary Islamic apologist Dr. Zakir Naik creatively argues that while Satan is grouped with the angels, he is never actually called an angel, and so there is no contradiction. He says that Satan, although a jinn, is nevertheless held responsible for disobeying a command that is addressed to the angels because Allah meant it collectively—all the angels as well as Satan should obey it.[4]

Such are the intellectual contortions to which true believers will sometimes subject themselves in order to decipher what is purported to be the direct word of Allah.

verily Hell will be the recompense of you (all)—an ample recompense. Lead to destruction those whom thou canst among them, with thy (seductive) voice; make assaults on them with thy cavalry and thy infantry; mutually share with them wealth and children; and make promises to them" (17:63–64). But all these gifts are illusory; Satan, the Koran tells us, "promises them nothing but deceit" (17:64).

Satan's first victim is Adam, not Eve, whose role in the Koran is substantially diminished from the pivotal one she plays in Genesis. Satan tempts Adam with the fruit of what is in one Koranic account an unidentified tree (7:19–20). But in another Koranic version of the same story, Satan tempts him by inviting him to eat from what is known in the Bible as the Tree of Life—not, as the account in Genesis has it, the Tree of the Knowledge of Good and Evil: "O Adam! Shall I lead thee to the Tree of Eternity and to a kingdom that never decays?" (20:120). The temptation, then, is not to moral awareness, and of becoming a moral arbiter, of being "like God, knowing good and evil" (Genesis 3:5), but to everlasting life. Yet they do not receive this, even though they eat from this tree: Satan's promise turns out to have been a lie. After both Adam and Eve sin by tasting the fruit, Allah chides them for heeding the words of their enemy, Satan, who had enticed the couple to eat the fruit of the tree by telling them that Allah had only forbidden them to eat it because if they did, they would become like the angels and live forever (7:22). Then he banishes them from the garden (7:24–25).

But Allah tells them that those who follow his guidance will not lose their way (20:123). There is no concept in Islam of Original Sin, or any idea that "in Adam all die" (I Corinthians 15:22). In the Koran, Adam succumbed to the lure of Satan, and that lure is always present, but if the believers heed Allah's words through his prophets, they will be rewarded with a place in Paradise. There is no indication in Islam of the Christian ideas of the brokenness of the world arising from sin, although Muhammad identified Jesus and his mother Mary as the only sinless human beings who had ever lived—and Islamic tradition adds Muhammad himself to that list. Still, although human beings have sinned, there is no idea that the kingdom of Allah is not of this world.

And Muslims throughout history have labored to establish it in this world.

Cain and Abel

Cain's murder of his brother Abel (5:30–35) is another Koranic story originating in the Bible. It departs from the Biblical narrative in recounting that after Cain killed Abel, "Allah sent a raven scratching up the ground, to show him how to hide his brother's naked corpse." At this strange sight Cain exclaimed, "Woe unto me! Am I not able to be as this raven and so hide my brother's naked corpse?" At this point, the Koran tells us, "he became repentant" (5:31).

Then follows one of the Koran's most famous verses—one that Presidents George W. Bush and Barack Obama have both cited in attempting to demonstrate that Islam is a religion of peace that abhors terrorism: "On that account We ordained for the Children of Israel that if any one slew a person—unless it be for murder or for spreading mischief in the land—it would be as if he slew the whole people: and if any one saved a life, it would be as if he saved the life of the whole people" (5:32).

The Koran doesn't explain why Cain's killing of Abel would lead to this equation of the killing of one person with the killing of the entire people. In fact, this injunction also comes from Jewish tradition. The great nineteenth-century Koranic historian William St. Clair Tisdall noted that the substance of this verse was taken from the *Mishnah Sanhedrin*: "As regards Cain who killed his brother, the Lord addressing him does not say, 'The voice of thy brother's blood crieth out,' but 'the voice of his bloods', meaning not his blood alone, but that of his descendants; and this to show that since Adam was created alone, so he that kills an Israelite is, by the plural here used, counted as if he had killed the world at large; and he who saves a single Israelite is counted as if he had saved the whole world."[5]

This exposition of Genesis makes the connection clear between the killing of Abel and the killing of the entire people, pointing out that the Biblical text refers to Abel's "bloods," that is, his descendants. But the Koran leaves this out, leaping without explanation from the murder of Abel to the warning about killing the whole people. Muhammad almost certainly didn't read these rabbinic texts, but he is likely to have heard them expounded by rabbis from the three powerful Jewish tribes of Medina, the Banu Nadir, Banu Qaynuqa, and Banu Qurayza. The Koran's account reads like a retelling of the story by a man who has listened to it attentively, but has nonetheless left out one salient detail.

King Solomon, the Queen of Sheba, talking ants, and hairy legs

Another Bible story found in the Koran is that of Solomon and the Queen of Sheba (27:16–44), though it is filled with curious elements that aren't mentioned in the Biblical account (I Kings 10:1–13). Allah gives Solomon the gift of understanding the speech of birds. The king can also understand the ants, overhearing when one ant warns the others to flee before Solomon and those with him trample them, as all the jinns, men, and birds come before him. Solomon is annoyed when he discovers that the hoopoe is not among the birds, and vows to punish him. However, the hoopoe comes in late with news of the Queen of Sheba, who has a magnificent kingdom— but she and her people are deceived by Satan and worship the sun.

The hoopoe himself is a pious Muslim; Solomon sends the bird with a letter for the Queen, largely to test the hoopoe's veracity. The letter begins with the standard Islamic invocation *Bismillah ar-Rahman ar-Rahim* (27:30)—In the name of Allah, the compassionate, the merciful—and calls the Queen and her people to accept Islam. The Queen consults with her advisers and resolves to send Solomon a gift. Ibn Kathir explains this passage as meaning, "I will send him a gift befitting for one of his status, and will wait and see what his response will be. Perhaps he will accept that and leave us alone, or he will impose a tax which we can pay him every year, so that he will not fight us and wage war against us."[6]

This idea seems modeled on the jizya, the tax prescribed for the dhimmis, the subject non-Muslim people who submit to the rule of Islamic law (9:29): the Queen seems prepared to pay a tax as a symbol of her submission to Solomon's authority. Qatadah, one of Muhammad's companions, marveled, "May Allah have mercy on her and be pleased with her—how wise she was as a Muslim and (before that) as an idolater! She understood how gift-giving has a good effect on people."[7]

But Solomon rejects the gifts, intent instead on converting the Queen to Islam. Ibn Kathir paraphrases his response to the gifts: "Are you trying to flatter me with wealth so that I will leave you alone with your *Shirk* [worshipping others besides Allah] and your kingdom?"[8] He is not disposed to leave them alone, as Muslims have never been disposed to leave Infidel kingdoms alone, when they had the means to confront them. Solomon asks one of his men to bring him her throne. The throne received, Solomon orders it altered slightly, to test the Queen's powers of recognition. Her recognition of it, according to Ibn Kathir, shows "the ultimate in intelligence and strong resolve."[9] She forsakes her other objects of worship and worships Allah alone.

Solomon devised a further test, in which the Queen had to uncover her legs; he did this, according to a venerable commentary on the Koran, the *Tafsir Al-Jalalayn*, because he "wanted to marry her but disliked the hair on her legs and so the *shaytans* [devils] prepared a depilatory and she removed the hair with it. He married her and loved her and confirmed her as the ruler over her kingdom."[10]

This Koranic story is based on the *Targum of Esther* which, although differing from the Koran in some detail, contains all the principal elements of the story: the talking animals, including one reluctant animal (a rooster in the Jewish tradition, rather than a hoopoe), the letter to the Queen of Sheba, who is a pagan (worshipping the sea in the Jewish tale, rather than the sun as in the Islamic version)—even the hairy legs.

St. Clair-Tisdall comments that this story "reminds one of such stories as we find in the 'Arabian Nights.' But strange that the Prophet could not have seen it so. Having heard it from his Jewish friends, he evidently fancied that it had been read by them in their inspired Scriptures, and as such introduced it, as we find, into the Koran."[11]

There are numerous other Jewish influences in the Koran, including specific lines. Allah says, "On the day when We say unto hell: Art thou filled? And it saith: Can there be more to come?" (50:30). St. Clair-Tisdall points out that a pre-Islamic Jewish author wrote, "The Prince of Hell shall say, day by day, give me food that I may be full." Moreover, during Ramadan, Muslims may eat and drink throughout the night "until the white thread of dawn appear to you distinct from its black thread" (2:187). In the *Mishnah Berakhoth*, "the beginning of the day is at the moment when one can but distinguish a blue thread from a white thread."[12]

Sleepy Christians become sleepy Muslims

The Koran shows traces of Christian influences as well. In the fifth, sixth, and seventh centuries, Christians who belonged to heretical sects left the Eastern Roman Empire, where they faced discrimination and hardship, and struck out east. In Muhammad's time, many of them could be found in Arabia—where they (and a smattering of orthodox Christians) unwittingly helped shape the Islamic view of Christianity as they told religious stories, some from the Bible and some embroidered from it, in the hearing of Muhammad, who duly incorporated them in the Koran.

Take, for example, the story of the "companions of the Cave and of the Inscription" (18:9–26). A group of young men sleep for around three hundred years, miraculously protected by Allah. These are, according to Ibn Kathir, "boys or young men" who are "more accepting of the truth and more guided than the elders who had become stubbornly set in their ways and clung to the religion of falsehood."[13] The men worship Allah alone, who protects them from wrathful idolaters by sheltering them in the cave.

Although the young men remain in the cave for three centuries, when they are asked how long they have been there, the Koran says they answer, "We have stayed (perhaps) a day, or part of a day." Allah "turned them on their right and on their left sides" (18:19)—presumably to preserve their bodies from decay while they slept. Ibn Abbas, Muhammad's cousin and a recognized early authority on the Koran, explains that "if they did not turn over, the earth would have consumed them."[15]

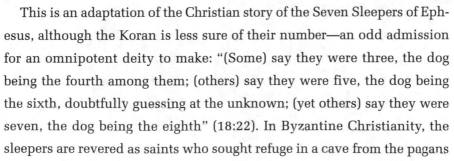

THE HADITH ILLUMINATES THE KORAN

Stifle that yawn, if you know what's good for you

"The Prophet said, 'Yawning is from Satan and if anyone of you yawns, he should check his yawning as much as possible, for if anyone of you (during the act of yawning) should say: '*Ha*', Satan will laugh at him."[14]

This is an adaptation of the Christian story of the Seven Sleepers of Ephesus, although the Koran is less sure of their number—an odd admission for an omnipotent deity to make: "(Some) say they were three, the dog being the fourth among them; (others) say they were five, the dog being the sixth, doubtfully guessing at the unknown; (yet others) say they were seven, the dog being the eighth" (18:22). In Byzantine Christianity, the sleepers are revered as saints who sought refuge in a cave from the pagans in the pre-Christian Roman Empire, were miraculously protected, and who woke up after the Empire had been Christianized. (Ibn Kathir, however, thinks the story is pre-Christian since, he says, the Jewish rabbis know of it and ask Muhammad about it as one of their tests of his prophethood.)[16]

The amazing story of Jesus and his flying clay birds

Jesus, in the Koran a Muslim prophet, explains that he will perform miracles, but only by the permission of Allah: "I have come to you, with a Sign from your Lord, in that I make for you out of clay, as it were, the figure of a bird, and breathe into it, and it becomes a bird by Allah's leave. And I heal those born blind, and the lepers, and I quicken the dead, by Allah's leave; and I declare to you what ye eat, and what ye store in your houses. Surely therein is a Sign for you if ye did believe" (3:49). Maulana Bulandshahri explains that the clause "by Allah's leave" is repeated in order to emphasize that only by Allah's permission does Jesus perform miracles—since "after witnessing these miracles, especially the raising of the dead, it is possible that a person may consider Sayyidina Isa [Master Jesus] to be Allah himself."[17]

The miracles of bringing clay birds to life does not appear in the canonical Gospels, but it is in the second-century Infancy Gospel of Thomas:

> And a certain Jew when he saw what Jesus did, playing upon the Sabbath day, departed straightway and told his father Joseph: Lo, thy child is at the brook, and he hath taken clay and fashioned twelve little birds, and hath polluted the Sabbath day. And Joseph came to the place and saw: and cried out to him, saying: Wherefore doest thou these things on the Sabbath, which it is not lawful to do? But Jesus clapped his hands together and cried out to the sparrows and said to them: Go!

and the sparrows took their flight and went away chirping. And
when the Jews saw it they were amazed, and departed and told
their chief men that which they had seen Jesus do.[18]

Other Koranic verses are also preoccupied with establishing Jesus' subordination to Allah. In the Koran, baby Jesus begins speaking from the
cradle, answering the reproaches of Mary's relatives (19:30–33). The baby
Jesus doesn't speak in the New Testament, but an Arabic Infancy Gospel
that dates from the sixth century says this: "Jesus spoke, and, indeed,
when He was lying in His cradle said to Mary His mother: I am Jesus, the
Son of God, the Logos, whom thou hast brought forth, as the Angel Gabriel
announced to thee; and my Father has sent me for the salvation of the
world." Of course, in the Koran he doesn't say he was the Son of God, but
rather the "slave of Allah" (19:30), for to have a son is not befitting for
Allah's majesty (19:35).

At one point in the Koran, the prophet Jesus asks Allah for a table laden
with food from heaven, which would be "a solemn festival and a sign from
thee" (5:114). This appears to be a vestige of the Christian Eucharist: the
consuming of the body and blood of Christ in the form of bread and wine,
which was central to all Christian groups in Muhammad's time, and which
was derived from the Last Supper accounts in the canonical Gospels, in
which the disciples sit at table with Jesus as he pronounces that the bread
is his body and the wine is his blood. In the Koran this incident seems
curious—a "solemn festival" of an unclear nature, shorn of its sacramen-
tal and salvific significance. But it is only intelligible at all as a vestige of
the Christian practice.

Wait a minute. . . . *That's* not from the Bible.

Besides relying heavily on Bible stories, Koranic stories also appear to
make use of Jewish and Christian legends, sometimes blending traditions

so that the origin becomes unclear. Take, for example, one of the Koran's most bizarre passages, and one that has become supremely important in Islamic mysticism, in which the Biblical prophet Moses figures prominently. But this particular passage appears nowhere in the Bible, and doesn't seem to have any direct antecedents in Judaism either, although some Jewish traditions do suggest themselves as possible sources.

The Koran tells of the strange journey of Moses and Khidr (18:60–82)—one of the all-time great road-trip stories. Moses, traveling with his servant, forgets the fish they had carried along for their meal. Returning to retrieve it, they encounter "one of Our servants, on whom We had bestowed Mercy from Ourselves and whom We had taught knowledge from Our own Presence" (18:65). In Islamic tradition this man is identified as Al-Khadir or Al-Khidr, or, more commonly, Khidr, "the Green Man." Some identify him as one of the prophets, others as a *wali*, a Muslim saint.

Moses asks Khidr, "May I follow thee," so that "thou teach me something of the (Higher) Truth which thou hast been taught?" (18:66) Leery, Khidr finally consents, provided Moses asks him no questions and that Moses shows patience if Khidr does something that Moses doesn't understand. Moses agrees. Khidr and Moses then get on a boat, which Khidr immediately scuttles—whereupon Moses breaks his promise and upbraids Khidr; Khidr reminds him of his promise. Shortly thereafter, Khidr murders a young man in an apparently random

THE HADITH ILLUMINATES THE KORAN

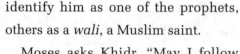

Shut up, you ass

"The Prophet said, 'When you hear the crowing of a cock, ask for Allah's Blessings for (its crowing indicates that) it has seen an angel. And when you hear the braying of a donkey, seek refuge with Allah from Satan for (its braying indicates) that it has seen a Satan.'"[19]

act, and Moses criticizes him again, and Khidr reminds him once again of his promise. Finally, Khidr rebuilds a wall in a town that had refused the two hospitality, and Moses scolds him yet again, telling Khidr that he could have gotten money for his work, which the two could have used to pay for food and lodging.

Informing Moses that their journey is over, Khidr finally explains his strange actions. (Even Muhammad wanted to hear more, commenting, "We wished that Moses could have remained patient by virtue of which Allah might have told us more about their story.")[20] Khidr damaged the ship because a king is seizing "every boat by force" (18:79), but not ones that are unserviceable—presumably the poor owners of the boat could repair it once the king passed by. Khidr killed the young man because he would grieve his pious parents with his "rebellion and ingratitude" (18:80), and Allah will give them a better son. And there was buried treasure beneath the wall that belonged to boys too young to inherit it yet—so repairing it gave them time to reach maturity while protecting the treasure from theft.

The twentieth-century Koran commentator Maulana Maududi finds a pietistic point in all this:

> You should have full faith in the wisdom of what is happening in the Divine Factory in accordance with the will of Allah. As the reality is hidden from you, you are at a loss to understand the wisdom of what is happening, and sometimes if it appears that things are going against you, you cry out, "How and why has this happened". The fact is that if the curtain be removed from the "unseen", you would yourselves come to know that what is happening here is for the best. Even if some times it appears that something is going against you, you will see that in the end it also produces some good results for you.[21]

The Koran translator Abdullah Yusuf Ali derives the lesson from the story that "even as the whole stock of the knowledge of the present day, the sciences and the arts, and in literature (if it could be supposed to be gathered in one individual), does not include all knowledge. Divine knowledge, as far as man is concerned, is unlimited." Furthermore, "There are paradoxes in life: apparent loss may be real gain; apparent cruelty may be real mercy; returning good for evil may really be justice and not generosity (18:79–82). Allah's wisdom transcends all human calculation."[22]

Perhaps understandably in light of the strangeness of the story and the mystery embedded within it, Khidr looms large in Islamic mystical tradition. The eighth-century Sufi mystic Ibrahim Bin Adham (Abou Ben Adhem) once claimed, "In that wilderness I lived for four years. God gave me my eating without any toil of mine. Khidr the Green Ancient was my companion during that time—he taught me the Great Name of God."[23] Some Koranic scholars, such as the famed medieval-era commentator Ibn Taymiyya, even consider Khidr to be immortal.[24]

And in Islamic tradition, Muhammad reinforces the importance of this story with reference to a concept that is itself straight out of the Hebrew Scriptures and Jewish tradition. In one story, a man was reciting this section of the Koran when "a cloud came down and spread over that man, and it kept on coming closer and closer to him till his horse started jumping (as if afraid of something). When it was morning, the man came to the Prophet, and told him of that experience. The Prophet said, 'That was *As-Sakinah* (tranquility or peace and reassurance along with angels) which descended because of (the recitation of) the Qur'an.'"[25] *As-Sakinah* is an adaptation of the Hebrew *Shekinah*, which refers in Jewish tradition to God's presence in the world, and the cloud clearly recalls the cloud that accompanies God's presence in Biblical passages such as Exodus 40:35.

The historic importance of the Khidr story is unfortunate, given another lesson that emerges from it in Islamic tradition: don't kill children, *unless you know they're going to grow up to be unbelievers.* One early Muslim, Najda, recalled, "The Messenger of Allah (may peace be upon him) used not to kill the children, so thou shouldst not kill them unless you could know what Khadir had known about the child he killed, or you could distinguish between a child who would grow up to be a believer (and a child who would grow up to be a non-believer), so that you killed the (prospective) non-believer and left the (prospective) believer aside."[26]

This interpretation may help to explain the persistent phenomenon of honor killing in Islamic countries and even among Muslims in the West, in which a Muslim kills a daughter or other relative who has "shamed" him by engaging in allegedly un-Islamic activity, such as dating a non-Muslim boy or adopting Western clothing. Muslims who take the Koran literally can find a justification in this passage for such acts by claiming his victim was turning into an unbeliever.

Alexander the Great—another Muslim without realizing it?

Besides Jewish and Christian traditions, Islam also contains some traces of pagan traditions. In fact, the Ka'aba, the Meccan shrine to which every Muslim, if able, is obligated to make at least one pilgrimage, was a pagan Arab shrine and a center of pilgrimage long before Muhammad began preaching Islam.

The Koran has its share of pagan-derived stories, even appropriating some pagan heroes as Muslims—notably, Alexander the Great.

According to Islamic tradition, at one point a group of skeptical rabbis devised a test for Muhammad's claim to be a prophet: "Ask him about a man who travelled a great deal and reached the east and the west of the earth. What was his story?"[27] Responding to this challenge, the Koran tells the story of that man, whom it calls Dhul-Qarnayn (18:83)—"the one with two horns." Ibn Kathir explains that Dhul-Qarnayn had "dominion over the east and the west, all countries and their kings submitted to him, and all the nations, Arab and non-Arab, served him."[28] He goes on to explain that Dhul-Qarnayn got his Koranic name "because he reached the two 'Horns' of the sun, east and west, where it rises and where it sets."[29]

But who was this great conqueror? The *Tafsir al-Jalalayn* says that "he was not a prophet" and that his name was Alexander—better known as Alexander the Great, who was depicted on coins with two ram's horns on his head.[30] Maududi notes that "early commentators on the Qur'an were generally inclined to believe" that Dhul-Qarnayn was Alexander.[31] The twentieth-century Egyptian scholar Muhammad Al-Ghazali says that Alexander the Great is "high on the list of possibilities."[32]

> ## THE HADITH ILLUMINATES THE KORAN
>
> ....
>
> ### Couldn't he have just gone behind a bush?
>
> "It was mentioned before the Prophet that there was a man who slept the night till morning (after sunrise). The Prophet said, 'He is a man in whose ears (or ear) Satan had urinated.'"[33]

Dhul-Qarnayn, however, seems to have been a pious Muslim, since he said, "Whoever doth wrong, him shall we punish; then shall he be sent back to his Lord; and He will punish him with a punishment unheard-of (before). But whoever believes, and works righteousness, he shall have a goodly reward, and easy will be his task as We order it by our Command" (18:87–88).

Modern-day Koran commentators show some embarrassment that earlier commentators insisted that the manifestly pagan Alexander the Great was identified as a Muslim in the Koran. Still, if the book can claim Abraham, Moses, all the other Biblical prophets, and Jesus as Muslims, why not claim Alexander the Great as well?[34]

There are alternative theories, however. Some have suggested instead that Dhul-Qarnayn was Cyrus the Great of Persia, or some other great ancient king. But as Muhammad Asad observes, all these pre-Islamic figures were pagans, whereas the Koran depicts Dhul-Qarnayn as a strict Muslim. The consensus today, therefore, is that his exact identification is unknown. Asad concludes that the Koranic account "has nothing to do with history or even legend, and that its sole purport is a parabolic discourse on faith and ethics, with specific reference to the problem of worldly power."[35]

As Asad notes, however, because so many commentators have identified Dhul Qarnayn with Alexander, it is not uncommon to find Muslims asserting this—and also because it does fit in neatly with the Koranic idea that Islam was mankind's original religion, and all other religions are simply later corruptions of it. Thus there were in every pre-Islamic age pure monotheists such as Dhul Qarnayn who were essentially proto-Muslims.

Muhammad the plagiarist?

The Koran's obvious repetition of pre-existing stories gave rise to charges during Muhammad's lifetime that he was passing off warmed-over Bible stories as new revelations from Allah. The Koran itself relates the objections of such skeptics: "We have heard this (before): if we wished, we could say (words) like these: these are nothing but tales of the ancients" (8:31). "Such things have been promised to us and to our fathers before! They are nothing but tales of the ancients!" (23:83) Allah, of course, defends Muhammad from such charges (25:4–6), and explains that Muhammad's detractors make this charge out of the hardness of their hearts (6:25). Allah even reacted with fury to one Muhammad skeptic, pointing out in a revelation that the man was illegitimate ("base-born") and promising to brand him on the nose (68:10–16).

But some other Koran passages suggest that Allah's anger may have stemmed from the prophet of Islam's credulity as he attempted to fill out his store of divine revelations with stories he heard from Jews and Christians in Arabia. Allah at one point complains about those who would disturb his prophet by claiming that "he is all ear"—i.e., that he is merely repeating as divine revelation what he heard from others: "Among them are men who molest the Prophet and say, 'He is (all) ear.' Say, 'He listens to what is best for you: he believes in Allah, has faith in the Believers, and is a Mercy to those of you who believe.'" Allah goes on to warn that those who dare to trouble Muhammad will be harshly punished: "But those who molest the Messenger will have a grievous penalty" (9:61).

The Koran also calls down divine woe upon those who may have tried to fool Muhammad—"those who write the Book with their own hands, and then say: 'This is from Allah,' to traffic with it for miserable price! Woe to them for what their hands do write, and for the gain they make thereby" (2:79). And when speaking of the People of the Book (which mostly refers to Jews and Christians), Allah tells Muhammad, "As for those who sell the faith they owe to Allah and their own plighted word for a small price, they shall have no portion in the Hereafter" (3:77). Some claim to be reading from the Scripture, when in fact they are reading something else: "There is among them a section who distort the Book with their tongues: (As they read) you would think it is a part of the Book, but it is no part of the Book; and they say, 'That is from Allah,' but it is not from Allah: It is they who tell a lie against Allah, and (well) they know it!" (3:78)

Did some people—particularly from among the "People of the Book"—mock Muhammad's prophetic pretensions by representing their own writings, or folkloric or apocryphal material, as divine revelation, and selling them to him? That suspicion persists.

Whatever the roots of Muhammad's prophecies, they were codified in the Koran and now form the core of the belief system of more than a billion Muslims across the world.

Chapter Four

UNDERSTANDING
THE KORAN

Lost in Translation

WHEN FOUR MUSLIMS were arrested in May 2009 for plotting to bomb two synagogues in New York, Fozia Khan of the American Muslim Women's Association declared, "We would like to stress that the people who commit these acts are misguided and confused and ignorant or unaware of Islam's ideology of peace and tolerance."[1]

This has become conventional wisdom—one might even call it unquestionable dogma—among those seeking to downplay the connection between Islam and terrorism: violent Muslim extremists, we are told, simply don't understand what the Koran says.

This axiom has a kernel of truth: large numbers of Muslims, in fact, have no firm idea of what is really in the Koran. As central as it is to Islamic faith and culture, the Koran is an Arabic book: its Arabic character is part of its essence. This notion comes from the book itself: "We have revealed the Koran in the Arabic tongue so that you may grow in understanding" (12:1). The Koran describes itself repeatedly as essentially and inherently an "Arabic Koran" (12:2; 20:113; 39:28; 41:3; 41:44; 42:7; and 43:3).

Indeed, with an eye apparently only on the local situation in Muhammad's time and not on the long-term picture, Allah says that it would not have made any sense to send down the Koran to Muhammad in any language other than Arabic, and to have done so would have incited the scorn of Infidels: "Had We sent this as a Qur'an (in the language) other than Arabic, they would have said: 'Why are not its verses explained in detail? What! (a Book) not in Arabic and (a Messenger) an Arab?'" (41:44)

All Muslims, whether or not they speak Arabic, are obligated to recite the Koran in Arabic. This means most Muslims worldwide recite their prayers from rote memory, since most Muslims worldwide today are not Arabs.

Thus, translations of the Koran occupy a curious position in the Islamic world. Muslims do not consider any translation of the Koran to be the Koran at all; it is only Allah's word when it is transmitted in Arabic. In Arabic, says English Muslim convert Mohammed Marmaduke Pickthall, the Koran is an "inimitable symphony, the very sounds of which move men to tears and ecstasy."[3] But that quality allegedly doesn't carry over to other languages—something essential is lost in translation.

THE HADITH ILLUMINATES THE KORAN

And pictures of dogs are definitely out

"The Prophet said, 'Angels do not enter a house which has either a dog or a picture in it.'"[2]

Still, translations of the Koran are tolerated for the sake of spreading Islam to non-Arabic speakers. Muslim groups worldwide work energetically to convert non-Muslims, offering Islamic materials such as translated Korans that are produced by Muslims themselves, despite the alleged impossibility of understanding the Koran except in Arabic. And yet Muslim scholars and apologists often dodge tough questions about the allegedly peaceful nature of Islam by dismissing all translations of the Koran and claiming that the book can only be truly understood in Arabic. Why they bother translating it and distributing these translations among non-Muslims remains unexplained.

According to Ibn Taymiyah, one of the most influential thinkers in Islamic history and an enduring paragon of Islamic orthodoxy, "The Arabic language is from the Religion, and the knowledge of it is an obligation. For surely the understanding of the Koran and Hadith is an obligation, and these two are not understood except with the understanding of the Arabic language, and whatever obligation is not fulfilled except by certain steps then those steps themselves become obligatory."[4]

A mainstream and influential commentator on the Koran, Ibn Kathir, further explains, "The Arabic language is the most eloquent, plain, deep and expressive of the meanings that might arise in one's mind. Therefore, the most honorable Book, was revealed in the most honorable language, to the most honorable Prophet and Messenger, delivered by the most honorable angel, in the most honorable land on earth, and its revelation started during the most honorable month of the year, Ramadan. Therefore, the Qur'an is perfect in every respect."[5]

The religious superiority of Arabic in Islam has led to an Arabic cultural hegemony in the non-Arabic Muslim world. Great non-Arab civilizations in lands that are now Muslim—most notably Iran—are not valued as part of the Muslim heritage, but are generally dismissed as products of the worthless time of *jahiliyya*, the "pre-Islamic period of ignorance." This view has led to a surprising lack of knowledge on the part of even faithful and devoted Muslims as to the precise contents of the Koran. Many recite it syllabically without any deep understanding of the meaning of the words they are pronouncing. A Pakistani Muslim once said to me, in all seriousness, "I am very proud of my religion, and have memorized almost all of the Koran. And one day I plan to get one of those translations and find out what it means."

The implications of this for contemporary debates about Islamic terrorism are profound. The point here is not that peaceful Muslims misunderstand their own religion and would become radicalized if they knew it better. But when the Koran is not immediately understood, those who believe in it understand it by means of how it is preached and presented in the local mosque. If the imams there do not preach hatred of Infidels and the necessity to fight and subjugate them, then these probably won't be live ideas in the minds of the devout—and such has long been the case in many areas of the world.

At the same time, however, the Koran says what it says, and so jihadist movements do point to chapter and verse to attempt to recruit peaceful Muslims to their cause, and to justify their actions within the Islamic community.

And when they do this, they can and do point to verses that appear benign or insignificant to non-Muslim readers.

It all depends on what the meaning of "is" is
I. "Strive in the way of Allah"

In a certain sense you really do have to understand Arabic, or at least be familiar with some Arabic concepts and terms, in order to understand the Koran fully. That's not because of the mystical qualities of the Arabic language, as Islamic apologists claim, but because many phrases that don't seem in English to be matters of particular concern for Infidels look very different when one examines their full Arabic meaning.

Take, for example, the Koran's repeated exhortation to "strive in the way of Allah" and its praise for those who do so (2:218; 4:95; 9:19–20; 9:41; 49:15; etc.) To the English-speaking reader, this sounds like a simple call to piety, to ascetical and spiritual effort. One might refer to the struggle to avoid sin as "striving in the way of Allah," and a believing and knowledgeable Muslim would consider that understanding entirely correct.

In Islamic tradition, however, to "strive in the way of Allah" refers to jihad warfare—that is, fighting to extend the boundaries of the Islamic world, called the House of Islam (*dar al-Islam*), at the expense of the non-Muslim world, called the House of War (*dar al-harb*). The Koran's declaration that those who "strive in the way of Allah...have hope of Allah's mercy" (2:218) is a call to jihad and a promise of reward for those who answer the call. "Strive" here is *jahadu,* which is a verbal form of the noun *jihad*, and in Islamic theology "jihad for the sake of Allah" or "jihad in the way of Allah" always refers to jihad warfare.

It is true that the word *jihad*, which means "struggle," has many connotations. In fact, there are as many "jihads" in Arabic as there are "struggles" in English. The Islamic Republic of Iran has a Department of Agricultural Jihad, and it has nothing to do with setting off bombs down on the farm. And as Islam's defenders unfailingly insist, "jihad" can mean an internal, spiritual struggle to lead a moral life. So when the Koran says that those who wage jihad in the way of Allah have hope of Allah's mercy, couldn't it just mean that Muslims who engage in the struggle to avoid sin will be rewarded with mercy?

It could, except that other passages make the martial implications unmistakable. Indeed, the Koran declares that the only true Muslims are those who have believed in Allah and his prophet Muhammad, "and have never since doubted, but have striven with their belongings and their persons in the Cause of Allah; such are the sincere ones" (49:15). It is hard to see how one could strive with his "belongings" and "person" in a spiritual struggle. Jihad—here, "fighting"—plainly refers to warfare in the Koran: "Those who believe in Allah and the Last Day ask thee for no exemption from fighting with their goods and persons. And Allah knoweth well those who do their duty" (9:44).

But when English translations depict the Koran as exhorting Muslims to "strive in the way of Allah," the implication to take up arms can be missed altogether.

II. "Persecution is worse than slaughter"

The Koran twice repeats that "persecution is worse than slaughter" (2:191; 2:217). This brief phrase has extraordinarily important implications but can easily be missed, since the Koran does not explain what it means. Islamic tradition fills in the details, relating that this all-important but opaque maxim was revealed to Muhammad during controversies over whether or not fighting was permissible during a sacred month.

The historical background is important here: Muhammad was born into the pagan Quryash tribe in Mecca. The Quryash rejected his prophecies, and after years of tension, in 622 Muhammad and a band of Muslims moved to Medina, where they raided Quryash caravans. At one point Muhammad sent out his trusted lieutenant, Abdullah bin Jahsh, and eight other Muslims with orders to watch for a Quraysh caravan at Nakhla, a settlement near Mecca, and "find out for us what they are doing." Abdullah and his band took this as an order to raid the caravan, which soon came along, carrying leather and raisins.

But it was the last day of the month of Rajab—a sacred month in which fighting was forbidden. This presented the Muslims with a dilemma: if they waited until the sacred month was over, the caravan would get away, but if they attacked, they would sin by desecrating the sacred month. They finally decided, according to Muhammad's first biographer, Ibn Ishaq, to "kill as many as they could of them and take what they had."

The raid, however, angered Muhammad, who refused his Koran-mandated share of the booty (one-fifth, according to Koran 8:41) and admonished the attackers that "I did not order you to fight in the sacred month."[6] But then Allah revealed Koran 2:217, explaining that the Quraysh's opposition to Muhammad was more offensive in his eyes than the Muslims' violation of the sacred month: the raid was therefore justified, "for persecution is worse than slaughter."

In other words, whatever sin the Nakhla raiders had committed in violating the sacred month was nothing compared to the Quraysh's sins. Ibn Ishaq elucidated the rationale, as explained to Muhammad by Allah: "They have kept you back from the way of God with their unbelief in Him, and from the sacred mosque, and have driven you from it when you were with its people. This is a more serious matter with God than the killing of those whom you have slain." Once he received this revelation, Muhammad accepted Abdullah's booty and prisoners, much to Abdullah's relief.

Bible vs. Koran

"Allah is only One Allah. Far is it removed from His Transcendent Majesty that He should have a son."
—Koran 4:171

"I am the Son of God."
—John 10:36

It was a watershed event, establishing a utilitarian morality that runs through Islamic theology: anything that benefits Muslims and Islam is good, and anything that harms them is evil. The twentieth century jihad theorist Sayyid Qutb accordingly explained that "Islam is a practical and realistic way of life which is not based on rigid idealistic dogma." Islam "maintains its own high moral principles," but only when "justice is established and wrongdoing is contained"—i.e., only when Islamic law rules a society—can "sanctities be protected and preserved."[7]

In other words, Muslims need not feel themselves bound by those "high moral principles" until Islamic law is established in the society where they live.

III. "Those whom your right hands possess"

The Koran allows a man to have four wives, but goes on to say that if a man cannot deal justly with multiples wives, then he should marry only one, or resort to "those whom your right hands possess" (4:3).

"Those whom your right hands possess" is another phrase that can sail right by the unwary reader. It is, in fact, the Koranic term for slave girls.

Slave girls? In his commentary on Koran 4:3, the twentieth-century Indian Islamic scholar Muhammad Aashiq Ilahi Bulandshahri explains the wisdom of this practice and longs for the good old days: "During Jihad (religion war), many men and women become war captives. The Amirul Mu'minin [Leader of the Believers, one of the titles of the caliph, the leader of the Sunni Muslims from the seventh century until 1924] has the choice of distributing them amongst the Mujahidin [jihad warriors], in which event they will become the property of these Mujahidin. This enslavement is the penalty for disbelief (kufr)."[8]

He goes on to explain that this is not ancient history—slavery has not been abolished in Islam:

> None of the injunctions pertaining to slavery have been abrogated in the Shari'ah. The reason that the Muslims of today do not have slaves is because they do not engage in Jihad (*religion war*). Their wars are fought by the instruction of the disbelievers (*kuffar*) and are halted by the same felons. The Muslim [sic]

have been shackled by such treaties of the disbelievers (*kuffar*) whereby they cannot enslave anyone in the event of a war. Muslims have been denied a great boon whereby every home could have had a slave. May Allah grant the Muslims the ability to escape the tentacles of the enemy, remain steadfast upon the Din (*religion*) and engage in Jihad (*religion war*) according to the injunctions of Shari'ah. Amin![9]

Muhammad owned slaves, and like the Bible, the Koran takes the existence of slavery for granted, even as it enjoins the freeing of slaves under certain circumstances, such as the breaking of an oath: "Allah will not call you to account for what is futile in your oaths, but He will call you to account for your deliberate oaths: for expiation, feed ten indigent persons, on a scale of the average for the food of your families; or clothe them; or give a slave his freedom" (5:89).

While the freeing of a few slaves here and there is encouraged, however, the institution itself is never questioned. The Koran even permits a man to have sexual relations with his slave girls as well as with his wives: "The believers must (eventually) win through, those who humble themselves in their prayers; who avoid vain talk; who are active in deeds of charity; who abstain from sex, except with those joined to them in the marriage bond, or (the captives) whom their right hands possess, for (in their case) they are free from blame...." (23:1–6).

A Muslim is not to have sexual relations with a woman who is married to someone else—except a slave girl: "And all married women (are forbidden unto you) save those (captives) whom your right hands possess. It is a decree of Allah for you" (4:24).

Slavery was taken for granted throughout Islamic history, as it was, of course, in the West up until relatively recent times. Yet the impetus to end slavery moved from Christendom into Islam, not the other way around.

Because the Koranic word cannot be questioned, and the book does not contain the Biblical principles that led to the abolition of slavery in the West, there has never been a Muslim abolitionist movement. Slavery ended in Islamic lands under pressure from the West.

In fact, when the British government began pressuring other regimes to abolish slavery in the nineteenth century, the Sultan of Morocco was incredulous. "The traffic in slaves," he noted, "is a matter on which all sects and nations have agreed from the time of the sons of Adam . . . up to this day." He said that he was "not aware of its being prohibited by the laws of any sect" and that the very idea that anyone would question its morality was absurd: "No one need ask this question, the same being manifest to both high and low and requires no more demonstration than the light of day."[10]

Sadiq al-Mahdi, former prime minister of Sudan, would agree. On March 24, 1999, he wrote to the United Nations High Commissioner for Human Rights, Mary Robinson, that "the traditional concept of JIHAD does allow slavery as a by-product."[11] And so slavery persists to this day in some areas of the Islamic world. The BBC reported in December 2008 that "strong evidence has emerged of children and adults being used as slaves in Sudan's Darfur region"—where a jihad rages today.[12]

Mauritanian human rights activist Boubakar Messaoud asserted in 2004 that in that country, people are born and bred as slaves: "A Mauritanian slave, whose parents and grandparents before him were slaves, doesn't need chains. He has been brought up as a domesticated animal."[13] Three years later, nothing had changed. Messaoud explained in March 2007, "It's like having sheep or goats. If a woman is a slave, her descendants are slaves."[14] Likewise in Niger, which formally abolished slavery only in 2003, slavery is a long-standing practice. Journalist and anti-slavery activist Souleymane Cisse explained that even Western colonial governments did nothing to halt the practice: "The colonial rulers preferred to ignore it because they wanted to co-operate with the aristocracy who kept these slaves."[15]

Islamic slavery has not been unknown even in the United States. When the Saudi national Homaidan Al-Turki was imprisoned for holding a woman as a slave in Colorado, he complained that "the state has criminalized these basic Muslim behaviors. Attacking traditional Muslim behaviors was the focal point of the prosecution."[16] Where did he get the idea that slavery was a "traditional Muslim behavior"? From the Koran.

Slavery: it's in the Koran. And if it's in the Koran, it is unquestionably right.

How's that again?

Who was the first Muslim?

Most people would probably answer that Muhammad himself was. After all, he was the first to receive the revelations and preach them—and indeed, Allah tells Muhammad to proclaim that he is: "Say: 'Nay! but I am commanded to be the first of those who bow to Allah (in Islam)" (6:14). "No partner hath He: this am I commanded, and I am the first of those who bow to His will" (6:163).

However, a series of contradictions is created by the Koranic dogma that the original religion of all the prophets was Islam, until their messages were corrupted by their self-serving, sinful followers. For Moses, when he meets Allah on the mountain, exclaims, "Glory be to Thee! To Thee I turn in repentance, and I am the first to believe" (7:143). Evidently some of those who hear Moses' message don't realize that he is a believer, for Pharaoh's sorcerers, overawed by Moses' miracles, say, "Lo! We ardently hope that our Lord will forgive us our sins because we are the first of the believers" (26:51).

But neither the sorcerers nor Moses may be able to claim the honors as the first Muslim, for before Moses there was Abraham who, when he and his son Ishmael were constructing the Ka'aba in Mecca, prayed, "Our Lord! Make of us Muslims, bowing to Thy (will), and of our progeny a people Muslim, bowing to Thy (will)" (2:127-128). Yet even before Abraham there was Adam, who was not only the first man but the first prophet: "Then learnt Adam from his Lord words of inspiration, and his Lord Turned towards him; for He is Oft-Returning, Most Merciful" (2:37).

Frames of reference

When reading the Koran, it is vitally important to keep in mind that Westerners, whether religious or not, and Muslims often have vastly differing frames of reference, even when considering the same individuals or concepts. Several years ago, former President George W. Bush and Karen Hughes, his former Under Secretary of State for Public Diplomacy and Public Affairs, issued greetings to the world's Muslims on the occasion of the Islamic Feast of Eid al-Adha, which commemorates the end of the pilgrimage to Mecca, the Hajj, and Abraham's willingness to sacrifice his son.

In December 2006, Bush issued a statement that read in part, "For Muslims in America and around the world, Eid al-Adha is an important occasion to give thanks for their blessings and to remember Abraham's trust in a loving God. During the four days of this special observance, Muslims honor Abraham's example of sacrifice and devotion to God by celebrating with friends and family, exchanging gifts and greetings, and engaging in worship through sacrifice and charity."[17]

And the previous January, Hughes had declared,

> Eid is a celebration of commitment and obedience to God and also of God's mercy and provision for all of us. It is a time of family and community, a time of charity.... I want to read to you a message from President Bush: "I send greetings to Muslims around the world as you celebrate Eid al-Adha. When God asked Abraham to sacrifice his son, Abraham placed his faith in God above all else. During Eid al-Adha, Muslims celebrate Abraham's devotion and give thanks for God's mercy and many blessings."[18]

In speaking of Abraham, even when doing so in the context of Eid al-Adha, Bush and Hughes were probably thinking of Genesis 22:15–18, in which Abraham is rewarded for his faith and told he will become a blessing to the nations: "By your descendants shall all the nations of the earth bless themselves, because you have obeyed my voice."

But the Muslim audiences that Bush and Hughes were addressing probably did not read Genesis. They read the Koran, in which Allah says that Abraham is an "excellent example" for the believers when he tells his family and other pagans that "there has arisen, between us and you, enmity and hatred for ever, unless ye believe in Allah and Him alone" (60:4). The same verse relates that Abraham is not an excellent example when he tells his father, "I will pray for forgiveness for you."

Thus the Koran, in the passages cited by Bush and Hughes, holds up hatred as exemplary, while belittling the virtue of forgiveness. Bush and Hughes were therefore inadvertently reinforcing a worldview that takes for granted the legitimacy of everlasting enmity between Muslims and non-Muslims—and doing so, naïvely, while attempting to build bridges between Muslims and non-Muslims. This demonstrates once again how crucial it is for American policymakers to have a detailed understanding of Islam's theological and cultural frame of reference, and of the actual teachings of the Koran. For lack of this understanding, careless statements continue to be made, and policy errors keep multiplying.

And sometimes, there's just no telling what it means

In the seventy-fourth chapter of the Koran comes a cryptic verse: "Above it are nineteen" (74:30).

That's it. "Above it are nineteen."

Above what? Nineteen what? The Koran doesn't say, and that is where the fun begins. There are innumerable theories regarding this verse, including that of the Koranic scholar Günther Lüling, who suggests a slight alteration of the text to make it a simple reference to the gates of hell—which works in context.[19]

However, Islamic scholars don't generally take kindly to suggestions that the Koranic text should be changed—it is supposed to have been delivered by the angel Gabriel to Muhammad in perfect form, and preserved in perfection ever after. Thus believers must make do with the existing cryptic verse—and they have. It has become the foundation for numerous elaborate flights of Islamic numerology, attempting to show that this verse contains a hidden, number-based key that demonstrates the Koran's miraculous character. The verse has also led to the development of mysticism surrounding the number nineteen—such that some have opined, despite the many nominees for the role of "twentieth hijacker," that there is no such person, and that precisely nineteen hijackers were chosen for the September 11 jihad missions because of the mystical significance of that number.

The verse that follows offers little help. It looks as if it dropped in from somewhere else, as it is lengthy and discursive in the middle of what is otherwise a sura full of clipped, poetic verses. It reinforces the mysticism surrounding the number nineteen, saying of the angels who act as "Guardians of the Fire" that Allah has "fixed their number only as a trial for unbelievers, in order that the People of the Book may arrive at certainty, and the believers may increase in Faith" (74:31). But if this means that the number of angels guarding hell is nineteen, how would that fact help the Jews, Christians, and other People of the Book become certain that Muhammad was a prophet, and strengthen the Muslims' faith?

The Koran leaves that question unanswered, and in Islamic history it is at that point that the numerological mysticism begins. Of course, the object of these exercises is always to demonstrate the truth of the Koran, so as to show the People of the Book that, as Ibn Kathir puts it, Muhammad "speaks according to the same thing that they have with them of heavenly revealed Scriptures that came to the Prophets before him."[21]

But ultimately Allah is absolutely sovereign regarding who will accept Muhammad's message and who won't; the verse concludes by repeating a common Koranic adage: "Allah leaves to stray those whom He pleases, and guides those whom He pleases."

THE HADITH ILLUMINATES THE KORAN

Baby looks like Mommy? Here's why

"When 'Abdullah bin Salam heard the arrival of the Prophet at Al-Madina, he came to him and said, 'I am going to ask you about three things which nobody knows except a Prophet:

(1) What is the first portent of the Hour?

(2) What will be the first meal taken by the people of Paradise?

(3) Why does a child resemble its father, and why does it resemble its maternal uncle (mother's brother)?'

"Allah's Messenger said, 'Jibril (Gabriel) has just now told me of their answers.' 'Abdullah said, 'He (i.e. Gabriel), from amongst all the angels, is the enemy of the Jews.' Allah's Messenger said, 'As for the first sign of the Hour, it will be a fire that will collect (or gather) the people from the east to the west; the first meal of the people of Paradise will be extra-lobe (caudate lobe) of fish-liver. As for the resemblance of the child to its parents: If a man has sexual intercourse with his wife and gets discharge first, the child will resemble the father, and if the woman gets discharge first, the child will resemble her.' On that 'Abdullah bin Salam said, 'I testify that you are the Apostle of Allah.'"[20]

Chapter Five

MUHAMMAD: IT'S ALL ABOUT HIM

Just another prophet— and much, much more

THE KORAN PRESENTS MUHAMMAD as the last in the line of the prophets, and the bearer of the same message his predecessors had brought to the world: "We have sent thee inspiration," Allah tells Muhammad, "as We sent it to Noah and the Messengers after him: we sent inspiration to Abraham, Isma'il, Isaac, Jacob and the Tribes, to Jesus, Job, Jonah, Aaron, and Solomon, and to David We gave the Psalms" (4:163). But his identification with the Biblical prophets doesn't end there. Most of the Koran's stories of the prophets before Muhammad are meant to demonstrate that Muhammad is experiencing the kind of opposition that the other prophets faced, and to warn the Infidels and Hypocrites who reject or deceive Muhammad that they will face the same judgment of Allah that the enemies of the earlier prophets faced.

Noah, for example, tells those who are skeptical about his flood warning that he is nothing but a "plain warner" (11:25; 26:115)—just as the Koran calls Muhammad a "warner" many times (5:19; 7:184; 7:188; 11:2; 11:12; 13:7; 15:89; 17:105). The Koran's Noah story also introduces a significant difference from the Biblical account—one that makes Noah resemble Muhammad. In Genesis 6–9, Noah has nothing to do with the unbelievers at all. God tells him, "I have determined to make an end of all flesh; for the earth is filled with violence through them; behold, I will destroy them with the earth" (Genesis 6:13), and tells him to build the ark, but he doesn't tell him to go warn the people about the flood. (However, II Peter 2:5 does call Noah a "preacher of righteousness," which suggests that Noah was indeed warning his neighbors about the impending judgment.) In the Koran, in any case, Noah comes to his people with a "clear warning" (11:25) that they should "serve none but Allah" (11:26). So in the Bible the people are punished for their corruption and violence, but in the Koran they are simply guilty of idolatry, or more precisely, *shirk*, the cardinal sin in Islam: the association of partners with Allah.

Of course, Muhammad also came to his people with a clear warning (14:52) that they should serve none but Allah (3:64), and so in the Koran Noah is a kind of proto-Muhammad, preaching a message identical to his. Even the reception Noah gets resembles how the pagan Quraysh received Muhammad. The unbelievers tell Noah he is just a man and charge him and his followers with lying (11:27), even claiming he is forging the messages he says are from Allah (11:35). Noah responds that it won't matter what he says to them if Allah has determined to lead them astray (11:34). This almost exactly replicates Muhammad's experience: Allah instructs him to tell the unbelievers that he is just a man (18:110); they charge him with lying (42:24) and with forging the Koran (11:13); and Muhammad also teaches that if Allah wills to lead someone astray, no one can guide him (7:186).

One of the unbelievers encountered by Noah is his own son, who declines to enter the ark and instead says, "I will betake myself to some mountain: it will save me from the water" (11:43). This son dies in the flood, and Noah reminds Allah that he promised to save Noah's family: "O my Lord! Surely my son is of my family!" (11:40, 11:45) But Allah tells him, "O Noah! He is not of thy family: for his conduct is unrighteous" (11:46). Ibn Kathir explains, "For his son, it had already been decreed that he would be drowned due to his disbelief and his opposition to his father."[1]

Ultimately, this offers up the same message as in the Koran's Abraham story, when the patriarch is upheld as exemplary after he disowns his relatives unless they worship Allah (60:4): belief and unbelief in Islam supersede even family ties.

Abraham . . . and Muhammad

Abraham, the father of what are fashionably known as the "three Abrahamic faiths," is presented in the Koran as a pious Muslim, another proto-Muhammad like Noah. Allah tells Muhammad to invoke Abraham in response to the attempts by the Jews and Christians of Arabia to convert him to their religion: "And they say: Be Jews or Christians, then ye will be rightly guided. Say (unto them, O Muhammad): Nay, but (we follow) the religion of Abraham, the upright, and he was not of the idolaters" (2:135). Allah directs Muhammad to underscore the unity of the messages of all the prophets: "Say ye: 'We believe in Allah, and the revelation given to us, and to Abraham, Isma'il, Isaac, Jacob, and the Tribes, and that given to Moses and Jesus, and that given to (all) prophets from their Lord: We make no difference between one and another of them: And we bow to Allah (in Islam)'" (2:136). Muhammad is directed to warn the people that those who turn away from "the religion of Abraham . . . debase their souls with folly" (2:130).

The Koran repeatedly insists that Abraham was neither a Jew nor a Christian. Allah at one point rebukes the Jews and Christians for arguing over the great patriarch's religion, about which they "have no knowledge" (3:66). Furthermore, Abraham couldn't have been a Jew or a Christian because "the Torah and the Gospel were not revealed till after him" (3:65). In reality, according to the Koran, he was a Muslim *hanif* (3:67)—the Koran commentary *Tafsir al-Jalalayn* explains that Abraham was "neither a Jew nor a Christian, but a man of pure natural belief, a *hanif* who inclines from all other religions to the Straight *Din* [religion]: a Muslim and affirmer of the Divine Unity."[2] The word "hanif" indicates one who held the original monotheistic religion that was later corrupted to create Judaism and Christianity.

What's more, Muhammad and the Muslims are "the nearest of kin to Abraham," as Ibn Kathir says in his explanation of Koran 3:67: "This Ayah [verse] means, 'The people who have the most right to be followers of Ibrahim are those who followed his religion and this Prophet, Muhammad, and his Companions.'"[3]

And Abraham's message, of course, is identical to Muhammad's. The Koran repeatedly features Abraham refusing to worship his father's idols. He confronts the idolaters among his own people, saying, "Do ye then worship, besides Allah, things that can neither be of any good to you nor do you harm?" (21:66) His words strongly resemble the ones Allah tells Muhammad to say to the Infidels: "Say: 'Do ye then take (for worship) protectors other than Him, such as have no power either for good or for harm to themselves?'" (13:16) This was to emphasize that all the prophets had the same message, and that Muhammad was one of those prophets.

It may seem strange that Allah tells Muhammad to consult with the Jews and Christians if he doubts the truth of what he has been receiving: "And if thou (Muhammad) art in doubt concerning that which We reveal unto thee, then question those who read the Scripture (that was) before thee.

Verily the Truth from thy Lord hath come unto thee. So be not thou of the waverers" (10:94).

But asking Muhammad to check with the Jews and Christians to assuage his doubts is perfectly reasonable in light of the Koranic assumption that his message was identical to the one they had received from their own prophets. The *Tafsir al-Jalalayn* says that this means Muhammad should "ask those who were reciting the Book (the Torah) before you—and they will tell you about its truthfulness."[4] This assumes, of course, that uncorrupted versions of the Jewish (and Christian) Scriptures were available in Muhammad's day—a contention that creates immense difficulties for the Islamic claim that they were corrupted at all, since copies that exist from that era are not different from the Jewish and Christian Scriptures that exist today.

Joseph . . . and Muhammad

In line with its overarching goal of bolstering Muhammad's prophetic claim, the Koran's version of the story of Joseph is essentially all about Muhammad. The focus of this story, which occupies the latter section of the Book of Genesis, is subtly changed in the Koran to transform it into a commentary on Muhammad's prophetic message and the cold reception it received from the pagan Arabs of Muhammad's Quraysh tribe. According to the twentieth-century Koranic scholar and leading jihad theorist Syed Abul Ala Maududi, one of the principal purposes of this account was to "warn [the Quraysh] that ultimately the conflict between them and the Holy Prophet would end in his victory over them. As they were then persecuting their brother, the Holy Prophet, in the same way the brothers of Prophet Joseph had treated him. . . . And just as the brothers of Prophet Joseph had to humble themselves before him, so one day the Quraish shall have to beg forgiveness from their brother whom they were then trying to crush down." Maududi points to 12:7, "Verily in Joseph and his brethren are signs for seekers," as referring to the Quraysh, who should heed the warning given them in this sura.[5]

The Koranic tale of Joseph in sura 12 is an abbreviated version of the story in Genesis 37–50, with some notable differences from the Biblical account. Joseph has a dream that eleven stars and the sun and the moon prostrate themselves to him and his family. This indicated that Joseph had been chosen as a prophet; according to Muhammad's cousin Ibn Abbas, "the dreams of Prophets are revelations from Allah."[6] Muhammad himself explained this as not applying just to the prophets, but as a general principle: "A good dream is from Allah, and a bad dream is from Satan." The prophet even recommends a ritual, involving puffing air through the lips, to defend against bad dreams: "So if anyone of you sees (in a dream) something he dislikes, when he gets up he should blow thrice (on his left side) and seek refuge with Allah from its evil, for then it will not harm him."[7]

Joseph's jealous brothers want to kill him, but finally decide to throw him down a well and tell their father, Jacob, that he is dead. In a departure from the Biblical account, Jacob doesn't believe them. Ibn Abbas explains that "he did not believe them because in another occasion they said that Joseph was killed by thieves."[8]

Joseph, sold into slavery in Egypt, becomes the target of an attempted seduction by his master's wife. Another detail missing from the Biblical account is that Joseph "would have desired her," except that Allah warded him off from "evil and lewdness. Lo! He was of Our chosen slaves" (12:24). The sharp dualism in Islam appears as Maududi sees a lesson in this: "Contrast the former characters [Jacob and Joseph] molded by Islam on the bedrock of the worship of Allah and accountability in the Hereafter with the latter [the master's wife] molded by kufr [unbelief] and 'ignorance' on the worship of the world and disregard of Allah and the Hereafter."[9]

The master's wife accuses Joseph of impropriety, but Joseph is proven innocent when his cloak is found to be torn in the back, not the front—he was, in other words, fleeing from her. Her husband laments that this is the kind of thing women do: "Lo! This is of the guile of you women. Lo! The guile of you is very great" (12:28).

The wife then holds a banquet for the women of the city, who are so awed by Joseph's good looks that they begin cutting their hands. Ibn Kathir explains, "They thought highly of him and were astonished at what they saw. They started cutting their hands in amazement at his beauty, while thinking that they were cutting the citron with their knives." The master's wife felt exonerated: "When they felt the pain, they started screaming and she said to them, 'You did all this from one look at him, so how can I be blamed?'"[10]

Joseph is ultimately imprisoned.

Bible vs. Koran

"Against them make ready your strength to the utmost of your power, including steeds of war, to strike terror into (the hearts of) the enemies of Allah and your enemies, and others besides, whom ye may not know, but whom Allah doth know. . . ."
—Koran 8:60

"You have heard that it was said, 'You shall love your neighbor, and hate your enemy.' But I say to you, love your enemies, and pray for those who persecute you in order that you may be sons of your Father who is in heaven. . . ."
—Matthew 5:43, 45

When two fellow prisoners ask him to interpret their dreams, he first tells them he is a good Muslim: he has "abandoned the ways of a people that believe not in Allah" (12:37). He follows the religion of Abraham, Isaac, and Jacob, and "never could we attribute any partners whatever to Allah" (12:38). He languishes in prison a while longer, but ultimately gets a chance to interpret the king's dream. His master's wife confesses her wrongdoing and so Joseph is freed and rewarded. Joseph's brothers later come to him for help during a famine, but they don't recognize Joseph, who demands that they bring their youngest brother, Benjamin.

A Western-oriented twentieth-century commentator on the Koran, Muhammad Asad, explains how the story then unfolds: "Joseph had wanted to keep Benjamin with himself, but under the law of Egypt he could not do this without the consent of his half-brothers." But when a goblet is discovered in his brother's bag, "Benjamin appeared to be guilty of theft, and under the law of the land Joseph was entitled to claim him as his slave, and thus to keep him in his house."[11]

The point of the Koranic story is that Allah orders all events, and none can thwart his will: "Thus did We contrive for Joseph. He could not have taken his brother according to the king's law unless Allah willed" (12:76). Joseph eventually reveals his identity to his brothers, who beg Allah's forgiveness and receive it. Jacob and his brothers go live with Joseph in Egypt.

The story ends with the declaration that all this is a warning—apparently, a warning for those who do not believe that Muhammad is a prophet. Allah tells Muhammad that he revealed the story of Joseph to him "by inspiration," for Muhammad was not present when Joseph's brothers plotted against him, so how could he know how it happened unless he is a true prophet? Thus, not only is the story of Joseph's rejection by his brothers reminiscent of Muhammad's rejection by his native tribe, but also Muhammad's knowledge of Joseph's story, presumably as he recited this sura for the first time, is itself held up as confirmation of his divine inspiration.

Moses, Pharaoh . . . and Muhammad

The Koran is considerably preoccupied with the story of Moses and particularly the confrontation between Moses and Pharaoh, retelling it in whole or part or alluding to it no fewer than twelve times. The twentieth-century Koran commentator Muhammad Al-Ghazali asserts that "every time the story appears different aspects of it emerge. Each version has details which are not included in any other version."[12] The story hews to the general outline of the Exodus account, but here again with an eye toward buttressing Muhammad's prophetic claims.

As with so many Biblically derived stories, the Koran tells this one in a way suggesting the audience has heard it before: for example, we see Moses telling Pharaoh to "send the Children of Israel with me" (7:105), and it is simply assumed that the reader will know that the Israelites were slaves in Egypt at this time.

Moses first encounters Allah in the Burning Bush, where he hears Allah's voice (20:10–17). Allah equips Moses with the staff that turns into a snake (20:20) and a hand that would turn brilliant white "without disease" (20:22), and sends him off to confront Pharaoh. Allah grants Moses' request to take Aaron along (20:36) and tells him the story of how he was plucked out of the river as a baby by "one who is an enemy to Me and an enemy to him" (20:39) and returned to his mother (20:40).

There are frequent, unmistakable comparisons to Muhammad's own story. When Allah tells Moses to go to preach to "the people of Pharaoh" (26:11), Moses replies, "I do fear

How's that again?

Allah commands Muhammad to say: "If I am astray, I only stray to the loss of my own soul" (34:50).

This, however, does not appear to be the case at all. Allah also tells the Muslims, that "in the messenger of Allah ye have a good example for him who looketh unto Allah and the Last Day, and remembereth Allah much" (33:21). Allah also says that "he who obeys the Messenger [Muhammad], obeys Allah" (4:80). The Koran tells Muslims numerous times to obey Allah and Muhammad (3:32; 3:132; 4:13; 4:59; 4:69; 5:92; 8:1; 8:20; 8:46; 9:71; 24:47; 24:51; 24:52; 24:54; 24:56; 33:33; 47:33; 49:14; 58:13; 64:12).

So if Muhammad is astray, his soul is by no means the only one at risk. With millions of Muslims looking to him as the supreme pattern of conduct and example to emulate, if he is astray, so, inescapably, are they.

that they will charge me with falsehood" (26:12)—just as they charged Muhammad (25:4). Moses is afraid the unbelievers will kill him (26:14), just as they plotted to kill Muhammad (8:30). When Allah tells Moses and Aaron again to go to Pharaoh (20:44), they respond that they're afraid "lest he hasten with insolence against us, or lest he transgress all bounds" (20:46). Allah responds that they should not be afraid, for he is with them, and sees and hears everything—recalling a message of consolation he gave to Muhammad (20:5–7). After Moses preaches to him, Pharaoh says Moses is a "veritable madman" (26: 27), just as the pagan Arabs said about Muhammad (15:6). The unbelievers ridicule Moses' signs (43:47), as they do Muhammad's (21:36), and they call Moses a sorcerer (7:109; 43:49), a slur repeated against Muhammad (10:2).

Moses and Aaron do their duty, telling Pharaoh that Allah is the only God and has "made for you the earth like a carpet spread out" (20:53), and that punishment awaits the disbelievers (20:48). Moses performs various miracles before Pharaoh, as in the Biblical account. But Pharaoh rejects their message (20:56) and says he can match their miracles (20:58). His magicians are impressed, however, and when they profess belief in "the Lord of the Worlds, the Lord of Moses and Aaron" (7:121–22; 20:70; 26:47–48), Pharaoh threatens to cut off their hands and feet on opposite sides and crucify them (7:124; 20:71; 26:49)—the same punishment that Allah commands for those who "wage war against Allah and His Messenger, and strive with might and main for mischief through the land" (5:33).

When Pharaoh threatens to kill Moses (40:26), an Egyptian believer asks him, "Will ye slay a man because he says, 'My Lord is Allah?'" (40:28) According to Maududi, this sura came to Muhammad when the unbelievers were plotting to kill him for asking this same question.[13] Likewise this unnamed believer and contemporary of Moses warns his people that they risk suffering the fate of those who rejected the earlier prophets (40:31, 34), as Muhammad does many times in the Koran (3:137; 6:11; 30:9; 43:25).

The magicians pray that Allah will "take our souls unto thee as Muslims" (7:126)—a portentous verse, reflecting the Koranic belief that Islam was the original religion of all the Biblical prophets, whose messages were later corrupted to create Judaism and Christianity.

As Pharaoh threatens Moses and his people, Moses tells the Jews, "It may be that your Lord is going to destroy your adversary and make you viceroys in the earth, that He may see how ye behave" (7:129)—a test the Jews later fail. But Allah does indeed destroy their adversary: he sends plagues upon the Egyptians, quickly enumerated as if, once again, the audience is already familiar with the story: "wholesale death, locusts, lice, frogs, and blood" (7:133). Allah saves the Israelites from Pharaoh by parting the sea so that they pass on dry land (20:77–79) and drowns Pharaoh's men (7:136). Moses prays that Allah show no mercy toward Pharaoh: "Deface, our Lord, the features of their wealth, and send hardness to their hearts, so they will not believe until they see the grievous penalty." Allah accepts their prayer, although when Pharaoh repents, Allah saves him (10:88–92).

Allah makes the Jews, "the folk who were despised," the inheritors of "the eastern parts of the land and the western parts thereof which We had blessed" (7:137). He "settled the Children of Israel in a beautiful dwelling-place," but "they fell into schisms" (10:93). The Jews, encountering idolaters in their new land, immediately turn to idolatry themselves (7:138). Moses goes up on Mount Tur (28:46) to converse with Allah and receive stone tablets promulgating laws which—in a very significant omission—the Koran does not enumerate (7:145). Allah tells him that he is testing Moses' people by allowing them to be led astray by Samiri, an extra-Biblical character introduced in the Koran (20:85).

Finding the Israelites worshipping the "image of calf" (7:148), Moses scolds Aaron for allowing them to go astray (20:92). After Samiri explains that he himself fashioned the calf from "a handful (of dust) from the footprint of the Messenger" (20:96)—widely thought to refer to a hoofprint left by the angel Gabriel's horse as Gabriel led the Israelites in battle—Moses punishes Samiri (20:97) and prays for Allah's forgiveness (7:155). Allah promises mercy "for those who do right, and practise regular charity, and those who believe in Our signs" (7:156). The words used for charity—*zakat*—and for signs—*ayat*—indicate that everyone involved in this story is a Muslim, for in the Koran's own context, only the Koran contains *ayat*, and only Muslims pay *zakat*.

The point of the story is that Allah shows mercy to "those who follow the messenger, the Prophet who can neither read nor write, whom they will find described in the Torah and the Gospel (which are) with them" (7:157). This is, of course, Muhammad, whom Muslims contend was prophesied and described in the Jewish and Christian Scriptures before

MIRACLES OF THE KORAN

NOAH'S STEAMBOAT!

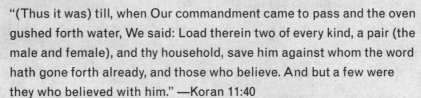

"(Thus it was) till, when Our commandment came to pass and the oven gushed forth water, We said: Load therein two of every kind, a pair (the male and female), and thy household, save him against whom the word hath gone forth already, and those who believe. And but a few were they who believed with him." —Koran 11:40

According to Masud Masihiyyen, a writer for the website Answering-Islam.org, some Islamic apologists have asserted that the oven gushing forth water refers to the way in which Noah's Ark was powered —making it a veritable pre-modern steamboat. In the context of the story, however, the gushing water actually refers to the beginning of the flood, not to the Ark at all.[14]

they were corrupted. Says Ibn Kathir, "This is the description of the Prophet Muhammad in the Books of the Prophets. They delivered the good news of his advent to their nations and commanded them to follow him. His descriptions were still apparent in their Books, as the rabbis and the priests well know."[15]

"The rabbis and priests well know"—here is assumed the Islamic belief that the Jews and Christians, or at least their leaders, know that Muhammad is a true prophet, but obstinately refuse to accept him.

Muhammad isn't crazy or demon possessed.... Really, he isn't.

While the Koran goes to great lengths to establish the legitimacy of Muhammad's prophecy, it also is compelled to defend Muhammad from charges that he was mentally unbalanced.

Allah tells Muhammad that he is a "bearer of glad tidings" and a "warner"—for "there never was a people without a warner having lived among them" (35:24; cf. 7:188; 48:8). But he is also a mere human being: Allah tells him that the Infidels would have tempted him away from the divine revelations he was receiving if Allah had not strengthened him (17:73–76) and directs him to pray for his own salvation (17:80). Allah rebukes his prophet for various shortcomings including, notoriously, for bowing to pressure from two of his wives and agreeing not to visit a favorite concubine: "O Prophet! Why holdest thou to be forbidden that which Allah has made lawful to thee? Thou seekest to please thy consorts. But Allah is oft-forgiving, most merciful" (66:1).

As a mere mortal, Muhammad, in general, does not "know what is hidden"—Allah tells him to say to the Infidels, "I but follow what is revealed to me" (6:50). He is also to disclaim any miraculous powers, saying, "I have no power over any good or harm to myself except as Allah willeth" (7:188). He must tell the Infidels, "I am but a man like yourselves"—

except for the fact that "the inspiration has come to me that your Allah is one Allah" (18:110).

Nevertheless, it is clear in the Koran that Muhammad is not an ordinary man, but is supremely important to Allah himself. "Allah and his angels send blessings on the prophet" and admonish believers to salute and bless him also, "with all respect" (33:56). Allah assures his prophet in a time of trouble that he "has not forsaken thee, nor is he displeased" (93:3) and reminds him of his many blessings—"Have We not...raised high the esteem (in which) thou (art held)?" (94:1, 4). "Did He"—that is, Allah, apparently speaking of himself in the third person, "not find thee (Muhammad) an orphan and give thee shelter" (93:6). Allah promises Muhammad a "reward unfailing" (68:3).

Allah also assures his prophet that Muhammad is not "mad or possessed" (68:2)—contrary to the claims of Muhammad's detractors who, Allah warns, will soon see who is really mad and who is sane (68:5–6). Allah directs his prophet to repeat this to his followers—that Muhammad "is neither astray nor being misled" (53:2).

Evidently the charge that Muhammad was mad was made repeatedly, for the Koran answers it numerous times. The Infidels say that Muhammad is peddling "medleys of dreams" (21:5) and claim that he is demon possessed (23:70; 37:36). But the Koran assures that he is no "soothsayer" and is not possessed (52:29). He is "not, by the grace of thy Lord, mad or"—once again—"possessed" (68:2). He is not "seized with madness. Rather, he is but a perspicuous warner" (7:184) who "was taught by one mighty in power" (53:5)—that is, Gabriel. Muhammad is—yet again—"not possessed," for "without doubt" he saw the angel Gabriel "in the clear horizon" (81:22–23).

Allah's solicitude for his prophet

Allah not only vouches for the sanity of his prophet; he also reassures him. He knows that the Infidels trouble Muhammad: "We know indeed the grief which their words do cause thee" (6:33). Indeed, Allah warns Muhammad that he is worrying about the Infidels too much: "Yet it may be, if they believe not in this statement, that thou (Muhammad) wilt torment thy soul with grief over their footsteps" (18:6). But Allah has consoling words for him: "Let not their speech then grieve thee. Verily, We know what they hide as well as what they disclose" (36:76).

Again, these consolations recur, with variations: "O Messenger! Let not those grieve thee, who race each other into unbelief." Those who do this include both the Hypocrites—a group of Muslims in name only who secretly opposed Muhammad—or those inveterate enemies of the Muslims, the Jews: "(whether it be) among those who say 'We believe' with their lips but whose hearts have no faith; or it be among the Jews, men who will listen to any lie" (5:41). Allah has not given Muhammad the Koran so that he will be saddened by the Infidels' rejection: "We have not sent down the Qur'an to thee to be (an occasion) for thy distress" (20:2).

> ## THE HADITH ILLUMINATES THE KORAN
>
> ### Yes, but which wing is which?
>
> "The Prophet said, 'If a housefly falls in the drink of anyone of you, he should dip it (in the drink), for one of its wings has a disease and the other has the cure for the disease.'"[16]

In the same spirit, Allah grants Muhammad special permission to gather an unlimited number of consorts:

> O Prophet! Lo! We have made lawful unto thee thy wives unto
> whom thou hast paid their dowries, and those whom thy right
> hand possesseth of those whom Allah hath given thee as spoils
> of war, and the daughters of thine uncle on the father's side and

the daughters of thine aunts on the father's side, and the daughters of thine uncle on the mother's side and the daughters of thine aunts on the mother's side who emigrated with thee, and a believing woman if she give herself unto the Prophet and the Prophet desire to ask her in marriage.

Here, Allah gives Muhammad a privilege that other Muslims do not enjoy, and emphasizes that Muhammad is not to be blamed for this, for it is "a privilege for thee only, not for the (rest of) believers—We are Aware of that which We enjoined upon them concerning their wives and those whom their right hands possess—that thou mayst be free from blame, for Allah is ever Forgiving, Merciful" (33:50).

On several occasions Allah even upbraids Muhammad for refusing gifts that he wants to give him—as in Muhammad's notorious marriage to Zaynab bint Jahsh, the beautiful ex-wife of Muhammad's adopted son, Zayd bin Harith. According to the *Tafsir al-Jalalayn*, after Zaynab married Zayd, Muhammad "looked at her and felt love for her whereas Zayd disliked her."[18] One day, seeking Zayd, Muhammad went to their house and chanced upon her wearing revealing clothing. Zaynab exclaimed, "He is not here, Messenger of God. Come in, you

THE HADITH ILLUMINATES THE KORAN

· ·

Water from fingertips and talking food

"Narrated 'Abdullah:...Once, we were with Allah's Messenger on a journey, and we ran short of water. He said, 'Bring the water remaining with you.' The people brought a utensil containing a little water. He placed his hand in it and said, 'Come to the blessed water, and the Blessing is from Allah.' I saw the water flowing from among the fingers of Allah's Messenger, and no doubt, we used to hear the meals (food) glorifying Allah, when it was being eaten (by him)."[17]

who are as dear to me as my father and mother!" But the Prophet of Islam hastened away in considerable agitation, murmuring something unheard and then adding audibly, "Glory be to God the Almighty! Glory be to God, who causes hearts to turn!"[19]

Zayd later goes to see Muhammad and makes a remarkable offer: "Messenger of God, perhaps Zaynab has excited your admiration, and so I will separate myself from her."

Muhammad's response is recorded in the Koran: "Keep thy wife to thyself, and fear Allah" (33:37). But then Allah himself intervened. According to the ninth-century Muslim historian Abu Ja'far Muhammad bin Jarir al-Tabari, one day Muhammad was talking with his young wife Aisha when "a fainting overcame him." Then he smiled and asked, "Who will go to Zaynab to tell her the good news, saying that God has married her to me?" He then recited the revelation Allah had just given him: "And when thou saidst unto him on whom Allah hath conferred favour and thou hast conferred favour: Keep thy wife to thyself, and fear Allah. And thou didst hide in thy mind that which Allah was to bring to light, and thou didst fear mankind whereas Allah hath a better right that thou shouldst fear Him" (33:37).

Apparently Allah had arranged the whole episode in order to teach that adopted sons were not like natural sons, and that it was thus permissible for men to marry the ex-wives of their adopted sons, an act which at the time was regarded as a form of incest: "So when [Zayd] had performed that necessary formality (of divorce) from her, We gave her unto thee in marriage, so that (henceforth) there may be no sin for believers in respect of wives of their adopted sons, when the latter have performed the necessary formality (of release) from them. The commandment of Allah must be fulfilled (33:37)."

Muhammad thus took Zaynab as his wife, protected by a direct revelation from Allah from the appearance of scandal.

Allah demonstrates a special solicitude for Muhammad on another notable occasion, related in just a few cryptic exhortations from Allah, who exclaims to Muhammad, "O Prophet! Why holdest thou to be forbidden that which Allah has made lawful to thee?" Allah further scolds his prophet for attempting to "please [his] consorts," but assures Muhammad that he is "oft-forgiving, merciful."

What's this about? It appears that Muhammad told something to one of his wives confidentially, but she told one of his other wives, who then confronted him with the secret. Allah, ever protective of Muhammad, warns them, "It may be, if he divorced you (all), that Allah will give him in exchange consorts better than you, who submit (their wills), who believe, who are devout, who turn to Allah in repentance, who worship (in humility), who travel (for Faith) and fast—previously married or virgins" (66:1–5).

Islamic tradition fills in the story. The two wives, we are told, were Aisha and Hafsa. Muhammad stayed the night with each of his wives on a rotating schedule, but one day Hafsa, on her scheduled night, caught Muhammad in bed with his concubine, Mary the Copt. Muhammad promised to stay away from Mary and asked Hafsa to keep the matter a secret, but Hafsa told Aisha. Then Allah stepped in with the revelation of the threat of divorce that we now find in sura 66, conveniently freeing Muhammad from his oath to stay away from Mary.[20]

Another tradition sanitizes this story, making it about Muhammad's bad breath after drinking some honey in the home of one of his other wives. After Hafsa and Aisha confronted him, Muhammad agreed not to drink honey anymore, leading to the revelation from Allah, "O Prophet! Why do you ban (for you) that which Allah has made lawful for you?" (66:1)[21] In this scenario the revelation concerns only Muhammad's wives' jealousy and his oath to stop drinking honey. In this case what Muhammad has held forbidden that Allah has made lawful for him would be honey: Muhammad tried to please his consorts by promising to give it up, and Allah is allowing him to break this oath and threatening the errant wives with divorce.

In any case, whether the Koranic passages concern Muhammad's honey or his *honeys*, Allah is going to great lengths to ensure that his prophet is not unduly inconvenienced by demanding wives. Readers of the Koran have two choices: they can either see passages like this as evidence that Muhammad was a false prophet who found that playing the prophetic game redounded to his earthly advantage, or they can see his life as pivotal and exemplary: the medium through which Allah revealed his commands to the human race. In the latter case, Muhammad would be by far the most important person who ever lived—and for Muslims, he is.

> # THE HADITH ILLUMINATES THE KORAN
>
> ....
>
> ## Weeping willow
>
> "The Prophet used to deliver his *Khutba* (religious talk) while standing beside a trunk of a date-palm. When he had the pulpit made, he used it instead. The trunk started crying and the Prophet went to it, rubbing his hand over it (to stop its crying)."[22]

Muhammad the "excellent example"

In light of Allah's tender solicitude for his prophet, it's no wonder the Koran and Islamic tradition are clear that Muhammad is the supreme example of behavior for Muslims to follow. The Koran calls him "an excellent model of conduct" (33:21) and repeatedly instructs Muslims to obey him (3:32; 3:132; 4:13; 4:59; 4:69; 5:92; 8:1; 8:20; 8:46; 9:71; 24:47; 24:51; 24:52; 24:54; 24:56; 33:33; 47:33; 49:14; 58:13; 64:12).

But aside from transmitting his revelations, the Koran provides only the sketchiest of information about Muhammad's words and deeds—to say nothing of his silences. So how are Muslims to find out how to "emulate and imitate their Prophet"? If Muhammad is the one who "commands them what is just and forbids them what is evil; he allows them as lawful what is good (and pure) and prohibits them from what is bad (and impure)" (7:157), how are Muslims to find out what he said?

This is one of the foundations for the authority of the Hadith—a voluminous collection of sayings of Muhammad, along with descriptions of his actions and related matters. The Hadith is verbose and detailed where the Koran is oblique and allusive, and together they form the foundation for Islamic legal reasoning. The Hadith, of course, also elucidates the Koran in many particulars—and in both, Muhammad is at the center, the standard by which all behavior is measured.

Chapter Six

WHY ALLAH HATES INFIDELS, AND WHAT HE HAS IN STORE FOR THEM

Who are the Infidels?

IN THE KORAN the Infidels (*kuffar*) are, simply, those who reject Islam. They are those who do not believe in Muhammad's message: they "treat it as a falsehood that they must meet Allah" (6:31) and "believe not in the Hereafter" (16:60). They "have bartered guidance for error" (2:16). They even dare to mock Muhammad in his proclamation of Islam. Allah tells his prophet, "When ye proclaim your call to prayer they take it (but) as mockery and sport; that is because they are a people without understanding" (5:58).

The Infidels are those who have made themselves enemies "to Allah, and His angels and His messengers, and Gabriel and Michael." Allah himself, in turn, "is an enemy to the disbelievers" (2:98). And Satan and his minions are their friends: "Lo! We have made the devils protecting friends for those who believe not" (7:27). They are also, naturally enough, the enemies of the Muslims. Allah gives permission to the believers to shorten their prayers while traveling "for fear the unbelievers may attack you: for the unbelievers are unto you open enemies" (4:101).

Who specifically are Infidels? First there are polytheists (*mushrikun*), whom Allah particularly disdains for committing the cardinal sin of shirk—associating partners with Allah. (Verses 2:105, 3:95, and many others identify the polytheists as apart from and opposed to Islam's central monotheism.)

There are also People of the Book—mostly Jews and Christians. Islamic apologists argue that Islam does not consider them Infidels, since the Koran never specifically identifies them as such. The Koran, they further note, speaks of the "unbelievers among the People of the Book" (59:2), implying that at least some People of the Book were believers, and therefore were not Infidels.

But who comprised this group among the People of the Book that the Koran identifies as believers? They were Jews and Christians who distinguished themselves by "believing" in one thing: that the Biblical prophets, as well as Jesus, preached Islam and anticipated Muhammad's arrival—and thus they became Muslims when they heard about Islam. In other words, they were proto-Muslims who recognized that the true teachings of Moses and Jesus were identical to Muhammad's teachings. Any Jews and Christians who rejected this idea and stayed true to their own religions were "unbelievers among the People of the Book"—and therefore Infidels.

Furthermore, the Koran portrays those who reject Islam as immensely, inveterately corrupt. They dare to "hide the proofs and the guidance which We revealed, after We had made it clear to mankind in the Scripture." Such people are "accursed of Allah and accursed of those who have the power to curse" (2:159). They invent "a lie against Allah," daring to claim that they have "received inspiration" as has Muhammad. They go so far as to say, "I can reveal the like of what Allah hath revealed" (6:93)—that is, they claim to be able to imitate the inimitable Koran itself. They even "spend their wealth to hinder (man) from the path of Allah, and so will they continue to spend" (8:36). Their "aim everywhere is to spread mischief through the earth and destroy crops and cattle" (2:205).

It is no surprise, then, that the Koran consistently assumes that the Infidels are not people who have come to a good faith decision that Islam is false—neither the Koran nor Islamic tradition allows for the existence of such people. The Koran declares that "the Religion before Allah is Islam," and that the People of the Book reject it only because of "envy of each other" (3:19). The Jews and Christians, says Maulana Bulandshahri, a twentieth-century Islamic scholar, recognized Muhammad "to be the final Prophet but their obstinate nature prevented them from accepting."[1]

In the Koran, those who reject Islam are never acting out of sincere conviction; rather, they are Hypocrites: "When they meet those who believe, they say: 'We believe;' but when they are alone with their evil ones, they say: 'We are really with you: We (were) only jesting'" (2:14).

Bible vs. Koran

"Let not the unbelievers think that our respite to them is good for themselves. We grant them respite that they may grow in their iniquity. But they will have a shameful punishment."

—Koran 3:178

"Bear in mind that our Lord's patience means salvation ...."

—2 Peter 3:15

The Hypocrites were a party of scheming false believers in Muhammad's day, and are spoken of many times in the Koran—so often, in fact, that their characteristics have become generally understood in Islamic thought as referring to all unbelievers throughout the ages. The bedrock assumption is that Islam is plainly and clearly true, and so anyone who rejects it must not be doing so out of intellectual or spiritual conviction, but out of narrow self-interest or desire for material gain. They "sell the faith they owe to Allah and their own plighted word for a small price" (3:77).

Thus, in the Koran the unbelievers know that Muhammad is a prophet, and yet, purely out of bad faith, they refuse to become Muslim and follow him. The Koran repeatedly emphasizes the oneness of Allah, and claims that "those to whom We have given the Book"—that is, the Jews and Christians—"know this"—that is, the truth of Muhammad's message—"as they know their own sons" (6:20). This is because, says Ibn Kathir, "they received good news from the previous Messengers and Prophets about the coming of Muhammad, his attributes, homeland, his migration, and the description of his *Ummah*."[2] In other words, their unbelief in Islam is not a sincere rejection based on honest conviction, but sheer perversity: they "lie against their own souls" (6:24). For "in their hearts is a disease; and Allah has increased their disease. And grievous is the penalty they (incur), because they are false (to themselves)" (2:10).

The worst sin of all

And in rejecting the message of Muhammad and refusing to worship Allah alone, Infidels commit the worst of all sins. "Who doth more wrong than he who inventeth a lie against Allah or rejecteth His signs?" (6:21). "Signs" in Arabic, as we have seen, is *ayat*, the name used for the verses of the Koran. This verse emphasizes that there can be no greater sin than shirk, the association of partners with Allah. The *Tafsir al-Jalalayn* asks, "Who could do greater wrong—no one does greater wrong—than someone who invents lies against Allah by ascribing a partner to Him, or denies His signs (the Qur'an)?"[3]

There is in Islam no greater evil. One modern-day Muslim writer wrote:

Murder, rape, child molesting and genocide. These are all some of the appalling crimes which occur in our world today. Many would think that these are the worst possible offences which could be committed. But there is something which outweighs all of these crimes put together: It is the crime of shirk.

Some people may question this notion. But when viewed in a proper context, the fact that there is no crime worse then shirk, will become evident to every sincere person.

There is no doubt that the above crimes are indeed terrible, but their comparison with shirk shows that they do not hold much significance in relation to this travesty. When a man murders, rapes or steals, the injustice which is done is directed primarily at other humans. But when a man commits shirk, the injustice is directed towards the Creator of the heavens and the earth; Allah. When a person is murdered, all sorts of reasons and explanations are given. But one thing that the murderer cannot claim, is that the murdered was someone who provided him with food, shelter, clothing and all the other things which keep humans aloft in this life.[4]

Consequently, "those who reject Faith, and die rejecting, on them is Allah's curse, and the curse of angels, and of all mankind" (2:161). They are destined for hell: "Verily Allah has cursed the unbelievers and prepared for them a blazing fire" (33:64).

The concept of shirk effectively delegitimizes all religious traditions except Islam. Christians associate "partners" with Allah by worshiping Jesus as the Son of God, as the Koran repeatedly admonishes them not to do. Even Jewish monotheism is not equivalent to Koranic monotheism—in part because the Koran claims that Jews hold Ezra to be the Son of God (9:30), and also because by rejecting Muhammad as a prophet they have introduced distinctions between the prophets, a practice that the Koran eschews (4:152). And Hindus and other polytheists, of course, are indisputably guilty of shirk.

So the only group that is free of shirk turns out to be the Muslims.

Are Jews and Christians saved? Sure—if they become Muslims

In arguing that the Koran does not consider Jews and Christians as Infidels, Islamic apologists point to passages like this one, claiming that the Koran teaches that even non-Muslims can be saved: "Those who believe (in the Qur'an), and those who follow the Jewish (scriptures), and the Christians and the Sabians, any who believe in Allah and the Last Day, and work righteousness, shall have their reward with their Lord; on them shall be no fear, nor shall they grieve" (2:62).

This passage, one of the Koran's celebrated "tolerance verses," seems to promise a place in Paradise to "those who follow the Jewish (scriptures), and the Christians and the Sabians"— or at least to those who are not "unbelievers among the People of the Book" (59:2). Muhammad Asad, whose popular twentieth-century commentary on the Koran struggles to make apparently unpalatable doctrines and concepts acceptable in Western eyes, exults in the spiritual generosity that the Koran appears to display to the Jews and Christians: "With a breadth of vision unparalleled in any other religious faith, the idea of 'salvation' is here made conditional upon three

---

THE HADITH ILLUMINATES THE KORAN

· ·

Convert to Islam, lose six intestines

"Ibn 'Umar reported Allah's Messenger (may peace be upon him) as saying that a non-Muslim eats in seven intestines whereas a Muslim eats in one intestine."[5]

elements only: belief in God, belief in the Day of Judgment, and righteous action in life."[6] Not, apparently, acceptance of Islam.

Asad then contradicts himself, however, by translating the beginning of this verse as "Verily, those who have attained to faith (in this divine writ)...." By adding in this parenthetical remark, Asad specifies that in order to be saved one must believe in the Koran ("this divine writ") as well as the earlier revelations. And indeed, Muslim commentators are generally not inclined to see this passage as an indication of divine pluralism. The translators Abdullah Yusuf Ali and Mohammed Marmaduke Pickthall, as well as Asad, all add parenthetical glosses that make the passage mean that Jews and Christians (as well as Sabians, whose identity is disputed) will be saved only if they become Muslims. And according to Ibn Abbas, this verse was abrogated by another verse: "If anyone desires a religion other than Islam (submission to Allah), never will it be accepted of him; and in the Hereafter he will be in the ranks of those who have lost (all spiritual good)" (3:85).[7]

Abrogation—when a Koranic verse is cancelled out by a latter, contradictory verse—is a concept acknowledged by mainstream Islamic tradition. And the "tolerant" verse hailed by Asad is seen by some to have been abrogated, since Muhammad was adamant that any fair-minded reader would find prophecies of his coming in the Scriptures of the People of the Book: "The Unbelievers say: 'No messenger art thou.' Say: 'Enough for a witness between me and you is Allah, and such as have knowledge of the Book'" (13:43). The sincere Jews and Christians would become Muslims: "Those to whom We sent the Book before this, they do believe in this (revelation)" (28:52). Those who did not convert to Islam should be reminded that Muslims, Jews, and Christians all worship the same deity (29:46).

Allah says, however, that the Muslims are superior: "Ye are the best of peoples, evolved for mankind, enjoining what is right, forbidding what is wrong, and believing in Allah." Only those Jews and Christians who become Muslims are on the right path: "If only the People of the Book had faith, it were best for them: among them are some who have faith, but most of them are perverted transgressors" (3:110).

In line with this, Sayyid Qutb opined that the verse promising salvation to Jews and Christians (2:62) applied only before Muhammad brought Islam to the world, a view supported by a saying of Muhammad recorded by Tabari, in which the Islamic prophet said that Christians who died before his coming will be saved, but those who have heard of him and yet rejected his prophetic claim will not be.[8]

Opening with hate

This view is reinforced by the traditional understanding of the most common prayer in Islam, which opens the Koran. The Fatiha (Opening) is the first chapter of the Koran and Islam's most common prayer—a pious Muslim who prays the five requisite daily prayers will recite the Fatiha seventeen times in the course of those prayers. According to Islamic tradition, Muhammad said that the Fatiha surpassed anything revealed by Allah in the Torah, the Gospel, or the rest of the Koran.[9] And indeed, it efficiently and eloquently encapsulates many of the principal themes of the Koran and of Islam in general: Allah as the "Lord of the Worlds," who alone is to be worshiped and asked for help, the merciful judge of every soul on the Last Day.

In Islamic theology, since Allah is the speaker of every word of the Koran, some have found it strange that Allah would say something like "praise be to Allah, Lord of the worlds," but the traditional Islamic understanding is that Allah revealed this prayer to Muhammad early in his career as a prophet, so that the Muslims would know how to pray.

It is for its last two verses that the Fatiha is of most concern to Infidels, and for which it has been in the news lately. A Shi'ite imam, Husham Al-Husainy, ignited controversy by paraphrasing this passage during a prayer at a Democratic National Committee winter meeting in 2007, giving the impression that he was praying that the assembled pols convert to Islam.[10] Then Imam Yusuf Kavakci of the Dallas Central Mosque prayed the Fatiha at the Texas State Senate, giving rise to the same concerns.[11]

The final two verses of the Fatiha ask Allah, "Show us the straight path, the path of those whom Thou hast favoured; not the (path) of those who earn Thine anger nor of those who go astray." The traditional Islamic understanding of this is that the "straight path" is Islam.[12] The path of those who have earned Allah's anger are the Jews, and those who have gone astray are the Christians.

Ibn Kathir explains that "the two paths He described here are both mis-guided," adding that the two paths

> are the paths of the Christians and Jews, a fact that the believer should beware of so that he avoids them. The path of the believ-ers is knowledge of the truth and abiding by it. In comparison, the Jews abandoned practicing the religion, while the Christians lost the true knowledge. This is why "anger" descended upon the Jews, while being described as "led astray" is more appro-priate of the Christians.[13]

Ibn Kathir's understanding of this passage is not a lone "extremist" inter-pretation. In fact, most Muslim commentators believe that the Jews are those who have earned Allah's wrath and the Christians are those who have gone astray.[14] One contrasting, but not majority view, is that of the Islamic scholar Nisaburi, who says that "those who have incurred Allah's wrath are the people of negligence, and those who have gone astray are the people of immoderation."[15]

Wahhabis drew criticism a few years back for adding, in parentheses, the phrases "such as the Jews" and "such as the Christians" to this passage in translated Korans printed in Saudi Arabia. Some Western commentators imagined that the Saudis made up this interpretation, and indeed the whole idea of Koranic hostility toward Jews and Christians. But in fact, Muslims all over the world learn what is the mainstream interpretation of the central prayer of their faith: that it anathematizes Jews and Christians.

The insertion of this interpretation into a translated Koran is a rather trivial matter anyway, since the Arabic text is always and everywhere normative, and since so many mainstream commentaries insist that the Jews and Christians are being criticized here—seventeen times a day, by the pious.

All this doesn't necessarily mean that the anti-Jewish and anti-Christian interpretation of the Fatiha is the "correct" one, however. While religious texts are not infinitely malleable, in this case Nisaburi's reading has as much to commend it as the other: there is nothing in the text itself that absolutely compels one to believe it is talking about Jews and Christians. And it is noteworthy that in his massive and evocatively named 30-volume commentary on the Koran, *Fi Zilal al-Qur'an* (*In the Shade of the Qur'an*), Sayyid Qutb doesn't mention Jews or Christians in connection with this passage. At the same time, however, the idea in Islam that Jews have earned Allah's anger and Christians have gone astray doesn't depend on this passage alone. The Jews have earned Allah's anger by rejecting

THE HADITH ILLUMINATES THE KORAN

No compulsion in religion, just chains

"The Verse: 'You [true believers in Islamic Monotheism, and real followers of Prophet Muhammad and his *Sunna*] are the best of peoples ever raised up for mankind. . .' means, the best for the people, as you bring them with chains on their necks till they embrace Islam (thereby save them from the eternal punishment in Hell-fire and make them enter Paradise in the Hereafter)."[16]

Muhammad (2:90), and the Christians have gone astray by holding to the divinity of Christ (5:72).

Islamic tradition also contains material linking Jews to Allah's anger and Christians to his curse, which result from their straying from the true path. (The Jews are accursed also, according to Koran 2:89, and both are accursed according to 9:30). One hadith recounts that an early Muslim, Zaid bin 'Amr bin Nufail, in his travels met with Jewish and Christian scholars. The Jewish scholar told him, "You will not embrace our religion unless you receive your share of Allah's Anger," and the Christian said, "You will not embrace our religion unless you get a share of Allah's Curse." Zaid, needless to say, became a Muslim.[17]

In light of these and similar passages it shouldn't be surprising that many Muslim commentators have understood the Fatiha to encapsulate these views.

The Infidels: They just can't help it

The Koran says that Allah ultimately controls the fate of the unbelievers. They do not accept Islam because Allah has "thrown veils on their hearts" so that they do not understand Muhammad's message (6:25–26, 30). Whenever Muhammad receives a fresh revelation, they dare to question the existence and omnipresence of Allah: "Whenever there cometh down a Sura, they look at each other, (saying), 'Doth anyone see you?' Then they turn aside: Allah hath turned their hearts (from the light); for they are a people that understand not" (9:127). Many jinns and men, says Allah, "We have made for hell: they have hearts wherewith they understand not, eyes wherewith they see not, and ears wherewith they hear not." Indeed, they're entirely bestial: "These are as the cattle—nay, but they are worse!" (7:179)

The believers shall guide mankind with Allah's truth and establish justice by means of it (7:181). In contrast, Allah says he has set barriers around the unbelievers so that they "cannot see" (36:9); the *Tafsir al-Jalalayn* says this is "another metaphor for how the path of faith is closed to them."[18] Another notable commentary agrees, arguing this verse means that Allah has "covered the insight of their hearts (so that they see not) the Truth and guidance."[19] An early Muslim also concurs: "Allah placed this barrier between them and *Islam* and *Iman* [faith], so that they will never reach it."[20] Ibn Kathir paraphrases this passage as "We [i.e., Allah] have blinded their eyes to the truth."[21] So whether Muhammad warns them or not, they will continue in unbelief (36:10). Thus only believers will benefit from Muhammad's warning (36:11). His message will profit "whoever among you wills to go straight" (81:28), but no one can so will "except as Allah wills" (81:29).

Yet despite the fact that Allah created some human beings expressly for hell, the Koran elsewhere suggests that people really do have free will: "Allah does not change a people's lot unless they change what is in their hearts" (13:11). The *Tafsir al-Jalalayn* explains that Allah does not remove "blessings from them" until they "exchange their good state for disobedience."[22] But it is hard to see how this fits in with the idea that "had Allah willed, He could have guided all mankind" (13:31); "those whom Allah leaves to stray, no one can guide" (13:33); and other passages stating that one's belief or unbelief is up to Allah.

At one point Allah tells his prophet, who is frustrated by the perversity of the unbelievers, that to change their minds is beyond Muhammad's power: "And We have put a bar in front of them and a bar behind them, and further, We have covered them up; so that they cannot see. The same is it to them whether thou admonish them or thou do not admonish them: they will not believe" (36:9–10). For even the unbelievers are manifesting the divine will: "If it had been thy Lord's will, they would all have believed, all who are on earth! Wilt thou then compel mankind, against their will, to believe? No soul can believe, except by the will of Allah, and He will place doubt (or obscurity) on those who will not understand" (10:99–100). Ibn Kathir explains, "Allah has decreed that they will be misguided, so warning them will not help them and will not have any effect on them."[23] Allah controls even the choices of individual souls to believe in him or reject him, yet even though the Infidels have no choice but to reject Allah, they will still pay the penalty in hell for this rejection: "As to those who reject Faith, it is the same to them whether thou warn them or do not warn them; they will not believe. Allah hath set a seal on their hearts and on their hearing, and on their eyes is a veil; great is the penalty they (incur)" (2:6–7).

Thus, those who reject faith do so because Allah wills it, as per these verses, not because they have free choice. Says Ibn Kathir, "These Ayat [verses] indicate that whomever Allah has written to be miserable, they shall never find anyone to guide them to happiness, and whomever Allah directs to misguidance, he shall never find anyone to guide him."[24] For "he for whom Allah hath not appointed light, for him there is no light" (24:40).

In light of Koranic verses like these, the idea of free will was declared heretical early in Islamic history. The twelfth-century Muslim jurist Ibn Abi Ya'la describes the Qadari sect, which affirmed free will:

> They are those who claim that they possess in full the capacity to act (*al-istitâ`a*), free will (*al-mashî'a*), and effective power (*al-qudra*). They consider that they hold in their grasp the ability to do good and evil, avoid harm and obtain benefit, obey and disobey, and be guided or misguided. They claim that human beings retain full initiative, without any prior status within the will of Allah for their acts, nor even in His knowledge of them. Their doctrine is similar to that of Zoroastrians and Christians. It is the very root of heresy.[25]

They will meet hellfire. . . . And then some

Even though "they would all have believed, all who are on earth" if Allah had so willed it, Allah still holds men responsible for their actions, for "on no soul doth Allah Place a burden greater than it can bear. It gets every good that it earns, and it suffers every ill that it earns" (2:286). Deathbed conversions are unacceptable: "Of no effect is the repentance of those who continue to do evil, until death faces one of them, and he says, 'Now have I repented indeed;' nor of those who die rejecting Faith: for them have We prepared a punishment most grievous" (4:18).

That grievous punishment shall be "the fire whose fuel is men and stones, which is prepared for those who reject Faith" (2:24). For soon Allah will "cast terror into the hearts of the unbelievers, for that they joined companions with Allah, for which He had sent no authority. Their abode will be the Fire, and evil is the home of the wrong-doers!" (3:151) There they will have "no defender" (10:27), but only "layers of fire above them, and layers (of fire) below them" (39:16).

On the Day of Judgment "it shall be said to them: 'Where are the (gods) ye worshipped besides Allah? Can they help you or help themselves?'" Then the Infidels will be "led to

How's that again?

The unbelievers, once damned to hell, will eat only food that increases their tortures: "No food for them save bitter thorn-fruit" (88:6).

Yet apparently the menu in hell is somewhat in flux, for another passage says that the damned will have only pus for food: "Nor hath he any food except the corruption from the washing of wounds" (69:36).

And yet despite the fact that both those verses say they are listing the *only* food the damned will eat, Allah declares elsewhere that he will also torture the damned by making them eat of "the Tree of Zaqqum," which he created as "a torment for wrong-doers." This tree springs up "in the heart of hell," and bears fruits that resemble "the heads of devils." Yet of this revolting tree the damned "must eat…and fill (their) bellies therewith" (37:62–66).

Hell in crowds." Once there, the gatekeepers will ask them, "Did not messengers come to you from among yourselves, rehearsing to you the signs of your Lord, and warning you of the meeting of this Day of yours?" And the answer will come, "True: but the Decree of Punishment has been proved true against the unbelievers!" (39:71) The Infidels will be thrown into the flames (26:92–94), amid "boiling water and in the shades of black smoke" (56:42–43).

Once cast into the flames of hell, the damned will have "food that chokes" (73:13) and "boiling water" to drink (56:54)—and that is just the beginning. Christianity and Islam share the concept of hell, but the Koran differs from the Bible in dwelling, with a certain relish, upon the tortures of the damned. The punishment of hell will be "humiliating" (4:14): the unbelievers will be "bound together in fetters" and made to wear "garments of liquid pitch" (14:49–50). The wealth that the Infidels accumulated on earth will be heated in hell's fires and fashioned into a brand for the backs of the unbelievers, reading, "This is the (treasure) which ye buried for yourselves: taste ye, then, the (treasures) ye buried!" (9:35)

The damned—the "Companions of the Fire"—will beg the blessed—the "Companions of the Garden"—for succor: "Pour down to us water or anything that Allah doth provide for your sustenance." But the blessed will tell them that "both these things hath Allah forbidden to those who rejected Him" (7:50). In fact, pleas for mercy will only bring on fiercer tortures: "if they implore relief they will be granted water like melted brass, that will scald their faces, how dreadful the drink! How uncomfortable a couch to recline on!" (18:29) Trying to get away will be useless, and the unbelievers will be forced back into the fire: "every time they wish to get away therefrom, they will be forced thereinto, and it will be said to them: 'Taste ye the penalty of the fire, the which ye were wont to reject as false'" (32:20).

The tortures of hell are unending. Allah says of the denizens of hell, their "faces covered with fire" (14:50), that "as often as their skins are roasted through, We shall change them for fresh skins, that they may taste the penalty: for Allah is exalted in power, wise" (4:56).

Unequal in this world, too

The Koran says Muslims are "the best community that hath been raised up for mankind," for they "enjoin right conduct and forbid indecency" and "believe in Allah" (3:110). By contrast, the unbelievers "among the People of the Book and among the Polytheists" are "the worst of created beings" (98:6).

And so the pious Muslim is not to treat both groups in the same way. The Infidels are bound for hell, but the punishments of the next world are not all they are to suffer: their unbelief will reap miserable dividends in this world also. Allah will go about this subtly: "Those who reject Our signs, We shall gradually visit with punishment, in ways they perceive not; respite will I grant unto them, for My scheme is strong (and unfailing)" (7:182–83). That respite from Allah's wrath is not meant to let them repent, but so that "they may grow in their iniquity" (3:178). The works of the Infidels "will bear no fruit in this world" as well as "in the Hereafter" (3:22). Allah promises, "As to those who reject faith, I will punish them with terrible agony in this world and in the Hereafter, nor will they have anyone to help" (3:56).

Apparently Muslims are to be the agents of the "terrible agony" Infidels are to experience in this world. The Koran tells Muslims to "make ready your strength to the utmost of your power, including steeds of war, to strike terror into (the hearts of) the enemies of Allah and your enemies" (8:60). For "Muhammad is the messenger of Allah," the Koran reminds Muslims, "and those with him are hard against the disbelievers and merciful among themselves" (48:29). As we shall see, this dichotomy runs through the whole of Islam.

Chapter Seven

THE MUSLIMS' WORST ENEMIES: THE KORAN ON THE JEWS

ANYONE WHO WONDERS WHY the Israeli–Palestinian conflict seems immune to any solution, and why the Palestinians perpetually disregard every agreement as soon as they sign it, should look into what the holy book of Islam says about the Jews. Reading the Koran, a believing Muslim will learn that the Jews are crafty, scheming deceivers, inveterate rebels against the authority of Allah, and above all, the fiercest enemies (along with the pagans) of the Muslims (5:82). It is hard to see how a Muslim, accepting the Koran as divine revelation, can possibly view the Jews as negotiating partners worthy of even the most basic human respect.

But how did it come to this?

Rejecting Muhammad

As we have seen, the Koran presents Muhammad as the last and greatest in the line of Biblical prophets, preaching a message identical to theirs. The authentic Torah supposedly commands Jews to follow Muhammad and recognize his prophecy—those who refuse to accept Muhammad as a prophet are, in the Muslim view, rejecting both Moses and the real prophecies of the Torah. It is no surprise, then, that in the Koran both David and Jesus curse the disbelieving Jews for their disobedience (5:78).

Yet of course, Torah-observant Jews did not and do not accept Muhammad as a prophet, and this enraged the prophet of Islam during his lifetime. Muhammad initially appealed energetically to the Jews, hoping they would accept his prophetic status. He even had the Muslims imitate the Jews by facing Jerusalem for prayers, and he adopted for the Muslims the Jews' prohibition of pork. But he was infuriated when the Jews rejected him, and Allah shared his fury in Koranic revelation: they had the Torah, and the Koran confirmed it, and yet they refused to accept the Koran! "And when there came to them a messenger from Allah, confirming

How's that again?

Shirk, the association of partners with Allah, is—as we have seen—the greatest sin in Islam. Indeed, it is unforgivable: "Allah forgiveth not that partners should be set up with Him; but He forgiveth anything else, to whom He pleaseth; to set up partners with Allah is to devise a sin Most heinous indeed" (4:48).

And yet in one notable case, Allah did indeed forgive those who associated partners with him in a most flagrant manner: "The people of the Book...worshipped the calf even after clear signs had come to them; even so We forgave them" (4:153).

Why Allah says in one place that he will not forgive those who worship others, and then in another place does so, is left unexplained.

what was with them, a party of the people of the Book threw away the Book of Allah behind their backs, as if (it had been something) they did not know!" (2:101)

Another Jewish leader noted that "no covenant was ever made with us about Muhammad." Allah again responded through his Prophet: "Is it ever so that when they make a covenant a party of them set it aside? The truth is, most of them believe not" (2:100).

Once his breach with the Jews solidified, Muhammad received a revelation instructing the Muslims to face Mecca instead of Jerusalem for prayers and declaring that the prayers in the direction of Jerusalem were only a test for the believers. The revelation even asserted that the Jews and Christians knew that the Muslims' new direction for prayer was the correct one: "The People of the Book know well that that is the truth from their Lord. Nor is Allah unmindful of what they do" (2:143–44). Dissenters were warned, "So from whencesoever thou startest forth, turn thy face in the direction of the sacred Mosque" (2:150).

Several traditions report that some rabbis at this point told Muhammad they would declare him a prophet and accept Islam if he turned his people's prayers back to Jerusalem.[1] Muhammad refused, and received another revelation: "The fools among the people will say: 'What hath turned them from the Qibla [direction for prayer] to which they were used?' Say: To Allah belong both East and West: He guideth whom He will to a Way that is straight" (2:142).

The "People of the Book:" Really a compliment?

In addition to the curses that fall on them specifically, the Jews share with Christians the opprobrium that the Koran heaps upon the "People of the Book." This comes in marked contrast to the "tolerant" attitude attributed to the Koran by many Islamophilic scholars. "Islam," writes Islamic apologist Harun Yahya, "is a religion of peace, love and tolerance. Today, however, some circles have been presenting a false image of Islam, as if there were conflict between Islam and the adherents of the two other monotheistic religions. Yet Islam's view of Jews and Christians, who are named 'the People of the Book' in the Koran, is very friendly and tolerant."[2]

Similarly, journalist Yvonne Ridley, a convert to Islam, wrote this in 2006, "We respect the people of the book. The Qur'an tells us that it is our duty to protect Jews and Christians and allow them to practice their faith in peace."[3]

Ridley didn't say anything about the Koran's directive to make the Jews and Christians "feel themselves subdued" (9:29), but other Muslims noticed it without her help. Supporters of the notorious one-eyed, hook-handed, British imam and jihad leader, Abu Hamza Al-Masri, maintained in the early 2000s a website called "Supporters of Shariah." In its Q&A section was once posted this question:

> I have been hearing some people say that the Jews and Christians are People of the Book. And since they are people of the book, we are not to call them kuffar, mushrikun (pagans) or any other derogatory terms, because Allah called them the People of the Book. May we call the Jews and Christians kuffar or pagans?

The answer was not particularly ecumenical-minded:

> Only the most ignorant and animal minded individuals would insist that prophet killers (Jews) and Jesus worshippers (Christians) deserve the same right as us. If you want to know the rights of Jews and Christians, read Surat ut-Tawba, ayah 29 [Koran 9:29, which mandates warfare against the People of the Book].[4]

And in fact, traditional Islamic law, based on verse 9:29, has never granted to the "People of the Book" the same rights as those enjoyed by

Muslims. Being designated "People of the Book" only accords to Jews, Christians, and a few others the ambiguous privilege of being allowed to practice their religions under the "protection" of Islamic law, which mandates severe restrictions to make them "feel themselves subdued" (9:29). There is some value to this, for though the "protected peoples" (*dhimmis*) do not enjoy equal rights with Muslims, at least they are allowed to maintain their religious identity. In a tradition, Muhammad directed his followers to "invite" non-Muslims to convert to Islam, and if they refuse, to call upon them to pay the jizya, the non-Muslim poll tax specified in verse 9:29—and if they refuse both, to go to war with them.[5] By contrast, those non-Muslims who do not qualify as People of the Book face the stark ultimatum to convert or die.

Thus People of the Book are allowed to enter into a state of subjugation vis-à-vis the Muslims that is not accorded to others. A dubious honor, to be sure, and one meant to enforce upon them a constant sense of degradation due to their rejection of Muhammad and Islam. The ninth-century Koranic scholar al-Tabari (838–923) emphasizes that the tax that the People of the Book must pay was meant to be humiliating and degrading: "Abasement and poverty were imposed and laid down upon them.... The dhimmis' posture during the collection of the *jizya*—[lowering themselves] by walking on their hands...."

This degradation falls especially on the Jews. Why? Because the Jews "used to kill the Messengers of God without God's leave, denying their messages and rejecting their prophethood."[6] This meme—the Jews as prophet killers—has become one of the dominant tropes of Islamic anti-Semitism. For all the Koran's repeated charges that the Jews killed their prophets (2:61; 2:87; 2:91; 3:21; 3:112; 3:181; 3:183; 4:155; 5:70), however, only one such victim is named, when the Koran depicts the Jews boasting that "we killed the Messiah, Jesus the son of Mary" (4:157). Yet, as we shall see, the same verse later states that the Jews did not actually kill Jesus, but only thought they did. So the Koran strangely declines to provide a single example to back up one of its most incendiary accusations against the Jews.

In any case, it's hardly appropriate for Muslims to act peaceably toward the Jews when the Jews, according to the Koran, are prone to war—especially against Muslims. Whenever the Jews "kindle the fire of war," says the Koran, "Allah doth extinguish it" (5:64). The *Tafsir al-Jalalayn* specified that this verse refers to "war against the Prophet."[7] And according to Bulandshahri, "The Jews make every effort to instigate wars against the Muslims, but Allah foils their attempts each time, either by instilling terror in their hearts or by their defeat in these battles."[8]

The Jews also "strive to do mischief on earth"—that is, *fasaad*, for which the punishment is specified in 5:33: "They will be killed or crucified, or have their hands and feet on alternate sides cut off, or will be expelled out of the land."

How the Jews tried to control Allah

The rebellion against Allah that has resulted in the Jews' degradation—the "terrible agony" that those who have rejected Islam are to feel "in this world" as well as in the next (3:56)—is a frequent preoccupation of the Koran. Departing from his earlier tendency to appeal to the Jews as the authorities on what Allah had revealed, Muhammad began to criticize them for concealing parts of that revelation. The Koran several times criticizes Jews for refusing to follow Muhammad, asking, "Why don't the Jews' rabbis stop their evil behavior?" (5:63)

In a particularly egregious transgression, the Jews even dare to say that "Allah's hand is fettered" (5:64). It is unclear what Jewish concept, if any, the Koran is referring to here, but the classic Islamic commentators on the Koran show no uncertainty as to what the verse is about. Ibn Kathir comments, "Allah states that the Jews, may Allah's continuous curses descend on them until the Day of Resurrection, describe Him as a miser. Allah is far holier than what they attribute to Him."[9]

According to Islam, Allah is free, with hand absolutely unfettered, and bound by no laws. He is not bound to govern the universe according to consistent and observable laws. As the Koran states, "He cannot be questioned concerning what He does" (21:23).

This theological tenet not only helped to cultivate anti-Semitism within mainstream Islam, but it also hindered the spread of science in Muslim societies. It seemed there was no point to observing the workings of the physical world; there was no reason to expect any consistent pattern. If Allah could not be counted on to be consistent, why waste time observing the order of things? It could change tomorrow. The idea that Allah had constructed the universe according to observable laws would have been for pious Muslims tantamount to saying, "Allah's hand is fettered."

Did Allah promise Israel to the Jews?

The Hamas Charter asserts that "the Islamic Resistance Movement believes that the land of Palestine is an Islamic Waqf consecrated for future Muslim generations until Judgement Day." A *waqf* is a religious endowment, a bestowal from Allah. Consequently, "it, or any part of it, should not be squandered: it, or any part of it, should not be given up. Neither a single Arab country nor all Arab countries, neither any king or president, nor all the kings and presidents, neither any organization nor all of them, be they Palestinian or Arab, possess the right to do that."[10]

In this the Charter is not unique or eccentric; rather, it represents a mainstream view among Muslims today. In recent years, however, several Muslim spokesmen have claimed that the Koran promises the land of Israel to the Jews, and that the Muslim claim to Israeli land is therefore illegitimate on Islamic grounds.

This is a comforting message that some of these spokesmen have taken to Jewish audiences, reinforcing in them the idea that the Islamic jihad imperative against Israel is simply the province of a tiny minority of extremists among Muslims, and that the voices of reason and moderation—and Koranic authenticity—will eventually prevail in the Islamic world.

Alas, these spokesmen are spreading a false message based on a partial and highly misleading reading of the Koran.

Those who make this argument usually base it primarily upon Koran 5:21, in which Moses declares, "O my people! Enter the holy land which Allah hath assigned unto you, and turn not back ignominiously, for then will ye be overthrown, to your own ruin." London-based imam Muhammad al-Husseini emphasizes the views of al-Tabari, who explains that this statement is "a narrative from God...concerning the saying of Moses...to his community from among the children of Israel and his order to them according to the order of God to him, ordering them to enter the holy land."[11]

And indeed, al-Tabari is not unique in this. Ibn Kathir says in his interpretation of 5:21 that the Jews "were the best among the people of their time"—a designation reminiscent of the Koran's calling the Muslims "the best of people" (3:110).[12] And the parallels Ibn Kathir imagines he sees

---

Bible vs. Koran

"Who is an enemy to Allah, and His angels and His messengers, and Gabriel and Michael! Then, lo! Allah (Himself) is an enemy to the disbelievers."

—Koran 2:98

"But I say to you, Love your enemies and pray for those who persecute you, so that you may be sons of your Father who is in heaven; for he makes his sun rise on the evil and on the good, and sends rain on the just and on the unjust."

—Matthew 5:44–45

between the Muslims and the Jews don't end there—he even has the Jews waging jihad:

> Allah states next that Musa [Moses] encouraged the Children of Israel to perform Jihad and enter Jerusalem, which was under their control during the time of their father Ya`qub [Jacob]. Ya`qub and his children later moved with his children and household to Egypt during the time of Prophet Yusuf [Joseph]. His offspring remained in Egypt until their exodus with Musa. They found a mighty, strong people in Jerusalem who had previously taken it over. Musa, Allah's Messenger, ordered the Children of Israel to enter Jerusalem and fight their enemy, and he promised them victory and triumph over the mighty people if they did so.

That is not the end of the story, however. Predictably, the Jews disobeyed Allah. Consequently, says Ibn Kathir, they "were punished for forty years by being lost, wandering in the land uncertain of where they should go. This was their punishment for defying Allah's command." In contrast stand the Muslims: "The Muslim Ummah [community] is more respected and honored before Allah, and has a more perfect legislative code and system of life, it has the most honorable Prophet, the larger kingdom, more provisions, wealth and children, a larger domain and more lasting glory than the Children of Israel."[13]

And the idea that the "glory" of the Children of Israel was not "lasting" undermines the entire argument that Allah promised the Land of Israel to the Jews. One might wonder why, if Allah gave Israel to the Jews, the Islamic world from Morocco to Indonesia manifests such hostility to Israel. Why have so few Muslims ever noticed that Allah actually wants the Jews to possess the Land of Israel? One reason may be that they read such

Koranic passages as 2:61, which says that some Jews who rebelled against Moses were "covered with humiliation and misery; they drew on themselves the wrath of Allah. This because they went on rejecting the Signs of Allah and slaying His Messengers without just cause. This because they rebelled and went on transgressing."

Meanwhile, those Jews who did not rebel or transgress converted to Islam. The idea that "good Jews" are those who convert to Islam is deeply rooted in Islamic tradition. In the 1970s, Muhammad Sayyid Tantawi, an Islamic scholar who is currently the grand sheikh of Al-Azhar University in Cairo, the most respected institution in Sunni Islam, wrote a 700-page treatise, *Jews in the Qur'an and the Traditions*, in which he concluded,

> [The] Qur'an describes the Jews with their own particular degenerate characteristics, i.e. killing the prophets of Allah, corrupting His words by putting them in the wrong places, consuming the people's wealth frivolously, refusal to distance themselves from the evil they do, and other ugly characteristics caused by their deep-rooted lasciviousness...only a minority of the Jews keep their word....[A]ll Jews are not the same. The good ones become Muslims, the bad ones do not.[14]

Finally, some cite another series of Koranic verses as proof that Allah promised Israel to the Jews—including, oddly enough, verses in which Muslims ("the best of peoples") are contrasted with the "perverted transgressors" among the People of the Book:

> Ye are the best of peoples, evolved for mankind, enjoining what is right, forbidding what is wrong, and believing in Allah. If only the People of the Book had faith, it were best for them: among them are some who have faith, but most of them are perverted

transgressors. They will do you no harm, barring a trifling annoyance; if they come out to fight you, they will show you their backs, and no help shall they get. Shame is pitched over them (like a tent) wherever they are found, except when under a covenant (of protection) from Allah and from men; they draw on themselves wrath from Allah, and pitched over them is (the tent of) destitution. This because they rejected the Signs of Allah, and slew the prophets in defiance of right; this because they rebelled and transgressed beyond bounds. (3:110–12)

Within this thunderous denunciation of Jews and Christians, some highlight the brief reference to some People of the Book being "under a covenant" from Allah. This most likely refers to the covenant of the dhimma, under which Jews and Christians live as subject peoples ruled by Islamic law. Some interpreters, however, argue that this refers to a covenant Allah made with the Jews to give them the Land of Israel.

But even if this were the case, the Koran also says the Jews broke whatever covenant with Allah they had made:

And because of their breaking their covenant, We have cursed them and made hard their hearts. They change words from their context and forget a part of that whereof they were admonished. Thou wilt not cease to discover treachery from all save a few of them. But bear with them and pardon them. Lo! Allah loveth the kindly. (5:13)

Being thus accursed according to the Koran, the Jews are not the legitimate inheritors of the promise made in verse 5:21. The ones who are the inheritors of that promise are those who have remained faithful to Allah—the Muslims—not those whom he has accursed—the Jews.

They didn't get it from Christianity: Koranic anti-Semitism

The Koran puts forward a clear, consistent image of the Jews: they are scheming, treacherous liars and the most dangerous enemies of the Muslims. Regardless of the actions of Jewish individuals today, and regardless of what policies the State of Israel follows, the Koran justifies an unrelenting form of anti-Semitism that will be extremely difficult to root out from the Muslim world.

An Egyptian imam, Muhammad Hussein Ya'qoub, summed up the theological argument for Islamic anti-Semitism in a January 2009 televised sermon:

> If the Jews left Palestine to us, would we start loving them? Of course not. We will never love them. Absolutely not. The Jews are infidels—not because I say so, and not because they are killing Muslims, but because Allah said: "The Jews say that Uzair is the son of Allah, and the Christians say that Christ is the son of Allah." These are the words from their mouths. They imitate the sayings of the disbelievers before. May Allah fight them. How deluded they are. [9:30] It is Allah who said that they are infidels.

And this is by no means confined to an "extremist" fringe. The Koranic impulse toward anti-Semitism is evident in the attacks on Jews emanating from Islamic preachers and scholars worldwide. Take, for example, "Jews as Depicted in the Qur'an," an article posted in 2004 on the website Islam Online. The website's founders include the prominent Islamic theologian Sheikh Yusuf al-Qaradawi, who is hailed as a moderate reformist by Western Islamic apologists.[15] The article, written by Sheikh 'Atiyyah

Saqr, formerly of Al-Azhar University, copiously cites the Koran in depicting the Jews as a gang of corrupt, deceitful cut-throats.

The Jews, he says, "used to fabricate things and falsely ascribe them to Allah." Supporting this, he quotes the verse condemning Jews for claiming Allah's hand was fettered (5:64) and another asserting that some People of the Book say "we have no duty to the Gentiles" and in doing so, "speak a lie concerning Allah knowingly" (3:75). He adds a third verse in which some Jews, asked for money, scoff that "Allah, forsooth, is poor, and we are rich!" (3:181)[16]

The Jews, continues Saqr, "love to listen to lies." This is essentially a straight rendering of the Koran's claim that the Jews are "men who will listen to any lie" (5:41). They also spread them: "There is a party of them who distort the Scripture with their tongues, that ye may think that what

MIRACLES OF THE KORAN

SEVEN EARTHS?

"Allah it is who hath created seven heavens, and of the earth the like thereof"—Koran 65:12.

"Of the earth the like thereof"? The *Tafsir al-Jalalayn* explains that this means there are seven earths as well as seven heavens.[17]

Of course, there *could* be seven earths, six as yet undiscovered. The evidence simply isn't all in yet. In any case, Ibn Abbas explains that there are indeed "seven earths but they are flat."[18] Belief in seven earths was a common feature of ancient cosmology, and thus contradicts claims that the Koran foreshadowed modern science.[19]

they say is from the Scripture, when it is not from the Scripture. And they say: It is from Allah, when it is not from Allah; and they speak a lie concerning Allah knowingly" (3:78). They dare to distort "Divine Revelation and Allah's Sacred Books. Allah says in this regard: 'Therefore woe be unto those who write the Scripture with their hands and then say, 'This is from Allah,' that they may purchase a small gain therewith. Woe unto them for that their hands have written, and woe unto them for that they earn thereby'" (2:79).[20]

Saqr also notes that in the Koran Allah says the Jews have broken "their covenant," and consequently he has "cursed them and made hard their hearts" (5:13). Indeed, says Saqr, "they never keep their promises or fulfill their words"—to demonstrate this, he quotes this Koranic passage: "Is it ever so that when ye make a covenant a party of you set it aside? The truth is, most of them believe not" (2:100).[21]

The Jews also refuse to believe in the prophets Allah has sent them, even Moses, telling him, "O Moses! We will not believe in thee till we see Allah plainly" (2:55). They are hypocrites (2:14; 2:44) who "grow arrogant" before the messengers of Allah, refusing to believe in some and killing others (2:87). They are so arrogant and haughty that they "claimed to be the sons and of Allah and His beloved ones"—a fault they share with the Christians: "The Jews and Christians say: We are sons of Allah and His loved ones" (5:18).[22]

All that represents damage the Jews do to their own souls, but Saqr—and the Koran itself—doesn't stop there. The Jews also wish "evil for people" and try to "mislead" them. "This is clear," says Saqr, "in the verse that reads: 'Many of the People of the Scripture long to make you disbelievers after your belief, through envy on their own account, after the truth hath become manifest unto them'" (2:109). They "feel pain to see others in happiness and are gleeful when others are afflicted with a calamity," as is demonstrated, according to Saqr, by this verse: "If a lucky chance befall you, it is evil unto them, and if disaster strike you they rejoice thereat" (3:120). The Koran, Saqr points out, accuses them of "taking usury when they were forbidden it, and of their devouring people's wealth by false pretences" (4:161).[23]

Even worse, "it is easy for them to slay people and kill innocents," for "nothing in the world is dear to their hearts than shedding blood and murdering human beings." Saqr grounds this on the Koran's assertion that the Jews "slew the prophets wrongfully" (2:61). The Jews are characterized, says Saqr, by "cowardice.... To this, the Qur'an refers when saying: 'Ye are more awful as a fear in their bosoms than Allah. That is because they are a folk who understand not. They will not fight against you in a body save in fortified villages or from behind walls'" (59:14). Saqr also excoriates the Jews for their "love for this worldly life"—as does the Koran: "And thou wilt find them greediest of mankind for life and (greedier) than the idolaters" (2:96).[24]

But Saqr concludes on an optimistic note, voicing hopes that some day Allah will help the Muslims to mete out divine punishment to their enemies; "Almighty Allah told us that He'd send to them people who'd pour on them rain of severe punishment that would last till the Day of Resurrection. All this gives us glad tidings of the coming victory of Muslims over them once Muslims stick to strong faith and belief in Allah and adopt the modern means of technology." [26]

THE HADITH ILLUMINATES THE KORAN

Rotting meat? Blame the Jews

"The Prophet said, 'But for the Israelis, meat would not decay, and but for Hawwa (Eve), wives would never betray their husbands.'"[25]

One should consider Saqr's interpretation in light of Iran's feverish attempts to acquire a nuclear bomb, alongside the repeated vows by Iranian president Mahmoud Ahmadinejad to wipe Israel off the map. For Ahmadinejad and his ilk, eliminating the Jewish state is not just a foreign policy goal; it is a religious imperative.

Jewish apes and pigs

Oddly, Saqr is silent about the infamous Koranic passages in which Allah transforms disobedient Jews into apes and pigs (2:63–66; 5:59–60; 7:166). Although some scholars argue that this curse only applied to a specific group of Jewish Sabbath-breakers, the Jews of today are commonly called "apes and pigs" throughout much of the Muslim world. Although Saudi authorities promised after the September 11 attacks to revise textbooks that taught hatred against Jews and Christians, as late as 2006 Saudi texts still referred to Jews as "apes" and Christians as "swine."[27] And in April 2008 a British employment tribunal awarded 70,000 pounds ($115,000) to a teacher who had been fired from a Saudi-funded Islamic school for exposing that the school's textbooks spoke of "the repugnant characteristics of the Jews" and asserted, "Those whom God has cursed and with whom he is angry, he has turned into monkeys and pigs. They worship Satan."[28]

There is an endless parade of similar examples. In March 2004 Sheikh Ibrahim Mudayris, speaking on official Palestinian Authority television, railed against "the Jews today taking revenge for their grandfathers and ancestors, the sons of apes and pigs."[29] And during the swine flu scare in May 2009, Sheikh Ahmad 'Ali 'Othman, the superintendent of da'wa [Islamic proselytizing] affairs at the Egyptian Ministry of Religious Endowments, declared that "all pigs are descended from the Jews whom Allah transformed into apes, swine and worshippers of Satan, and must therefore be slaughtered." Othman based his argument on Koran 5:60, one of the Koran's notorious "apes and pigs" passages.[30]

In his televised sermon denouncing the Jews regardless of their actions in Israel or elsewhere, Muhammad Hussein Ya'qoub also invoked this theme: "As for you Jews—the curse of Allah upon you. The curse of Allah upon you, whose ancestors were apes and pigs.... Allah, we pray that you transform them again, and make the Muslims rejoice again in seeing them as apes and pigs. You pigs of the earth! You pigs of the earth! You kill the Muslims with that cold pig [blood] of yours."[31]

Jews as apes and pigs: it's in the Koran, holy book of the religion of peace.

What the Jews have to do

Yet the Jews need not suffer their fate passively, for the Koran offers them a way out. Its second sura contains an extended meditation on all that Allah did for the Jews, and the ingratitude with which they repaid him. Allah warns them to "part not with My revelations for a trifling price" (2:41), which Islamic commentators generally interpret as an exhortation to put the service of Allah before the concerns of this world. Maududi says this verse "refers to the worldly benefits for the sake of which [the Jews] were rejecting God's directives."[32] Many have speculated, however, that this verse amounts to Muhammad's rebuke of those who sold him material that they told him was divine revelation, but wasn't (2:79).

At any rate, the one thing the Jews can do to get back into Allah's good graces is to convert to Islam (2:43). This might sail right by the English-speaking reader, since the translations exhort them to be "steadfast in prayer" and to "practise regular charity" (as Abdullah Yusuf Ali has it), but in Arabic the word used here for prayer is *salat*, and for charity *zakat*; these refer specifically to Islamic prayer and almsgiving. Non-Muslims cannot pray *salat* or pay *zakat*. Ibn Kathir is forthright about the need for this conversion: Allah "commands the People of the Book to be with, and among the *Ummah* of Muhammad."[33] Likewise, Sayyid Qutb observes that here Allah "invites the Israelites to join the Muslims in their religious practices, and to abandon their prejudices and ethnocentric tendencies."[34]

The Koran goes on, Maududi explains, to refer to "the best-known episodes of Jewish history. As these episodes were known to every Jewish child, they are narrated briefly rather than in detail. The reference is intended to remind the Jews both of the favours with which the Israelites had been endowed by God and of the misdeeds with which they had responded to those favours."[35] The favors include the Israelites being rescued from Pharaoh (2:49–50) and the feeding of the people with manna and quails in the wilderness (2:57; 61), which were matched by Jewish misdeeds such as the golden calf episode (2:54–55), all culminating in the avowal that, as we have seen, the Jews "were covered with humiliation and misery; they drew on themselves the wrath of Allah. This because they went on rejecting the Signs of Allah and slaying His Messengers without just cause. This because they rebelled and went on transgressing" (2:61).

THE HADITH ILLUMINATES THE KORAN

Jewish trees?

"Abu Huraira reported Allah's Messenger (may peace be upon him) as saying: 'The last hour would not come unless the Muslims will fight against the Jews and the Muslims would kill them until the Jews would hide themselves behind a stone or a tree and a stone or a tree would say: Muslim, or the servant of Allah, there is a Jew behind me; come and kill him; but the tree Gharqad would not say, for it is the tree of the Jews.'"[36]

Ibn Kathir applies these words to all Jews: "This Ayah [verse] indicates that the Children of Israel were plagued with humiliation, and that this will continue, meaning that it will never cease. They will continue to suffer humiliation at the hands of all who interact with them, along with the disgrace that they feel inwardly."[37]

Thus, the Koranic view of the Jews can be summarized quite succinctly: they're doomed to disgrace, unless they become Muslims.

What about Jerusalem?

When discussing the Israeli–Palestinian conflict, pundits and politicians often tell us that Jerusalem is one of the holy cities of Islam—indeed, its third holiest city, right after Mecca and Medina.

But in reality, the Islamic claim to Jerusalem is extremely tenuous, based only on a legendary journey of Muhammad—a journey that is at best a dream and at worst a fabrication. The Koran refers to this journey only obliquely and in just one place; Islamic tradition fills in the details and connects Jerusalem with the words of the Koran. But the Koran itself never mentions Jerusalem even once—an exceptionally inconvenient fact for Muslims who claim that the Palestinians must have a share of Jerusalem because the city is sacred to Islam.

Muhammad's famous Night Journey is the basis of the Islamic claim to Jerusalem. The Koran's sole reference to this journey appears in the first verse of sura 17, which says that Allah took Muhammad from "the Sacred Mosque" in Mecca "to the farthest [al-aqsa] Mosque." There was no mosque in Jerusalem at this time, so the "farthest" mosque probably wasn't really the one that now bears that name in Jerusalem, the Al-Aqsa mosque located on the Temple Mount. Nevertheless, Islamic tradition is firm that this mosque was in Jerusalem.

That's all the Koran says, but according to Islamic tradition, Muhammad's vision of this journey was as dramatic as anything that happened during his prophetic career. His first biographer, Ibn Ishaq, records that Muhammad described the journey as beginning "while I was lying in Al-Hatim or Al-Hijr," that is, an area in Mecca opposite the Ka'bah, identified by Islamic tradition as the burial place of Hagar and Ishmael, when "Gabriel came and stirred me with his foot."[38] Soon after that "someone came to me and cut my body open from here to here"—and he gestured from his throat to his pubic area. The one who had come to him, Muhammad continued, "then took out my heart. Then a golden tray full of Belief was brought to me and my heart was washed and was filled (with Belief) and then returned to its original place."[39] At that point Muhammad was presented with the Buraq, an animal he described as "half mule, half donkey, with wings on its sides with which it propelled its feet."[40]

"When I came up to mount him," Muhammad reported according to Ibn Ishaq, "he shied. Gabriel placed his hand on its mane and said, 'Are you not ashamed, a Buraq, to behave in this way? By God, none more honorable before God than Muhammad has ever ridden you before.' The animal was so ashamed that he broke out into a sweat and stood still so that I could mount him."[41]

They went to the Temple Mount, and from there to Paradise itself. According to a hadith, Muhammad explained,

> I was carried on it, and Gabriel set out with me till we reached the nearest heaven. When he asked for the gate to be opened, it was asked, "Who is it?" Gabriel answered, "Gabriel." It was asked, "Who is accompanying you?" Gabriel replied, "Muhammad." It was asked, "Has Muhammad been called?" Gabriel replied in the affirmative. Then it was said, "He is welcomed. What an excellent visit his is!"

Muhammad entered the first heaven, where he encountered Adam. Gabriel prods Muhammad, "This is your father, Adam; pay him your greetings." The Prophet of Islam duly greets the first man, who responds, "You are welcome, O pious son and pious Prophet." Gabriel then carries Muhammad to the second heaven, where the scene at the gate is reenacted, and once inside, John the Baptist and Jesus greet him: "You are welcome, O pious brother and pious Prophet." In the third heaven, Joseph greets him in the same words, and Muhammad and Gabriel go on, greeted by other prophets at other levels of heaven.

In the sixth heaven is Moses, occasioning another dig at the Jews. "When I left him," Muhammad says, "he wept. Someone asked him, 'What makes you weep?' Moses said, 'I weep because after me there has been sent (Muhammad as a Prophet) a young man, whose followers will enter Paradise in greater numbers than my followers.'"

In the seventh heaven, Muhammad meets Abraham, has further visions, and receives the command that the Muslims pray fifty times daily. But returning, Muhammad passes by Moses, who tells him to go back and argue Allah down to a more manageable number. Muhammad complies, finally agreeing with Allah on five daily prayers.[43]

Muhammad's account of his journey to Paradise met with considerable skepticism—perhaps abetted by his wife Aisha's statement that "the apostle's body remained where it was but God removed his spirit by night."[44] Nonetheless, it forms the basis of the Muslim claim to Jerusalem to this day.

THE HADITH ILLUMINATES THE KORAN

How to identify Jewish rats

"The Prophet said, 'A group of Israelites were lost. Nobody knows what they did. But I do not see them except that they were cursed and transformed into mouses or rats, for if you put the milk of a she-camel in front of a mouse or a rat, it will not drink it, but if the milk of a sheep is put in front of it, it will drink it.'"[42]

Abraham sacrifices...Ishmael

The claim to Jerusalem is by no means the sole instance of Islamic appropriation of things Jewish, even while casting curses on the Jewish people themselves. Muslims generally believe that the famous episode in which the patriarch Abraham almost sacrificed his beloved son—presented in Genesis as an object lesson in obedience to God and a prohibition of human sacrifice—featured Abraham's son Ishmael, the father of the Arabs, not Isaac, the father of the Jews. Islamic scholars argue that one sign that the Jews corrupted the Scriptures they received from Allah is that they changed the famous story to suit their own purposes by claiming Isaac was the son who was almost sacrificed.

In the Koranic account (37:102–12), Abraham sees in a dream that he must sacrifice his son, but—similar to the Biblical story—Allah stops him just before he is about to do it; it was all a test. Which son did Abraham almost sacrifice? The son is not actually named in the Koranic text, but Isaac's birth follows the story of the near-sacrifice, thus implying that the son almost sacrificed was Ishmael. Ibn Kathir explains that—surprise, surprise!—the Jews got the story all wrong, wrong, wrong:

> According to their Book, Allah commanded Ibrahim [Abraham] to sacrifice his only son, and in another text it says his first-born son. But here they falsely inserted the name of Ishaq [Isaac]. This is not right because it goes against what their own Scripture says. They inserted the name of Ishaq because he is their ancestor, while Isma'il [Ishmael] is the ancestor of the Arabs. They were jealous of them, so they added this idea and changed the meaning of the phrase "only son" to mean "the only son who is with you," because Isma'il had been taken with his mother to Makkah [Mecca]. But this is a case of falsification and distortion, because the words "only son" cannot be said except in the case of one who has no other son. Furthermore, the firstborn son has a special status that is not shared by subsequent children, so the command to sacrifice him is a more exquisite test.[45]

So once again, the Jews are guilty of falsifying and distorting what they have received from Allah. And as the Koran says, they will pay the penalty for their disobedience, arrogance, and obstinacy in this world as well as in the next (3:56).

Chapter Eight

THE KORAN ON CHRISTIANS: THEY'RE NOT SO HOT, EITHER

"Muslims respect and revere Jesus?"

Like Christians, Muslims respect and revere Jesus. Islam teaches that Jesus is one of the greatest of God's prophets and messengers to humankind.

Like Christians, every day, over 1.3 billion Muslims strive to live by his teachings of love, peace, and forgiveness. Those teachings, which have become universal values, remind us that all of us, Christians, Muslims, Jews, and all others have more in common than we think.

S O READ AN ADVERTISEMENT that the Council on American Islamic Relations (CAIR) placed in California newspapers in March 2004 as part of one of its much-touted "bridge building" efforts. And it all sounds great. Muslims often approach Christians in this way, explaining to them that there is a whole chapter of the Koran named after

Jesus' mother Mary (sura 19), and that the Koran teaches the Virgin Birth of Christ and other Christian doctrines. It's a great way to build bridges—by emphasizing what Christians and Muslims hold in common, rather than what divides them. But will this bridge collapse if any weight is put on it?

Maybe not. CAIR is at least partially right: Jesus has a prominent place in the Koran. The Islamic holy book refers to Jesus frequently, usually either as "Jesus Christ" or as "Jesus the Son of Mary" (although it uses a form of the name Jesus, *Isa*, that is not used by Arabic-speaking Christians, and which in reality is closer to "Esau" than to "Jesus"). The references to the "Son of Mary" reflect the Koran's acceptance of the Virgin Birth—everyone in antiquity was referred to as the son of his father, not of his mother, unless his father was unknown. And the Koran also affirms the Virgin Birth directly (3:47). Furthermore, besides "Son of Mary," Jesus is called Christ (3:45; 4:157; 4:171–72; 5:17; 5:72; 5:75; 9:30–31) and the "Word" of Allah (3:45; 4:171), recalling the Gospel of John, which also identifies Jesus as God's Word in a striking passage that also says that "the Word was God" (John 1:1; 1:14).

But the Koran and the New Testament also disagree, quite profoundly, about Jesus Christ. Yes, Jesus is the Word of Allah in the Koran, but the Word is not Allah. Allah explains, "The similitude of Jesus before Allah is as that of Adam; He created him from dust, then said to him: 'Be.' And he was" (3:59).

There is a remnant in this of the Christian doctrine that Christ is the New Adam who brings to life all those who died in the old Adam (see, for example, I Corinthians 15:22). The Koran, however, never ventures into that territory; rather, it limits the meaning of the Divine "Word" to signifying that Jesus came into existence by the express command of Allah—not that Jesus shares in any way in the divine nature.

Similarly, in the Koran, "Christ" (*al-Masih*) is essentially a proper name, not a title; Jesus is not the "anointed one" promised to the Jews or to anyone else. Islamic scholars explain that the name is derived from the Arabic verb *Massaha*, which means to anoint someone with oil for healing. So then is Jesus the Messiah, the anointed one? Not in the Christian sense—they say he bears this name solely because he healed others.

Instead of the Messiah and the Savior of the world, Jesus in the Koran is only one among many prophets—even if he is favored above his fellow prophets, for Allah has given him "clear (signs), and strengthened him with the holy spirit" (2:253). In fact, another passage says that Jesus is himself a "spirit proceeding from" Allah (4:171).

The spirit of a being is, of course, its very life, but Muslim theologians have never considered the implications of this title, any more than they have considered the implications of calling Jesus Allah's "word." The Koran repeats twelve times that Allah has no son, saying that to claim that he does would impugn his transcendent majesty (2:116; 10:68; 17:111; 18:4; 19:35; 19:88; 19:91; 19:92; 21:26; 23:91; 39:04; 43:81). It also specifically rejects the Christian idea that Jesus is the Son of God (4:171; 9:30), at one point implying, remarkably, that Muhammad thought of the question in purely physical terms: "How can [Allah] have a Son when He has no consort?" (6:101)

Ultimately, the Koran concludes that Christians have departed from the truth by teaching the Trinity and the Divinity of Christ: "So believe in Allah and His messengers, and say not 'Three.' Cease! (It is) better for you! Allah is only One Allah. Far is it removed from His Transcendent Majesty that He should have a son" (4:171).

Setting the Christians straight

Indeed, Islamic tradition presents itself as the correction to the errors of the faction-ridden Christians. According to Ibn Ishaq, the first eighty verses of the Koran's third chapter were revealed after a delegation of Christians came from the Yemeni city of Najran. This group included a bishop, Abu Haritha ibn 'Alqama, who received money, servants, and other favors from "the Christian kings of Byzantium." Abu Haritha, says Ibn Ishaq, knew that Muhammad was a prophet, but refused to accept him for fear of losing the loot that the Byzantines were lavishing upon him.

Ibn Ishaq records that the delegation "differed among themselves in some points, saying [Jesus] is God; and He is the son of God; and He is the third person of the Trinity, which is the doctrine of Christianity." They presented arguments defending these propositions to Muhammad, but he would have none of it. When they told him that they had submitted to God, he responded, "You lie. Your assertion that God has a son, your worship of the cross, and your eating pork hold you back from submission." Allah then revealed much of sura 3, refuting their assertions and—in the Muslim view—giving the world the truth about Jesus and Christianity.[1]

Jesus' mother, Aaron's sister?

That chapter—sura 3—relates the story of Mary's birth and early life, telling us that her mother was the "wife of Imran"—that is, Amram, the father of Moses and Aaron (3:35). This verse, along with 19:27, in which Mary is called "sister of Aaron," has given rise to the charge that Muhammad confused Miriam the sister of Moses with Mary the Mother of Jesus, since the names are identical in Arabic: Maryam. When confronted about this, Muhammad had a ready answer: "The (people of the old age) used to give names (to their persons) after the names of Apostles and pious persons who had gone before them."[2] While this may explain why Mary is called "Sister of Aaron," it doesn't explain why she is clearly depicted as the daughter of Imran.

In any case, Imran's wife dedicates the child in her womb to the service of Allah; when she gives birth, she says of Mary, "I crave Thy protection for her and for her offspring from Satan the outcast" (3:36). Every child, according to Muhammad in a hadith, is "pricked by the Satan" after he is born—that's why newborn babies cry. But Mary and Jesus were preserved from Satan's touch. Although the child is a female and "the female is not like the male" (3:36), the wife of Imran fulfills her vow: Mary is dedicated to Allah's service. Maulana Bulandshahri says that she went to live in the Temple in Jerusalem, which he calls the *Baitul Muqaddas* ("Holy House") and, in keeping with the Islamic idea that the original message of all the Jewish prophets was Islam, identifies as a mosque.[3] There Mary is miraculously fed (3:37).

This story recalls one told in the *Protoevangelium of James*, a second-century Christian document: in it, Mary's parents, Joachim and Anne, prayed to God for an end to their childlessness, and dedicated the child they subsequently conceived to the Lord in thanksgiving.[4] Later, when Mary was three, she went to live in the Temple, where she was fed by an angel. This is the sort of thing that earned Muhammad the charge that he was just retelling "fables of the men of old" (6:25; 8:31; 16:24; 23:83; 25:5; 27:68; 46:17; 68:15; 83:13), not divine revelation. But Muslims respond that the Koran is sorting out the true from

How's that again?

Allah has sent prophets—"warners"—to every nation on earth: "There never was a people, without a warner having lived among them (in the past)" (35:24).

Yet before Muhammad, no warner had ever come to the Arabs. Muhammad brings "the Truth from thy Lord, that thou mayest admonish a people to whom no warner has come before thee, in order that they may receive guidance" (32:3).

The Koran, however, also speaks of the prophet Hud, who was sent to the 'Ad people (7:65) of southern Arabia, and of the prophet Salih, who preached to the Thamud people, kin of the 'Ad (26:142–43). What's more, Ishmael, who is identified with the Arabs as a people, is included in the Koran's roster of prophets (19:54).

the false about Christianity among the revelations that were corrupted by the followers of Jesus.

John the Baptist: Preparing the way for... no one, actually

Like the Gospel of Luke, the Koran also recounts the birth of John the Baptist in the context of the birth of Jesus (19:2–40). The Koranic account hits the highlights of Luke 1:5–80, but with numerous important differences. In both books, an angel tells John's father, Zechariah, that he will become a father despite his old age and his wife's barrenness. In the Koran, however, when the great event is announced, there is no hint that, as Luke's Gospel says, "many will rejoice" at the birth of John the Baptist. The Koran does not depict John as the messenger sent to prepare the way of the Lord; he is simply pious ("meaning that he was pure and had no inclination to do sins," says Ibn Kathir, in an echo of some Christian traditions that John committed no sins), devout, and kind to his parents (19:13–14).[5] Nor does the Koran say that John will, as the angel tells Zechariah in Luke, be "great before the Lord" and "filled with the Holy Spirit, even from his mother's womb," and the Muslim holy book gives no hint whatsoever that John will "make ready for the Lord a people prepared" (Luke 1:14–15, 17).

Instead, Zechariah is only told that the boy's name is to be John, and that "we have given the same name to none before (him)" (19:7). But why John enjoys this unique name is left unexplained. Once John is born, Allah gives him "the book" and "wisdom," indicating that he is a prophet, but there is no hint that he is to prepare the way for the coming of Jesus.

Still, John seems to be set aside for a particular purpose in a way others were not. Allah even gives him an effusive benediction: "Peace on him the day he was born, and the day he dieth and the day he shall be raised alive!" (19:15). Oddly enough, Jesus pronounces this same benediction upon himself later in the same Koranic chapter: "Peace on me the day I was born, and the day I die, and the day I shall be raised alive!" (19:33) And in both the Gospel (Luke 1:20) and the Koran (19:10), Zechariah is unable to speak after his vision, although the Koran presents this only as a sign of Allah's power, while the Gospel depicts it as punishment for Zechariah's unbelief.

Nevertheless, even after all this the Koran says nothing about why John has received this singular treatment. The Koranic account thus subtly contradicts the Christian view of Christ, and of John the Baptist as his precursor, as presented in Luke's Gospel. There is nothing in the Koran paralleling the Gospel's connection of Zechariah's son John with Elijah (Luke 1:17), the prophet who was to return before the Lord's coming (Malachi 4:5–6).

And the same thing happens in the Koran's account of the birth of Christ.

Christ, who is not the Savior, is born

The Koran begins one of its accounts of Jesus' birth with a reaffirmation of Muhammad's prophethood. Allah tells Muhammad that he is about to give him "tidings of things hidden," and reminds him that he was not present at the events to be recounted (3:44). Ibn Kathir explains the point of this: even though Muhammad wasn't present at these events, "Allah disclosed these facts" to him as if he had been an eyewitness.[6] Thus the account in itself is presented as evidence of Muhammad's prophethood. The resemblance to the familiar Christian story is, of course, passed over in silence, but that story was most likely familiar enough to at least some of Muhammad's audience that it may have given rise to the charge that so infuriated both Muhammad and Allah: that the prophet of Islam was merely retailing "tales of the ancients" (6:25; 8:31; 23:83).

The angels' announcement of Jesus' birth in the Koran differs from Gabriel's annunciation in Luke 1:30–35 in several key particulars: in the Muslim book, Jesus is identified as a "word" from Allah (3:45) and is called "Messiah," or Christ, but not "Son of the Most High." Muslim exegetes explain that Jesus is Allah's word not in the sense of being divine, as in

Bible vs. Koran

"O Zachariah! Lo! We bring thee tidings of a son whose name is John; we have given the same name to none before (him)."

—Koran 19:7

"Do not be afraid, Zechariah, for your prayer is heard, and your wife Elizabeth will bear you a son, and you shall call his name John. And you will have joy and gladness, and many will rejoice at his birth; for he will be great before the Lord, and he shall drink no wine nor strong drink, and he will be filled with the Holy Spirit, even from his mother's womb. And he will turn many of the sons of Israel to the Lord their God, and he will go before him in the spirit and power of Elijah, to turn the hearts of the fathers to the children, and the disobedient to the wisdom of the just, to make ready for the Lord a people prepared."

—Luke 1:13–17

John 1:1, but because he was created without a human father by Allah's word, as was Adam (3:59).

The angel tells Mary only that she will be the mother of a "holy son" (19:19). Given the Koran's frequent, vehement denials that Allah has a son, it is unsurprising that there is no hint of Mary's son also being the "Son of the Most High" (Luke 1:32). Indeed, the concept of divine sonship is rejected again in Koran 19:35.

Although Jesus is not presented as divine, the Koran does say that he was virginally conceived (19:20). This has been interpreted in a somewhat—one might say—unusual way. As Ibn Kathir notes, "Many scholars of the predecessors (Salaf) have mentioned that at this point the angel [Gabriel] blew into the opening of the garment that she was wearing. Then the breath descended until it entered into her vagina and she conceived the child by the leave of Allah."[7]

But just as the Koran sketches out a singular place for John the Baptist but leaves it essentially unexplained, so it does for Jesus in many ways, including the Virgin Birth. There is no explanation offered for why Jesus, but not any other prophet (including

Muhammad), would be born of a virgin. The Virgin Birth doesn't indicate that Jesus was divine; if anything, it is simply another sign of Allah's power, given gratuitously and without explanation to one prophet but not to the others.

At any rate, despite the miraculous nature of Jesus' birth, in the Koran Mary still suffers the pains of childbirth (19:23)—while in some Christian traditions she does not, since those are the result of the sin (Genesis 3:16) that Jesus is taking upon himself and expiating (I Corinthians 15:22). Here, Mary gives birth to Jesus as Allah comforts her in her pains with dates (19:24–26). A voice cries out from beneath her, "Grieve not! For thy Lord hath provided a rivulet beneath thee" (19:24); many early and influential Islamic authorities say that the speaker was Gabriel, while others maintain that it was the baby Jesus himself—who speaks soon enough anyway (19:30–33).

A tradition has it that when Jesus told Mary in this verse not to grieve, she responded, "How can I not grieve when you are with me and I have no husband nor am I an owned slave woman?"[8] To avoid the embarrassment of having to explain how she came to have a newborn, he instructs her to tell people she is fasting and not speaking with anyone (19:26).

Allah says that he will teach Jesus "the Scripture and wisdom, and the Torah and the Gospel" (3:48): in the Koran, the Gospel is not the news about Jesus, but a book that he is given by Allah. Jesus later performs a series of miracles, each one "by Allah's leave" (3:49). As Bulandshahri explains, the clause "by Allah's leave" is repeated in order to emphasize that Jesus is human, not divine, and does miracles only by Allah's permission.[9]

The uncrucified Christ

We have seen that some Koranic stories of Jesus borrow from Gnostic gospels and other heretical Christian material that was apparently circulating in seventh-century Arabia: the Koranic Jesus speaks while still a baby in his cradle (19:29–33) and breathes life into clay birds (5:110). The most significant Koranic appropriation from Christian Gnosticism, however, is a denial of the reality of the crucifixion of Christ: "They did not kill him, nor crucify him, but they thought they did [or literally, it appeared so to them]" (4:157).

For the Gnostics, this denial was rooted in an abhorrence of the material world and the flesh, which led to their denying altogether the reality of the Incarnation; Muslims, on the other hand, deny the Crucifixion because, in their view, God's prophet cannot suffer defeat.

In the Koran, the Jews boast that they killed Jesus—but they only think they did (4:157). In fact, Jesus escaped crucifixion, though how he did so is the source of some dispute. Ibn Kathir argues that "when Allah sent 'Isa [Jesus] with proofs and guidance, the Jews, may Allah's curses, anger, torment and punishment be upon them, envied him because of his prophethood and obvious miracles...." Consumed by this envy, Ibn Kathir continues, the Jews stirred up "the king of Damascus at that time, a Greek polytheist who worshipped the stars" to order his deputy in Jerusalem to arrest Jesus. Jesus, perceiving this, asked those with him, "Who volunteers to be made to look like me, for which he will be my companion in Paradise?" A young man volunteered, whereupon "Allah made the young man look exactly like 'Isa, while a hole opened in the roof of the house, and 'Isa was made to sleep and ascended to heaven while asleep." Then "those surrounding the house saw the man who looked like 'Isa, they thought that he was 'Isa. So they took him at night, crucified him and placed a crown of thorns on his head. The Jews then boasted that they killed 'Isa and some Christians accepted their false claim, due to their ignorance and lack of reason."[10]

Other sources offer different theories. Some Islamic authorities claim Jesus was with seventy of his disciples when the guards came to arrest him, and all seventy were made to look just like Jesus; one stepped forward and was crucified. The *Ruhul Ma'ani*, however, identifies the one who was made to look like Jesus and crucified as the one who betrayed him for thirty dirhams—Judas. Another Muslim source says it was a sentry who was guarding Jesus after his arrest.[11]

The Koran asserts in this context that "there is none of the People of the Book but must believe in him before his death" (4:159). This rather odd statement has been taken to mean that Jesus will return to earth—and when he does, according to Muhammad in an Islamic tradition, he will "break the Cross and kill the pig and abolish the Jizya"—the tax taken from the non-Muslims subjugated under Islamic rule.[12] That is, he will abolish the subservient dhimmi status of the non-Muslims and Islamize the world: "During his time, Allah will destroy all religions except Islam and Allah will destroy Al-Masih Ad-Dajjal (the False Messiah)."[13]

Jesus not divine

The Koran emphasizes that Jesus was a prophet of Allah, who did all his mighty works by order of Allah—and is thus not himself divine. Interestingly, unlike Muhammad, Jesus is depicted performing various miracles. But after these miracle stories, Allah again stresses that Jesus is not divine, asking him point blank: "O Jesus, son of Mary! Didst thou say unto mankind: Take me and my mother for two gods beside Allah?" (5:116)

The Koran here seems to be criticizing the Christian doctrine of the Trinity, which it apparently envisions as consisting of Allah along with a deified Jesus and Mary. Ibn Kathir says the same thing, claiming the Christians elevated Jesus "and his mother to be gods with Allah." The actual Christian Trinity of God the Father, Son, and Holy Spirit is not envisioned in the Koran.

In any case, Jesus denies having told his followers to worship him and his mother, and the passage concludes by repeating that those who believe otherwise will, of course, be punished (5:116).

The Koran even asserts that those who believe that Jesus is divine are themselves Infidels—and hell-bound to boot: "They surely disbelieve who say: Lo! Allah is the Messiah, son of Mary. The Messiah (himself) said: O Children of Israel, worship Allah, my Lord and your Lord. Lo! Whoso ascribeth partners unto Allah, for him Allah hath forbidden paradise. His abode is the Fire. For evil-doers there will be no helpers" (5:72).

Jesus, far from being divine, is a "slave of Allah" (*Abdullah:* 4:172; 19:30; 43:59). This designation, of course, puts Jesus on the same level as all created beings—for the master–slave relationship is the primary paradigm in Islam for human relations with the divine. Despite his Virgin Birth, despite

THE HADITH ILLUMINATES THE KORAN

Jesus is coming back—to break the Cross

"Allah's Messenger said, 'By Him (Allah) in Whose Hands my soul is, surely ['Isa (Jesus)], the son of Maryam (Mary) will shortly descend amongst you (Muslims) and will judge mankind justly by the law of the Qur'an (as a Just Ruler); he will break the Cross and kill the pigs and there will be no *Jizya* (i.e. taxation taken from non Muslims). Money will be in abundance so that nobody will accept it, and a single prostration to Allah (in prayer) will be better than the whole world and whatever is in it.' Abu Hurairah added: 'If you wish, you can recite (this Verse of the Qur'an): 'And there is none of the people of the Scriptures (Jews and Christians), but must believe in him (i.e., 'Isa, son of Maryam, as only a Messenger of Allah and a human being) before his ['Isa, or a Jew's or a Christian's] death; (at the time of the appearance of the angel of death) And on the Day of Judgment he ('Isa) will be a witness against them.' (V. 4:159)"[14] his miracles, despite his being favored above the other prophets, Jesus is, in the final analysis, simply another created being, a slave of Allah.

In case the point is not clear, Allah directs Muhammad to say that Allah could destroy Jesus, his mother, and the entire earth if he so wished (5:17)—thereby vividly reasserting Allah's absolute sovereignty, which the Koran appears to regard as threatened by the idea of the divinity of Christ.

A sign left unexplained

Jesus is also "a sign for mankind and a mercy from Us" (19:21)—and his mother Mary is also a sign (21:90; 23:50). Once again, the word for sign is *aya*, the word used also for the verses of the Koran—for each verse, you see, is a sign of Allah's presence and power. But why are Jesus and Mary signs of Allah's action in the world in a way that other prophets are not?

Here again the Koran accords Jesus a special status and then leaves it unexplained. Jesus is, despite all his singular gifts, privileges, and powers, presented simply as a Muslim prophet. When the Jews reject him, he gathers disciples who say, "Do thou bear witness that we are Muslims" (3:52). And while Jesus' enemies plotted against him, Allah, "the best of schemers" (3:54), plotted also, revealing that he would cause Jesus "to ascend to Me." This, says Ibn Ishaq, refuted "what they assert of the Jews in regard to his crucifixion"—that is, their claim that Jesus was crucified at all.[15]

Nevertheless this, says the Koran, "is the true account: There is no god except Allah." (3:62)—in other words, Jesus is not divine. Allah tells Muhammad to challenge those who believe otherwise: since "knowledge hath come to thee," he should say to dissenters, "Come! Let us gather together, our sons and your sons, our women and your women, ourselves and yourselves. Then let us earnestly pray, and invoke the curse of Allah on those who lie!" (3:61)

According to Ibn Ishaq, when the Christian delegation from Najran heard this, they asked Muhammad for time to confer among themselves. Then one of their leaders told the rest,

> O Christians, you know right well that Muhammad is a prophet sent (by God) and he has brought a decisive declaration about the nature of your master. You know too that a people has never invoked a curse on a prophet and seen its elders live and its youth grow up. If you do this you will be exterminated. But if you decide to adhere to your religion and to maintain your doctrine about your master, then take your leave of the man and go home.[16]

So they went to Muhammad, declined his challenge, and went home, obstinate renegades confirmed in their rebellion against Allah.

Away under the palm tree

Hold the Christmas carols: according to the Koran, Jesus was not born in a manger, but under a palm tree: "And the pains of childbirth drove her to the trunk of a palm-tree. She cried (in her anguish): 'Ah! Would that I had died before this! Would that I had been a thing forgotten and out of sight!'" (19:23)

Jesus: not the Son of God, not the Savior, not crucified and therefore not resurrected, and born not in a manger but under a palm tree. The Koran presents all this as a corrective to the beliefs of the Christians since, after all, they "forgot a good part of the message that was sent them." As punishment, Allah divided them into warring sects: "We estranged them, with enmity and hatred between the one and the other, to the day of judgment. And soon will Allah show them what it is they have done" (5:14).

Paradoxically, the Koran professes to correct Christian beliefs while affirming the truth of the Gospel:

> We sent Jesus the son of Mary, confirming the Law that had come before him. We sent him the Gospel; therein was guidance and light, and confirmation of the Law that had come before him, a guidance and an admonition to those who fear Allah. Let the people of the Gospel judge by what Allah hath revealed therein. If any do fail to judge by (the light of) what Allah hath revealed, they are (no better than) those who rebel. (5:46–47)

Thus Christians are to judge Muhammad's message by their own Scriptures. Yet when Muslims began to have extended contact with Christians, this passage put them in an uncomfortable position: they were sure the Gospel contained "guidance and light" and also bore witness to Muhammad's prophetic status—so that accordingly, if Christians judged by it rightly, they would become Muslims. But instead, Muslims found that the New Testament affirmed the Christian understanding of Jesus that the Koran repudiated, and contained no trace of an idea that a later prophet would come with a final revelation.

Thus Muslims began to teach that Christians had corrupted the pure Gospel that was given to Jesus by Allah. This idea is still common in the Islamic world today. Islamic scholars explain that the true "Gospel," the book that, according to the Koran, Allah gave to Jesus, is nowhere to be found. Abdullah Yusuf Ali includes an explanatory note in his Koran about the Gospel: "The *Injil* [Gospel] mentioned in the Qur'an is certainly not the New Testament, and it is not the four Gospels, as now received by the Christian Church, but an original Gospel which was promulgated by Jesus as the *Tawrah* [Torah] was promulgated by Moses and the Qur'an by Muhammad al Mustafa."[17]

Yet there is no indication that such a book ever existed at all: there is no textual evidence whatsoever for a pre-Islamic Christian text that reflected Islamic beliefs about Jesus or the Biblical prophets. Christianity, of course, regards "the Gospel" as the message of Christ, not a book.

In the Islamic scenario, the authentic Gospel is lost, while the corrupted version alone remains. This idea accords with passages of the Koran saying that established Christian doctrines—such as the mainstream Christian idea that Jesus is the Son of God—are nothing more than "a saying from their mouth" by which the Christians "imitate what the unbelievers of old used to say" (9:30).

Did Jesus predict the coming of Muhammad?

The Koran declares that, just as Muhammad's message confirmed that of the Gospel before it, Jesus told the Jews that his message confirmed that of the Torah. Jesus also said, according to the Koran, that he was the precursor of a messenger who would come after him, whose name would be Ahmad. But the people would dismiss Jesus' miracles as "sorcery" (61:6)—recalling their dismissal of Moses (28:36) and Muhammad (28:48).

"Ahmad" means "the Most Praised One," and it is etymologically related to Muhammad, which means "Praised One." Mohammed Marmaduke Pickthall, a British Islamic scholar and convert to Islam, drove the connection home by translating "Ahmad" simply as "Praised One." And Muslims universally understand the verse as depicting Jesus predicting the coming of Muhammad.

Muslims contend that this prophecy is the uncorrupted version of the words of Jesus that survive in corrupted form in John 14:16–17, where Jesus says, "And I will pray the Father, and he will give you another Counselor, to be with you for ever, even the Spirit of truth, whom the world cannot receive, because it neither sees him nor knows him; you know him, for he dwells with you, and will be in you."

"Counselor" here is *parakletos,* or Paraclete. Some Islamic apologists have claimed this is a corruption of *periklytos*, which means "famous" or "renowned," i.e., "Praised One." However, there is no textual evidence whatsoever for this: no manuscripts of the New Testament exist that use the word *periklytos* in this place. Nor is it likely that the two words might have been confused. That kind of confusion may be theoretically possible in Arabic, which does not write vowels and hence would present two words with identical consonant structures. But Greek does write vowels, so the words would never have appeared in Greek as even close to identical.

The true Christians and those false worshippers of Christ

In light of all this, it is clear that when the Koran refers to Jesus, it has in mind a figure who is strikingly different from the one in the New Testament—one that fully qualifies as "another Jesus than the one we preached," as the apostle Paul puts it (II Corinthians 11:4).

Consequently, when Muslims today say they revere Jesus and even that they recognize Christianity as a legitimate faith, they are being disingenuous. For the Christianity that the Koran recognizes is not Christianity as millions practice it around the world today.

This is a key source of much of the enduring suspicion and mistrust between Muslims and Christians. The Saudi Sheikh Abd Al-Muhsin Al-Qadhi expatiated on the Koranic view of mainstream Christianity in a recent sermon, in which he also elaborated a contemptuous view of Christian charity:

> Today we will talk about one of the distorted religions, about a faith that deviates from the path of righteousness...about Christianity, this false faith, and about the people whom Allah described in his book as deviating from the path of righteousness. We will examine their faith, and we will review their

history, full of hate, abomination, and wars against Islam and the Muslims. In this distorted and deformed religion, to which many of the inhabitants of the earth belong, we can see how the Christians deviate greatly from the path of righteousness by talking about the concept of the Trinity. As far as they are concerned, God is the Father, the Son, and the Holy Ghost: three who are one.

... They see Jesus, peace be upon him, as the son of Allah.... It is the Christians who believe Jesus was crucified. According to them, he was hanged on the cross with nails pounded through his hands, and he cried, "My God, why have you forsaken me?" According to them, this was so that he would atone for the sins of mankind.... Regardless of all these deviations from the path of righteousness, it is possible to see many Muslims... who know about Christianity only what the Christians claim about love, tolerance, devoting life to serving the needy, and other distorted slogans.... After all this, we still find people who promote the idea of bringing our religion and theirs closer, as if the differences were miniscule and could be eliminated by arranging all those [interfaith] conferences, whose goal is political.[18]

The idea that Christianity is a "distorted, deformed religion" created by people who were bent on rejecting the prophet Muhammad fuels a great deal of Muslim hatred for Christianity, Christians, and the West to this day.

No Christian friends, please, we're Muslims

The Koran warns Muslims that the Jews and pagans will be their worst enemies, but "nearest among them in love to the believers wilt thou find those who say, 'We are Christians,' because amongst these are men devoted to learning and men who have renounced the world, and they are not arrogant" (5:82).

One Muslim interpretation of this passage holds that it refers not to all Christians, but only to those who accept Islam; this is made clear by the following two verses, in which those Christians accept Muhammad's message. But even if one takes the text at face value, the totality of the Koranic record suggests that while Christians may themselves feel "nearest in love" to the Muslims, Muslims are not to return the favor. For Allah commands them, "O ye who believe! Take not the Jews and the Christians for your friends and protectors: they are but friends and protectors to each other. And he amongst you that turns to them (for friendship) is of them. Verily Allah guideth not a people unjust" (5:51).

> # THE HADITH ILLUMINATES THE KORAN
>
> ....
>
> ## Not that there's anything wrong with that
>
> "The Prophet said to Abu-Dhar, 'Listen and obey (your chief) even if he is an Ethiopian with a head like a raisin.'"[19]

The Jews and Christians will never make adequate friends and protectors for Muslims because they will never be satisfied with Muslims "unless thou follow their form of religion." Allah tells Muhammad to say to them in response, "The guidance of Allah, that is the (only) guidance," and he warns his prophet, "Wert thou to follow their desires after the knowledge which hath reached thee, then wouldst thou find neither Protector nor helper against Allah" (2:120).

Thus, according to the Koran, the only legitimate friends for Muslims are . . . other Muslims.

Chapter Nine

THE KORAN ON WOMEN: CROOKED AND INFERIOR

The Koran values women?

TWO KORANIC SCHOLARS, Amatul Rathman Omar and Abdul Mannan Omar, in an article entitled "Introduction to the Study of the Holy Qur'an," assert that "the concept of some Christians about the rights of women in Islam is based upon colossal ignorance of the teachings of the Qur'an and Islam."[1]

I would agree. Some Westerners, Christian and non-Christian, have a completely distorted and inaccurate view about the rights of women in Islam, and these misconceptions are indeed based on ignorance of the Koran and Islam.

But who are ignorant: the ones who believe the Koran is a marvelous, progressive tract advancing women's rights, or those who believe the Koran has been used all too often to justify the oppression of women?

To find out, let's look at the eighty-first chapter of the Koran, which begins with a stark litany of the cataclysmic events of the Day of Judgment:

> When the sun is overthrown,
>
> And when the stars fall,
>
> And when the hills are moved,
>
> And when the camels big with young are abandoned,
>
> And when the wild beasts are herded together,
>
> And when the seas rise,
>
> And when souls are reunited . . . (81:1–7)

The image that immediately follows is even more arresting: "And when the girl-child that was buried alive is asked for what sin she was slain" (81:8–9). Both Muslim and non-Muslim apologists for Islam point proudly to this passage to show that the Koran put an end to the pagan Arab practice of female infanticide. And indeed, this is a minor preoccupation of the Koran. In another place the book excoriates those whose faces become "darkened" when they receive news of the birth of a girl, and who consider burying her "beneath the dust. Verily evil is their judgment" (16:58–59). Allah tells the Muslims, "Slay not your children because of penury" (6:151).

The same apologists often make sweeping claims about the Koran's supposedly benevolent teachings on women. Late in 2005, English judge Marilyn Morington spoke in Islamabad at a seminar entitled "Violence against Women and Criminal Justice System: Challenge and Response." Morington stated there that "Islam is a religion which lays emphasis on giving the women their due rights."[2] Similarly, the U.S.-based Muslim Women's League asserts that "spiritual equality, responsibility and accountability for both men and women is a well-developed theme in the Quran. Spiritual equality between men and women in the sight of God is not limited to purely spiritual, religious issues, but is the basis for equality in all temporal aspects of human endeavor."[3]

Former British prime minister Tony Blair would probably agree, as he once remarked, "To me, the most remarkable thing about the Koran is how progressive it is.... The Koran is inclusive. It extols science and knowledge and abhors superstition. It is practical and far ahead of its time in attitudes toward marriage, women, and governance."[4]

Even Allah himself is cited as supporting equality, assuring the believers in the Koran that "never will I suffer to be lost the work of any of you, be he male or female" (3:195). All will be rewarded: "Whoever works righteousness, man or woman, and has faith, verily, to him will We give a new life, a life that is good and pure, and We will bestow on such their reward according to the best of their actions" (16:97).

And it seemingly gets even better. The Koran says that Allah created men and women from a "single soul" (4:1). Many Muslims in the West have pointed to this verse as evidence that Islam recognizes the full human dignity of women. A twentieth-century Iranian Shi'ite scholar, Ayatollah Murtada Mutahhari, says that "other religions also have referred to this question, but it is the Qur'an alone which in a number of verses expressly says that woman has been created of the species of man, and both man and woman have the same innate character." He then quotes verse 4:1.[5]

Crooked women

But once again, other verses and traditions undermine the Koran's ostensibly progressive injunctions. In this case, the "single soul" from which mankind was created was Adam's, and while the Biblical story of Eve's creation from Adam's rib is not repeated here, the prophet of Islam refers to that story in a hadith, suggesting that while men and women may have the same "innate character," that doesn't mean they are equal in dignity, for women are... crooked: "Woman has been created from a rib and will in no way be straightened for you; so if you wish to benefit by her, benefit by her while crookedness remains in her. And if you attempt to straighten her, you will break her, and breaking her is divorcing her."[6]

Women are inherently crooked? Certainly some Muslim clerics think so—or at least, they do not believe in legal equality for women. Bangladeshi Islamic cleric Mufti Fazlul Haq Amini read the same Koran that Tony Blair found so progressive and yet complained about attempts in his native country to establish equal property rights for women. The problem? That would be "directly against Islam and the holy Koran."[7]

And where do Muslims get such ideas? They stem from the overall inferior status of women promulgated in the Koran, which specifically refutes the notion that women have as much basic human dignity as men. To the contrary, Allah says men are superior. When giving regulations for divorce, Allah stipulates that women "have rights similar to those (of men) over them in kindness." Similar, but not identical, for "men are a degree above them" (2:228).

Far from mandating equality, the Koran portrays women as essentially possessions of men. The Koran likens a woman to a field (tilth), to be used by a man as he wills: "Your women are a tilth for you (to cultivate) so go to your tilth as ye will" (2:223). And in a tradition Muhammad details the qualities of a good wife, including that "she obeys when instructed" and "the husband is pleased to look at her."[8]

The Koran decrees women's subordination to men in numerous other verses:

- It declares that a woman's legal testimony is worth half that of a man: "Get two witnesses, out of your own men, and if there are not two men, then a man and two women, such as ye choose, for witnesses, so that if one of them errs, the other can remind her" (2:282).

- It allows men to marry up to four wives, and also to have sex with slave girls: "If ye fear that ye shall not be able to deal justly with the orphans, marry women of your choice, two or three or four; but if ye fear that ye shall not be able to deal justly (with them), then only one, or (a captive) that your right hands possess, that will be more suitable, to prevent you from doing injustice" (4:3).

- It rules that a son's inheritance should be twice the size of that of a daughter: "Allah (thus) directs you as regards your children's (inheritance): to the male, a portion equal to that of two females" (4:11).

- It allows for marriage to pre-pubescent girls, stipulating that Islamic divorce procedures "shall apply to those who have not yet menstruated" (65:4).

Even some passages that appear to benefit women don't end up doing so. The Koran requires a husband to give his wife a dowry (4:4). The wife, however, may choose to free the husband from this obligation: "If the wife gives him part or all of that dowry with a good heart, her husband is allowed to take it...."[9] In reality, this supposed choice is sometimes forced on women and justified by this Koranic verse.

These passages are not archaisms or dead letters; they are imposed wherever Islamic law is enforced—as in the Islamic Republic of Iran, where large numbers of women turned out during the June 2009 post-election demonstrations. Clearly, these women's grievances went far beyond a single rigged election. One explained, "I see lots of girls and women in these demonstrations. They are all angry, ready to explode, scream out and let the world hear their voice. I want the world to know that as a woman in this country, I have no freedom." This was not surprising, since Iranian law was formulated in scrupulous adherence to the Koran and Islamic tradition and law.

Even the Ayatollah Khomeini's granddaughter, Zahra Eshraghi, declared that under Islamic law, "a woman is there to fill her husband's stomach and raise children." And just weeks after President Barack Obama defended the right of women in non-Muslim countries to cover their heads, brave Iranian women were throwing off their head coverings as a sign of protest against the Islamic regime—with no peep of support from Obama. Journalist Azadeh Moaveni, author of the feminist book *Lipstick Jihad*, noted that "while it's not at the top of women's grievances, the hijab is symbolic. Taking it off is like waving a red flag. Women are saying they are a force to be reckoned with."[10]

The deficiency of a woman's mind

Laying out rules of evidence, the Koran directs those trying to make a legal case to "get two witnesses, out of your own men, and if there are not two men, then a man and two women, such as ye choose, for witnesses, so that if one of them errs, the other can remind her" (2:282).

Muhammad used this verse to argue that women were deficient in intelligence as well as in religious faith. According to an Islamic tradition, Muhammad was on his way to offer prayer one day when he passed by a group of women. He stopped to exhort them to charity, basing his exhortation upon a warning: "O women! Give alms, as I have seen that the majority of the dwellers of hell-fire were you (women)." Asked to explain his comments, he responded, "You curse frequently and are ungrateful to your husbands. I have not seen anyone more deficient in intelligence and religion than you. A cautious sensible man could be led astray by some of you." When pressed further, he invoked Koran 2:282: "Is not the evidence of two women equal to the witness of one man?" When the women admitted that this was indeed the case, Muhammad drove his case home: "This is the deficiency in her intelligence. Isn't it true that a woman can neither pray nor fast during her menses?" When they admitted this also, he concluded, "This is the deficiency in her religion."[11]

Such attitudes, enunciated by the prophet of Islam himself, are pervasive—and corrosive—in the Islamic world.

And for women, it gets worse.

Easy divorce and temporary husbands

A Muslim man may divorce his wife simply by saying, "*Talaq*"—I divorce you—but unsurprisingly, women may not divorce their husbands in this way. After a Muslim husband tells his wife he is divorcing her, the Koran directs that "divorced women shall wait concerning themselves for three monthly periods" in order to determine whether or not they are pregnant. (If the divorcing couple has children, they ordinarily go with the father, and he owes his wife no financial or any other kind of support.)[12] During that time span, "their husbands have the better right to take them back ... if they wish for reconciliation." Women "shall have rights similar to the rights against them,

How's that again?

The Koran instructs children to be good to their parents. This command holds true even if they are unbelievers: "But if they strive to make thee join in worship with Me things of which thou hast no knowledge, obey them not." This refusal to follow them into idolatry, however, doesn't mean one should be unkind to them: "Yet bear them company in this life with justice (and consideration)" (31:14–15).

And yet maybe it does. The Koran elsewhere commands Muslims not to love unbelievers, even if they are among one's closest relatives: "Thou wilt not find folk who believe in Allah and the Last Day loving those who oppose Allah and His messenger, even though they be their fathers or their sons or their brethren or their clan" (58:22).

Bible vs. Koran

"Verily for the righteous there will be a fullfilment of (the heart's) desires; gardens enclosed, and grapevines; and voluptuous women of equal age."

—Koran 78:31–33

"And they will be honoured in the gardens of delight, on couches facing one another. A cup from a gushing spring is brought round for them, white, delicious to the drinkers, wherein there is no headache nor are they made mad thereby. And with them are those of modest gaze, with lovely eyes, (pure) as they were hidden eggs (of the ostrich)."

—Koran 37:42–49

"We shall join them to fair women with beautiful, big, and lustrous eyes."

—Koran 44:54

"Therein are those of modest gaze, whom neither man nor jinni will have touched before them."

—Koran 55:56

"We have created (their Companions) of special creation and made them virgin, pure (and undefiled), beloved (by nature), equal in age, for the Companions of the Right Hand."

—Koran 56:35–38

"What no eye has seen, nor ear heard, nor the heart of man conceived, what God has prepared for those who love him...."

—I Corinthians 2:9

according to what is equitable," but "men have a degree (of advantage) over them" (2:228).

Talaq. It's that easy. And that very simplicity gives rise to abuses—some of which the Koran anticipates. A man may, after all, pronounce *talaq* upon his wife in a fit of temper, but then reconsider. Accordingly, the Koran says that "a divorce is only permissible twice: after that, the parties should either hold together on equitable terms, or separate with kindness" (2:229). This passage seems to envision marriage, at least for Muslim women, as something akin to a hostage situation, for the Koran goes on to direct that if the couple "would be unable to keep the limits ordained by Allah," then "there is no blame on either of them if she give something for her freedom," or, in Pickthall's translation, "ransom herself."

But after three *talaqs*, the divorce is irrevocable—until a certain condition is met. After a man divorces his wife three times, "he cannot, after that, remarry her until after she has married another husband and he has divorced her" (2:230). This has led to the phenomenon of "temporary husbands," who marry and divorce thrice-divorced women at the behest of Islamic clerics, so that these poor women can then return to their original husbands.

This practice is sanctioned by no less an authority than Muhammad himself. A woman once came to him with an unusual problem: she had been divorced by her husband, had married another man, and now wanted to remarry her first husband—but her second husband was impotent. Unyielding, Muhammad told her that she could not remarry her first husband "unless you had a complete sexual relation with your present husband and he enjoys a complete sexual relation with you."[13]

Predictably, this odd requirement has resulted in all kinds of strange and abusive situations. In India in 2006, a drunk man divorced his wife three times. Afterward he tried to keep his rash *talaqs* a secret, but word got out in the village—whereupon the local Islamic clerics declared the divorce binding and stipulated that he and his wife could not lawfully reconcile until she married and divorced another man.[14] In the Maldives five years earlier, a temporary husband spent the night with his new wife, only to renege on his agreement to divorce her after one night—much to her fury and that of her original husband.[15]

Temporary wives, too (at least for Shi'ites)

Koran 4:24 says, "And those of whom ye seek content (by marrying them), give unto them their portions as a duty. And there is no sin for you in what ye do by mutual agreement after the duty (hath been done)." From the phrase "what ye do by mutual agreement," Shi'ite Muslims have gleaned permission to enter into marriages that have a time limit: the couple may marry one another for one night, or a weekend, or a month, or any limit they choose. One tradition stipulates that a temporary marriage "should last for three nights, and if they like to continue, they can do so, and if they want to separate, they can do so."[16] In a temporary marriage, or *nikah mut'a*, the duration of the marriage is specified at its beginning, and after it ends the couple parts without further ado.

Unsurprisingly, "temporary wives" often congregate in seminary towns (such as the holy city of Qom), where many lonely young men with a bit of money can be found. One young seminarian in the early 1900s recounted his experience with a woman he married "for a while." After he had paid her and the marriage expired, he remembered the experience with satisfaction, and made an arresting comparison: "It is reported that the Imams have said that whoever makes love legitimately has in effect killed an infidel. That means killing the lascivious spirit."[17]

How reassuring for Infidels!

Marrying young—*very* young

The Koran takes child marriage for granted in its directives about divorce. Discussing the waiting period required in order to determine if a woman is pregnant, it says, "If you are in doubt concerning those of your wives who have ceased menstruating, know that their waiting period shall be three months. The same shall apply to *those who have not yet menstruated*" (65:4, emphasis added). Allah thus gives instructions for a situation in which a pre-pubescent woman is not only married, but is being divorced by her husband.

Such a verse might have made its way into the Koran because of the notorious fact that Muhammad himself had a child bride. According to *Sahih Bukhari*, the hadith collection that Muslims consider most reliable, "The Prophet married her when she was six years old and he consummated his

THE HADITH ILLUMINATES THE KORAN

Avoiding cross-eyed children

I must ask the reader's pardon: the hadiths in this chapter are, shall we say, a bit R-rated. Reader's discretion is advised.

According to Islamic tradition, the Koranic verse calling women a "tilth" for men was revealed because of the Jews, who "used to say that when one comes to one's wife through the vagina, but being on her back, and she becomes pregnant, the child has a squint"—or, according to other sources, is cross-eyed.[18] To refute this, Allah revealed that it didn't matter whether she was lying on her back: "Your wives are your tilth; go then unto your tilth as you may desire" (2:223). Sayyid Qutb says the use of the word "tilth," with its "connotations of tillage and production, is most fitting, in a context of fertility and procreation"—or, as Maududi puts it, Allah's "purpose in the creation of women is not merely to provide men with recreation."[19]

Not merely recreation: women were also created in order to provide men with children.

marriage when she was nine years old, and then she remained with him for nine years (i.e., till his death)." Another tradition recalls that at the age of nine, she was playing on a swing with some of her friends when Muhammad came for her.[20]

This behavior by the man whom hundreds of millions of Muslims regard as the exemplary standard of conduct has brought suffering to untold numbers of women and girls.

One Islamic land where child marriage is common—in fact, more common than anywhere else in the world—is northern Nigeria, where Sharia is in force. The Nigerian government has tried to stamp out the practice, passing a law in 2003, the Child Rights Act, that set the minimum age for marriage at eighteen. Islamic clerics have been the fiercest opponents of this law: Imam Sani, a Nigerian cleric, explained, "Child marriage in Islam is permissible. In the Koran there is no specific age of marriage." Consequently, "the Muslim clerics have a problem with this Child Rights Act and they decried it, they castigate it, they reject it and they don't want it introduced in Nigeria." If the government enforced the law, Sani said, "There will be violent conflict from the Muslims, saying that 'no, we will not accept this, we'd rather die than accept something which is not a law from Allah.'"[21]

Nigeria is made up of thirty-six states, of which eighteen have passed the Child Rights Act; however, only one of Nigeria's majority-Muslim states has passed the law, and that with a change that set "puberty," rather than the age of eighteen, as the minimum requirement for lawful marriage. The result? As many as 800,000 Nigerian women are afflicted with fistula, a disease resulting from early intercourse and pregnancy.[22]

Nigeria is not alone, either in the prevalence of child marriage or in attempts to end the practice. In September 2008, Moroccan officials closed sixty Koranic schools operated by Sheikh Mohamed Ben Abderrahman Al-Maghraoui, because he issued a decree justifying marriage to girls as young as nine. "The sheikh," according to Agence France-Presse, "said his decree was based on the fact that the Prophet Mohammed consummated his marriage to his favourite wife when she was that age."[23]

It should come as no surprise, then, given the words of the Koran about divorcing prepubescent women and Muhammad's example in marrying Aisha, that in some areas of the Islamic world the practice of child marriage enjoys the blessing of the law. *Time* magazine reported in 2001 that "in Iran the legal age for marriage is nine for girls, fourteen for boys," and notes that "the law has occasionally been exploited by pedophiles, who marry poor young girls from the provinces, use and then abandon them. In 2000 the Iranian Parliament voted to raise the minimum age for girls to fourteen, but this year, a legislative oversight body dominated by traditional clerics vetoed the move."[24] Likewise, the *New York Times* reported in 2008 that in Yemen, "despite a rising tide of outrage, the fight against the practice is not easy. Hard-line Islamic conservatives, whose influence has grown enormously in the past two decades, defend it, pointing to the Prophet Muhammad's marriage to a 9-year-old."[25] (The characterization of proponents of Islamic law as "conservatives" is notable—the *Times* doesn't seem fazed by the fact that "conservatives" in the U.S. are not typically advocates of child marriage.)

And so child marriage remains prevalent in many areas of the Islamic world. In 2007, photographer Stephanie Sinclair won the UNICEF Photo of the Year competition for a wedding photograph of an Afghani couple: the groom was said to be forty years old but looked older; the bride was eleven. UNICEF Patroness Eva Luise Köhler explained, "The UNICEF Photo of the Year 2007 raises awareness about a worldwide problem. Millions of girls are married while they are still under age. Most of theses child brides are forever denied a self-determined life."[26] According to UNICEF, about half the women in Afghanistan are married before they reach the age of eighteen.[27]

Like Brigham Young, only more so

The Koran allows a man to take as many as four wives, as long as he believes he can "deal justly" with all of them (4:3). For according to one hadith, Muhammad said, "The person who has two wives, but is not just between them, shall appear on the Day of Judgment in such a condition that one half of his body will be collapsing."[28]

Nonetheless, what constitutes "just" behavior is in the eye of the beholder. And Muslim theologians have noticed that the Koran says that one must treat all one's wives *justly*, not *equally*. Thus, Ibn Kathir surmises that this requirement is really no big deal: "It is not obligatory to treat them equally, rather it is recommended. So if one does so, that is good, and if not, there is no harm on him."[29]

Muhammad Asad justified this inequality by pointing to biological realities:

> One might ask why the same latitude has not been given to women as well; but the answer is simple. Notwithstanding the spiritual factor of love which influences the relations between man and woman, the determinant biological reason for the sexual urge is, in both sexes, procreation: and whereas a woman can, at one time, conceive a child from one man only and has to carry it for nine months before she can conceive another, a man can beget a child every time he cohabits with a woman. Thus, while nature would have been merely wasteful if it had produced a polygamous instinct in woman, man's polygamous inclination is biologically justified.[30]

Enjoying divine sanction, polygamy is legally practiced in a majority of Islamic countries worldwide.[31] And with large-scale Islamic immigration to the West, polygamy is increasing throughout Europe as well, with estimates of polygamous arrangements reaching up to 16,000 in Italy alone.[32] Britain appears to be a bit behind the curve; the *Toronto Sun* reported in 2008 that "the British government recently admitted that nearly a thousand men are living legally with multiple wives in Britain."[33]

It is perhaps unsurprising that polygamy is vociferously defended in the West by some Muslim immigrants; in 2004, the Islamic Cultural Centre of Norway (which receives money from the Norwegian government) declared that polygamy is "advantageous, and ought to be practiced where conditions lend themselves to such a practice."[34] What does come as a rude surprise, however, is the blithe acceptance of the practice by supine, politically correct Western governments; in February 2008, for example, the British government allowed men with multiple wives to claim extra welfare benefits.[35]

North America is not exempt from this trend. In Canada, Mumtaz Ali, president of the Canadian Society of Muslims, spoke approvingly of the spread of polygamy, declaring in 2008 that "polygamy is a regular part of life for many Muslims. Ontario recognizes religious marriages for Muslims and others." He said there were "several hundred" Muslim men practicing polygamy in the Toronto area.[37]

Koranic polygamy has also come to the United States. In November 2007, a Muslim woman sent a letter to Board of Directors of the Islamic Center of New England complaining that her husband "was able to marry illegally and secretly and without my knowledge three [A]merican [M]uslim women, and because of that my self

THE HADITH ILLUMINATES THE KORAN

....

Long before Monica's blue dress

"I asked 'Aishah about the clothes soiled with semen. She replied, 'I used to wash it off the clothes of Allah's Messenger and he would go for the *Salat* (prayer) while water spots were still visible.'"[36]

and my children have suffered and still suffering tremendously." She laid some of the responsibility at the feet of the leaders of the Islamic Center: "Because of the failure of the Islamic center as well the Imams to prevent such misconduct, I had no choice but to file for divorce." She threatened to "expose this misconduct to the court and media if I have to, I also hope through this letter that you will make sure that this victimizations [sic] doesn't happen to any other sisters."[38]

This was no isolated case. According to researcher David Rusin, "estimates for the United States typically run into the tens of thousands of polygamous unions."[39] In May 2008 researchers estimated that between 50,000 and 100,000 Muslims were living in polygamous arrangements in the United States.[40]

And Muslim imams don't seem concerned about U.S. laws forbidding the practice: Ibrahim Hooper of the Council on American-Islamic Relations asserted that a "minority" of Muslims in America were polygamous, and that "Islamic scholars would differ on whether one could do so while living in the United States."[41] He didn't say anything about the necessity of obeying U.S. laws in this regard. Toronto imam Aly Hindy explained that such laws would have no force for Muslims: "This is in our religion and nobody can force us to do anything against our religion. If the laws of the country conflict with Islamic law, if one goes against the other, then I am going to follow Islamic law, simple as that."[42]

The Koran has further gifts for men as well. As we have seen, it stipulates that if a man cannot deal justly with multiples wives, then he should marry only one, or resort to "the captives that your right hands possess"—that is, slave girls (4:3).

Divinely sanctioned wife-beating

"There is no basis in Islamic theology to support domestic abuse of any kind," declared Qanta A. Ahmed, author of *In the Land of Invisible*

Women: A Female Doctor's Journey in the Saudi Kingdom, in May 2009.[43] But it all depends on one's definition of "abuse:" wife-beating exists in all cultures, but only in Islam does it enjoy divine sanction. The Koran tells men to beat their disobedient wives after first warning them and then sending them to sleep in separate beds (4:34)—a punishment that suggests the Koran regards women as sexually insatiable and needing to be kept under control. This is, of course, an extremely controversial verse, so it is worth noting how several translators render the key word here, *waidriboohunna*:

> Pickthall: "and scourge them"
>
> Yusuf Ali: "(and last) beat them (lightly)"
>
> Al-Hilali/Khan: "(and last) beat them (lightly, if it is useful)"
>
> Shakir: "and beat them"
>
> Sher Ali: "and chastise them"
>
> Khalifa: "then you may (as a last alternative) beat them"
>
> Arberry: "and beat them"
>
> Rodwell: "and scourge them"
>
> Sale: "and chastise them"
>
> Asad: "then beat them"
>
> Dawood: "and beat them"

In a new, widely-publicized translation of the Koran, however, Muslim feminist Laleh Bakhtiar translates it as "go away from them." In light of the unanimity among translators, both Muslim and non-Muslim, this seems difficult to sustain—it is hard to believe that all these authorities on Koranic Arabic, spanning several centuries, got the passage wrong until Bakhtiar. But her impulse to mitigate the brute force of this verse is understandable, as many Muslims today regard it with acute embarrassment. Asad adduces numerous traditions in which Muhammad "forbade the beating of any woman," concluding that wife-beating is "barely permissible, and should preferably be avoided."[44]

Unfortunately, however, this is not a unanimous view. In his Koranic commentary *Ruhul Ma'ani*, Sheikh Syed Mahmud Allusi gives four reasons that a man may beat his wife: "if she refuses to beautify herself for him," if she refuses sex when he asks for it, if she refuses to pray or perform ritual ablutions, and "if she goes out of the house without a valid excuse."[45]

What's more, the propriety of wife-beating is reinforced in the hadith. Western apologists for Islam like to point to a hadith in which Muhammad held up a toothbrush in response to a question from his followers about the proper implement for beating one's wife. (He was brushing his teeth when they approached him.) In practice, however, Muhammad himself didn't always counsel such gentleness, and the early Muslims certainly didn't practice it. Muhammad's favorite wife, Aisha, said it herself: "I have not seen any woman suffering as much as the believing women." Muhammad was once told that "women have become emboldened towards their husbands," whereupon he "gave permission to beat them."[46] He was unhappy with the women who complained, not with their husbands who beat them.

Also, Aisha reports that Muhammad struck her—and remember, Muhammad's example is normative for Muslims, since he is an "excellent example of conduct" (33:21). Once he went out at night after he thought she was asleep, and she followed him surreptitiously. Muhammad saw her and, as Aisha recounts, "He struck me on the chest which caused me pain, and then said: 'Did you think that Allah and His Apostle would deal unjustly with you?'"[47]

Many influential Muslims take all this seriously. In spring 2005, when the East African nation of Chad tried to institute a new family law that would outlaw wife beating, Muslim clerics protested that the measure was un-Islamic.[48] A 2007 survey of hospital workers in Turkey found 69 percent of the women and 85 percent of the men agreed that under some circumstances a husband was justified in beating his wife. Among the acceptable circumstances were "criticising the male."[49] As many as 20 percent of women even in the "moderate" land of Tunisia are victims of spousal abuse.[50]

In September 2007, the Islamic cleric Muhammad Al-'Arifi explained on Saudi and Kuwaiti television, in line with the three-tiered approach counseled by Koran 4:34: "Admonish them—once, twice, three times, four times, ten times. If this doesn't help, refuse to share their beds." And if that doesn't work? Al-'Arifi asked his audience; one young man replied, "Beat them."

"That's right," Al-'Arifi responded.

Then he explained the parameters:

> Beating in the face is forbidden, even when it comes to animals. Even if you want your camel or donkey to start walking, you are not allowed to beat it in the face. If this is true for animals, it is all the more true when it comes to humans. So beatings should be light and not in the face.... If he beats her, the beatings must be light and must not make her face ugly. He must beat her where it will not leave marks. He should not beat her on the hand.... He should beat her in some places where it will not cause any damage. He should not beat her like he would beat an animal or a child—slapping them right and left.[51]

In January 2009, Australian Islamic cleric Samir Abu Hamza likewise echoed the Koranic injunction:

> First of all advise them. You beat them...but this is the last resort. After you have advised them (not to be disobedient) for a long, long time then you smack them, you beat them and, please, brothers, calm down, the beating the Mohammed

showed is like the toothbrush that you use to brush your teeth.
You are not allowed to bruise them, you are not allowed to
make them bleed.[52]

Unfortunately, men have differing ideas about what constitutes a light
beating. Sanctioning the beating of women in the first place will
inevitably lead to serious violence.

A prominent American Muslim leader, Dr. Muzammil H. Siddiqi, former president of the Islamic Society of North America (ISNA), has said
that "in some cases a husband may use some light disciplinary action in
order to correct the moral infraction of his wife.... The Koran is very clear
on this issue."[53]

Indeed it is.

Stoning adulterers—not in the Koran!

Allah mandates home imprisonment until death—unless "Allah ordain
for them some (other) way"—for women found guilty of "lewdness" on the
testimony of four witnesses (4:15). According to Islamic law, these four
witnesses must be male Muslims; women's testimony is inadmissible in
cases of a sexual nature, even in rape cases in which she is the victim. If a
woman is found guilty of adultery, she is to be stoned to death; if she is
found guilty of fornication, she gets a hundred lashes (cf. 24:2).

But why should a woman be stoned to death for adultery when the
Koran doesn't mandate this punishment? Because even though this verse
has dropped out of the perfect and eternal book, it has not dropped out of
the memories of Islamic jurists. As we have seen, the penalty of stoning
does not appear in the Koranic text as it stands now, but adulterers in
Islamic lands are still risking their lives: Umar, one of Muhammad's early
companions and the second caliph, insisted that it had originally been in
the Koran, had been practiced by Muhammad, and was the will of Allah.[55]

MIRACLES OF THE KORAN

THE KORAN FORESHADOWS EMBRYOLOGY!

"Then We made the sperm into a clot of congealed blood; then of that clot We made a (foetus) lump; then we made out of that lump bones and clothed the bones with flesh; then we developed out of it another creature. So blessed be Allah, the best to create!"—Koran 23:14

Islamic apologists argue that in this passage, the Koran predicted the stages of development of the fetus long before the advent of modern embryology. Dr. Keith Moore, an anatomy expert who has taught at King Abdulaziz University in Jeddah, Saudi Arabia, has stated that this passage is an exact description of the development of the human fetus, insisting that it contains "an appropriate description of the human embryo from days 7–24 when it clings to the endometrium of the uterus."[54]

Aside from his fanciful exegesis, Dr. Moore does not mention that the Koran speaks of Allah forming this new being from "sperm"—in accord with the ancient world's understanding that the fetus developed entirely from a man's "seed," once that seed was planted in a woman's womb. Uterine eggs were discovered later and are not mentioned in the Koran.

For men, however, the atmosphere is very different. "If two men among you are guilty of lewdness," says the Koran, "punish them both. If they repent and amend, leave them alone; for Allah is Oft-returning, Most Merciful" (4:16). The *Tafsir Al-Jalalayn* says that "lewdness" refers to men who commit "fornication or sodomy." They are to be punished "by cursing them and beating them with sandals; and if they repent of it and reform their behaviour, leave them alone and do not harm them." However, men don't get off entirely scot-free: the commentary adds that this verse "was abrogated by the *hadd* [prescribed] punishment for fornication," that is, stoning. The Islamic jurist al-Shafi'i, it goes on, says that someone who is guilty of sodomy "is not to be stoned, in his view, even if he has been married." Instead, "he is to be flogged and banished."[56]

Cover up—or else

In his much-praised June 4, 2009, speech in Cairo reaching out to the Islamic world, President Barack Obama declared, "I reject the view of some in the West that a woman who chooses to cover her hair is somehow less equal." He also noted that "the U.S. government has gone to court to protect the right of women and girls to wear the hijab [headscarf], and to punish those who would deny it."[57]

One may legitimately wonder, however, if Muslim women who wish to cover their heads in the United States really face the same kind of obstacles that both Muslim and non-Muslim women in the Islamic world often face when they refuse to cover their heads. As women's rights activist Phyllis Chesler notes, in Algeria, "as in Iran, 'unveiled,' educated, independent Algerian women have been seen as 'military targets' and increasingly shot on sight."[58] In February 2007, Zilla Huma Usman, the Pakistani government's minister for social welfare in Punjab province, was shot dead by a Muslim because her head was uncovered. The murderer, Mohammad Sarwar, declared, "I have no regrets. I just obeyed Allah's commandment. I will kill all those women who do not follow the right path, if I am freed again."[59]

Allah's commandment comes in the Koranic injunction that women should "draw their veils over their bosoms and not display their beauty except to their husbands, their fathers, their husbands' fathers, their sons, their husbands' sons, their brothers or their brothers' sons, or their sisters' sons, or their women, or the slaves whom their right hands possess, or male servants free of physical needs, or small children who have no sense of the shame of sex" (24:31)—in other words, they should be covered whenever they venture out in public. Ibn Kathir explains that this is not a matter of choice: "This is a command from Allah to the believing women, and jealousy on His part over the wives of His believing servants. It is also to distinguish the believing women from the women of the Jahiliyyah [the society of unbelievers] and the deeds of the pagan women."[60]

But what exactly should they cover?

The *Tafsir al-Jalalayn* explains that this verse instructs women to cover everything except "the face and the hands" when in public.[61] In a hadith, Aisha recounts that Muhammad said that "when a woman reaches the age of menstruation, it does not suit her that she displays her parts of body except this and this, and he pointed to her face and hands." Even today some Muslims use this hadith to justify mandating the hijab for women. In another hadith, a woman with a veil over her face came to see Muhammad; she was looking for her son, who had been killed in battle. Muhammad asked her, "You have come here asking for your son while veiling your face?"

She responded, "If I am afflicted with the loss of my son, I shall not suffer the loss of my modesty."

Pleased, Muhammad told her, "You will get the reward of two martyrs for your son," because "the people of the Book have killed him."[62]

The same Koranic verse mandating that women veil themselves also says, "And let them not stamp their feet so as to reveal what they hide of their adornment." Ibn Kathir continues, "During Jahiliyyah, when women walked in the street wearing anklets and no one could hear them, they would stamp their feet so that men could hear their anklets ringing. Allah forbade the believing women to do this." Furthermore, "Women are also prohibited from wearing scent and perfume when they are going outside the home, lest men should smell their perfume."[63]

Can't have that.

Chapter Ten

THE KORAN TEACHES NONVIOLENCE— OH, AND VIOLENCE, TOO

Relax: the Koran teaches nonviolence!

Ever since the September 11 attacks, the fate of millions of people has depended upon our policymakers' unquestionable dogma that, as the *Detroit Free Press* put it, "the Quran teaches nonviolence."[1] Fedwa Wazwaz of the Minnesota-based Islamic Resource Group insists that "any allegation that the Qur'an teaches violence and religious hatred is totally unfounded and violate [sic] the textual, historical, linguistic and broader context of the Qur'anic teachings and amounts to serious distortions of its teachings."[2]

True Islam, we are told, has nothing to do with the terrorism practiced around the globe in the name of Islam, and so there is no need to worry about what is going on in U.S. mosques and Islamic schools, no problem with large-scale Muslim immigration into the United States, and nothing to be concerned about in showering billions upon "moderate" regimes in Pakistan and elsewhere.

The Koran teaches nonviolence. What could go wrong?

And it's true—or almost true. Within the Koran one can indeed find verses that teach, if not outright nonviolence, then at least tolerance. Foremost among these is the brief chapter 109, entitled "The Unbelievers:" "Say: O disbelievers! I worship not that which ye worship; Nor worship ye that which I worship. And I shall not worship that which ye worship. Nor will ye worship that which I worship. Unto you your religion, and unto me my religion."

According to most scholars this is a Meccan sura, revealed during the first part of Muhammad's career as a prophet, when he still lived in his native city of Mecca. At this time, the Muslims were a small, weak, embattled band, feeling threatened by the pagan Quraysh. This opens up the possibility that this chapter is a plea for tolerance *for the Muslims*, not a magnanimous granting of tolerance to others.

As Islamic scholar Al-Wahidi explains, this sura was a rejection of an invitation from the Quraysh. The Quraysh approached Muhammad and made him this offer: "Come follow our religion and we will follow yours. You worship our idols for a year and we worship your Allah the following year. In this way, if what you have brought us is better than what we have, we would partake of it and take our share of goodness from it; and if what we have is better than what you have brought, you would partake of it and take your share of goodness from it."

But Muhammad rejected the offer: "Allah forbid that I associate anything with Him."[3] And then, apparently, Allah revealed sura 109—which would reinforce the likelihood that it is a request for tolerance from the Quraysh, not a granting of tolerance to them.

In any case, the *Tafsir al-Jalalayn* says that this sura was revealed "before the command to fight" against Infidels came to Muhammad.[4] And the twentieth-century Egyptian Koranic scholar Muhammad al-Ghazali, who is often cited as a reformist, writes ominously about the limits of tolerance in his commentary on this sura in his *Journey Through the Qur'an*: "Oppressing Islam and denying it the right to life cannot be tolerated. It must be explicitly stated that blood will continue to flow until this evil desire is removed and the power of Islam is restored and its Shari'a protected and its complete implementation guaranteed. Do the oppressors understand?"[5] Thus, in his view

How's that again?

"**And We did try Solomon.** We placed on his throne a body (without life); but he did turn (to Us in true devotion). He said, 'O my Lord! Forgive me, and grant me a kingdom which, (it may be), suits not another after me: for Thou art the Grantor of Bounties (without measure).'" (38:34–35)

Apparently Allah tests Solomon by placing a body on his throne, whereupon Solomon repents and asks for Allah's forgiveness. But what was it about this body that caused Solomon to repent? Whose body was it? Why would placing it on Solomon's throne lead Solomon to ask Allah to forgive him?

This passage has puzzled even Muslim commentators on the Koran. Ibn Kathir scratches his head and writes, "Allah does not explain exactly what this *Jasad* [body] was which He placed on his throne. We believe that Allah tested him by placing this *Jasad* on his throne, even though we do not know what it was. Everything that has been said concerning it has been taken from the *Isra'iliyat* [Jews], and we do not know what is true. (Since the word means 'corporeal,' interpretations centered around some form of *Jinn*.) Allah knows best."[6]

The *Tafsir al-Jalalayn* explains, just about as helpfully, that this body was a "jinn, disguised as Solomon," and that the incident was part of Allah's punishment of Solomon "because he had married a woman [solely] out of his desire for her." But why seeing a jinn disguised as himself on his throne would move Solomon to repentance is left unexplained.

one may tolerate a non-Muslim's religion only insofar as no obstacles are placed in the way of full implementation of Sharia.

But in any case, taken at face value, at least sura 109 does seem to grant Infidels some freedom to practice their religion—even if other Koranic passages connect this tolerance to the fact that Allah will ultimately judge the unbelievers and cast them into hell. Allah tells Muhammad not to waste his time arguing with those who reject his message, but to leave them in peace until that terrible day: "So leave them alone until they encounter that Day of theirs, wherein they shall (perforce) swoon (with terror)" (52:45–47). Muhammad is instructed to bear the Infidels' skepticism and insults, for ultimately Allah will deal with them in his own inimitable way: "And have patience with what they say, and leave them with noble (dignity). And leave Me (alone to deal with) those in possession of the good things of life, who (yet) deny the Truth; and bear with them for a little while" (73:10–11).

And in a directive that anticipated CAIR's Christian-directed ad campaigns by 1,400 years, Allah even tells Muhammad not to argue with the People of the Book, but rather to emphasize to them that they all worship the same deity: "And dispute ye not with the People of the Book, except with means better (than mere disputation), unless it be with those of them who inflict wrong (and injury): but say, 'We believe in the revelation which has come down to us and in that which came down to you; Our Allah and your Allah is one; and it is to Him we bow (in Islam)'" (29:46).

Allah tells Muhammad to be a good ambassador for Islam: to present his message in an attractive manner and preach it with patience. He is to "invite (all) to the Way of thy Lord with wisdom and beautiful preaching; and argue with them in ways that are best and most gracious: for thy Lord knoweth best, who have strayed from His Path, and who receive guidance. And if ye do catch them out, catch them out no worse than they catch you out: But if ye show patience, that is indeed the best (course) for those who are patient" (16:125–26).

Who can argue with that? Preach, and if your hearers refuse to listen, be patient with them.

Unfortunately, that is not all that the Koran says about the matter.

Blurring the line between defensive and offensive warfare

Other passages don't imply that believers should leave Infidels alone and let Allah judge them—particularly if the Infidels are not willing to leave the Muslims alone. Osama bin Laden's October 6, 2002, letter to the American people begins by quoting the Koran granting "permission to fight" to those "who are fought against, because they have been wronged" (22:39). Bin Laden doesn't quote the entire verse, which identifies those who "have been wronged" as "those who have been driven from their homes unjustly only because they said: Our Lord is Allah"—in other words, the Muslims (22:39–40).

Thus is mandated defensive warfare, a command the Koran reinforces elsewhere. Allah tells the Muslims to stand and fight against the Infidels, not to flee: "O ye who believe! When ye meet the Unbelievers in hostile array, never turn your backs to them. If any do turn his back to them on such a day—unless it be in a stratagem of war, or to retreat to a troop (of his own)—he draws on himself the wrath of Allah, and his abode is Hell, an evil refuge (indeed)!" (8:15–16)

This follows a passage in which Allah directs the angels to strengthen the Muslims and promises to "instill terror" in the Infidels' hearts. He tells the Muslims to "smite ye above their necks and smite all their finger-tips off them" (8:12). Here again, this is all characterized as a defensive action: "This is because they contended against Allah and His Messenger. If any contend against Allah and His Messenger, Allah is strict in punishment" (8:13). And the Infidels will end up in hell: "Thus (will it be said): 'Taste ye then of the (punishment): for those who resist Allah, is the penalty of the Fire'" (8:14).

Other passages reinforce the proposition that this defensive struggle should not be limited in scope. Muslims should respond to provocations in kind: "And one who attacketh you, attack him in like manner as he attacked you" (2:194). Allah even instructs Muhammad to take no prisoners: "It is not fitting for a prophet that he should have prisoners of war until he hath thoroughly subdued the land."

This verse comes in the context of warning the Muslims not to fight simply for booty: "Ye look for the temporal goods of this world; but Allah looketh to the Hereafter: And Allah is Exalted in might, Wise" (8:67). At the battle of Uhud against the pagan Quraysh tribe of Mecca, the Muslims failed utterly to destroy their enemies because of their lust for the spoils of war: "Allah did indeed fulfill His promise to you when ye with His permission were about to annihilate your enemy, until ye flinched and fell to disputing about the order, and disobeyed it after He brought you in sight (of the booty) which ye covet."

The Koran further explains that fighting for Islam is not optional: "Fighting is prescribed for you, and ye dislike it. But it is possible that ye dislike a thing which is good for you, and that ye love a thing which is bad for you. But Allah knoweth, and ye know not" (2:216). And not only is this warfare mandatory, but it is to be waged without quarter:

> And slay them wherever ye catch them, and turn them out from where they have turned you out; for tumult and oppression are worse than slaughter; but fight them not at the Sacred Mosque, unless they (first) fight you there; but if they fight you, slay them. Such is the reward of those who suppress faith. But if they cease, Allah is Oft-forgiving, Most Merciful. And fight them on until there is no more tumult or oppression, and there prevail justice and faith in Allah; but if they cease, let there be no hostility except to those who practice oppression. (2:191–93)

Despite the violence of such injunctions, this warfare still appears to be defensive. One key passage exhorts Muslims to "fight in the cause of Allah those who fight you, but do not transgress limits; for Allah loveth not transgressors" (2:190). A prominent translation by Pickthall renders this as "begin not hostilities. Lo! Allah loveth not aggressors."[7]

Western Islamic apologists today often invoke the words "begin not hostilities" to show that jihad is strictly defensive. For example, Muhammad Asad argues that "this and the following verses lay down unequivocally that only self-defence (in the widest sense of the word) makes war permissible for Muslims."[8]

All these mandates that warfare be defensive, however, are undermined by other Koranic passages. A long-standing interpretation holds that the verse counseling "begin not hostilities" was abrogated by verse 9:1, which voids every treaty between the Muslims and Infidels. The *Tafsir al-Jalalayn* declares that "Allah and His messenger" have "freedom from obligation" toward the idolaters "with whom ye made a treaty"—and thus need not feel themselves bound by any restriction on offensive warfare. The *Tafsir al-Jalalayn* also suggests that the words "slay them wherever you catch them" in the very next verse (2:191) abrogate the defensive nature of the conflict.[9]

Ibn Kathir, however, denies the verse was abrogated.[10] But even if that

Bible vs. Koran

"And one who attacketh you, attack him in like manner as he attacked you."
—Koran 2:194

"But if any one strikes you on the right cheek, turn to him the other also; and if any one would sue you and take your coat, let him have your cloak as well; and if any one forces you to go one mile, go with him two miles. Give to him who begs from you, and do not refuse him who would borrow from you."

—Matthew 5:39–42

were true, the key phrase "begin not hostilities" doesn't necessarily mean what many Westerners assume or hope it means. The command to fight until "there prevail justice and faith in Allah" suggests there is an aspect to the warfare that is not purely defensive: Muslims must continue the war until Allah's law prevails over the world, which implies a conflict without end. The passage concludes, "And fight them until persecution is no more, and religion is for Allah" (2:193).

Ibn Ishaq explains that this means that Muslims must fight against unbelievers "until God alone is worshipped."[11] Ibn Kathir also contends that the verse instructs Muslims to fight "so that the religion of Allah becomes dominant above all other religions."[12] Bulandshahri puts it in starker terms: "The worst of sins are Infidelity (Kufr) and Polytheism (shirk) which constitute rebellion against Allah, The Creator. To eradicate these, Muslims are required to wage war until there exists none of it in the world, and the only religion is that of Allah."[13]

That bears repeating.

"The worst of sins are Infidelity (Kufr) and Polytheism (shirk) which constitute rebellion against Allah, The Creator. To eradicate these, Muslims are required to wage war until there exists none of it in the world, and the only religion is that of Allah."

That's an open-ended declaration of war against every non-Muslim, in all times and in all places.

A similar exhortation is found in sura 8, when Allah discusses the perversity of the pagan Quraysh, whom the Muslims have just defeated in the Battle of Badr (8:31–40). They reject Muhammad's preaching as "tales of the ancients" (8:31) and keep the Muslims out of the Sacred Mosque in Mecca (8:34). Allah tells Muhammad to call them to accept Islam, "and fight them on until there is no more tumult or oppression [*fitnah*], and there prevail justice and faith in Allah altogether and everywhere; but if they cease, verily Allah doth see all that they do" (8:39).

According to numerous Islamic authorities, the statement that Muslims must fight until there is no more fitnah means they must fight "so that there is no more Shirk."[14] Shirk, as we have seen, is the cardinal sin in Islam, the association of partners with Allah—i.e., calling Jesus the Son of God. So this verse, although it was revealed in the aftermath of a seventh-century battle between Muslims and pagans, has a universal application. The *Tafsir al-Jalalayn* glosses it this way: "Fight them until there is no more fitna (shirk) and the din [religion] is Allah's alone—meaning that only He is worshipped."[15]

And mind you, Muslims would still regard this onslaught as essentially *defensive*—a defensive action against the aggressions of unbelief. If Muslims must fight until unbelief does not exist, the mere presence of unbelief constitutes sufficient aggression to commence hostilities. This is one of the foundations for the supremacist notion that Muslims must wage war against unbelievers until those unbelievers are either converted to Islam or subjugated under the rule of Islamic law, as verse 9:29 states explicitly.

As Muhammad puts it in an Islamic tradition: "I have been commanded to fight against people, till they testify to the fact that there is no god but Allah, and believe in me (that) I am the messenger (from the Lord) and in all that I have brought. And when they do it, their blood and riches are guaranteed protection on my behalf except where it is justified by law, and their affairs rest with Allah."[16]

Thus, if one does not accept Muhammad as a prophet, the sanctity of one's life and possessions ("blood and riches") is not guaranteed.

Collecting the Jizya

And indeed, several Koranic verses enjoin Muslims to fight Infidels, with no hint that they are only to respond to provocations. Allah directs Muhammad to "strive hard [*jahidi*, a verbal form of the noun *jihad*] against the unbelievers and the hypocrites, and be firm against them. Their abode is Hell, an evil refuge indeed" (9:73). And the believers in general are to "fight the unbelievers who gird you about, and let them find firmness in you: and know that Allah is with those who fear Him" (9:123).

The command applies first to fighting polytheists: "Then, when the sacred months have passed, slay the idolaters wherever ye find them, and take them (captive), and besiege them, and prepare for them each ambush. But if they repent and establish worship and pay the poor-due, then leave their way free. Lo! Allah is Forgiving, Merciful" (9:5).

But Muslims must also fight the People of the Book, as is made clear in the famous verse 9:29: "Fight those who believe not in Allah nor the Last Day, nor hold that forbidden which hath been forbidden by Allah and His Messenger, nor acknowledge the religion of Truth, (even if they are) of the People of the Book, until they pay the Jizya with willing submission, and feel themselves subdued."

This is the one place in the Koran where Muslims are directed explicitly to make war against and subjugate Jews and Christians. Once they are subjugated, they enter the dhimma, the protection of the Muslims, and become dhimmis, protected (or guilty) people. According to several early Islamic authorities, this verse "was revealed when the Messenger of Allah was commanded to fight the Byzantines. When it was sent down, the Messenger of Allah prepared for the expedition to Tabuk."[17]

The fight was religious in nature. Ibn Kathir explains, "Allah commanded His Messenger to fight the People of the Scriptures, Jews and Christians, on the ninth year of Hijrah, and he prepared his army to fight the Romans and called the people to Jihad announcing his intent and destination."[18]

This was Muhammad's last military expedition—an inconclusive foray in 631 against the Byzantines, who had left the area by the time he got there. Still, it was his first attempt to take on the great Christian empire that the Muslims would chip away at for centuries and ultimately destroy. And the verse—9:29—is far more momentous than the battle.

What is of paramount importance is that Muslims collect jizya—a special poll tax—from their Jewish and Christian subjects. As Ibn Juzayy notes, "scholars agree about accepting jizya [a religious-based poll tax] from the Jews and Christians," which signifies their "submission and obedience."[19]

Though Islamic law stipulates that the jizya is not to be collected from women and children, such limitations have often been ignored in practice, as the jizya became an onerous tool for the oppression of non-Muslims by Islamic rulers. In the Ottoman Empire, according to the pioneering historian of dhimmitude, Bat Ye'or,

> the poll tax was extorted by torture. The tax inspectors demanded gifts for themselves; widows and orphans were pillaged and despoiled. In theory, women, paupers, the sick, and the infirm were exempt from the poll tax; nevertheless, Armenian, Syriac, and Jewish sources provide abundant proof that the jizya was exacted from children, widows, orphans, and even the dead. A considerable number of extant documents, preserved over the centuries, testify to the persistence and endurance of these measures. In Aleppo in 1683, French Consul Chevalier Laurent d'Arvieux noted that ten-year-old Christian children paid the jizya. Here again, one finds the disparity and contradiction between the ideal in the theory and the reality of the facts.[20]

Similarly, a contemporary account of the Muslims' conquest of Egypt in the 640s says of one conquered locale that the jizya payments were set way beyond the means of the local dhimmis: "It is impossible to describe the lamentable position of the inhabitants of this town, who came to the point of offering their children in exchange for the enormous sums that they had to pay each month."[21]

The nineteenth-century Koranic scholar Sheikh Ahmed as-Sawi specifies that the purpose of the jizya is for non-Muslims to show they are "humble and obedient to the judgements of Islam." This was a manifestation of the "state of abasement" specified by this verse and spelled out by the Bedouin commander al-Mughira bin Sa'd when he met the Persian Rustam. Said al-Mughira, "I call you to Islam or else you must pay the jizya while you are in a state of abasement."

Rustam replied, "I know what jizya means, but what does 'a state of abasement' mean?"

Al-Mughira explained, "You pay it while you are standing and I am sitting and the whip is hanging over your head."[22]

THE HADITH ILLUMINATES THE KORAN

. . . .

Merciful and compassionate

"Allah's Messenger entered (Makkah) in the year of the Conquest (of Makkah) wearing a helmet over his head. After he took it off, a man came and said, 'Ibn Khatal is clinging to the curtains of the Ka'bah.' The Prophet said, 'Kill him.'"[23]

Similarly, Ibn Kathir says that the dhimmis must be "disgraced, humiliated and belittled. Therefore, Muslims are not allowed to honor the people of *Dhimmah* or elevate them above Muslims, for they are miserable, disgraced and humiliated."[24] The seventh-century jurist Sa'id ibn al-Musayyab stated, "I prefer that the people of the dhimma become tired by paying the jizya since He says, 'until they pay the jizya with their own hands in a state of complete abasement.'" The fifteenth-century Koranic scholar Jalaluddin as-Suyuti elaborates that this verse "is used as a proof by those who say that it is taken in a humiliating way, and so the taker sits and the dhimmi stands with his head bowed and his back bent. The jizya is placed in the balance and the taker seizes his beard and hits his chin." He adds, however, that "this is rejected according to an-Nawawi who said, 'This manner is invalid.'" Nevertheless, Zamakhshari actually agreed that the jizya should be collected "with belittlement and humiliation."[25]

What have Jews and Christians done to deserve such humiliation? Ibn Kathir relates that the People of the Book were in bad faith when they rejected Muhammad, and that they are not true believers even in their own religions:

> Therefore, when People of the Scriptures disbelieved in Muhammad, they had no beneficial faith in any Messenger or what the Messengers brought. Rather, they followed their religions because this conformed with their ideas, lusts and the ways of their forefathers, not because they are Allah's Law and religion. Had they been true believers in their religions, that faith would have directed them to believe in Muhammad, because all Prophets gave the good news of Muhammad's advent and commanded them to obey and follow him. Yet when he was sent, they disbelieved in him, even though he is the mightiest of all Messengers. Therefore, they do not follow the religion of earlier Prophets because these religions came from Allah, but because these suit their desires and lusts. Therefore, their claimed faith in an earlier Prophet will not benefit them because they disbelieved in the master, the mightiest, the last and most perfect of all Prophets.[26]

Predictably, Asad, Daryabadi, and other Western-oriented commentators downplay the religious significance of the jizya, arguing that it was merely a tax for exemption from military service. Asad explains, "Every able-bodied Muslim is obliged to take up arms in jihad (i.e., in a just war in God's cause) whenever the freedom of his faith or the political safety of his community is imperiled.... Since this is, primarily, a religious obligation, non-Muslim citizens, who do not subscribe to the ideology of Islam, cannot in fairness be expected to assume a similar burden."[27] Of course, this benign interpretation is hard to square with the mandate in verse 9:29 that non-Muslims pay the jizya "with willing submission, and feel themselves subdued"—Islamic apologists tend to pass over that command in silence.

The Pact of Umar

In explaining how the Jews and Christians must "feel themselves subdued," Ibn Kathir quotes a saying of Muhammad: "Do not initiate the Salam [greeting of peace] to the Jews and Christians, and if you meet any of them in a road, force them to its narrowest alley."[28] He then outlines the notorious Pact of Umar, an agreement made, according to Islamic tradition, between the caliph Umar, who ruled the Muslims from 634 to 644, and a Christian community. This pact is worth close examination, because it became the foundation for Islamic law regarding the treatment of the dhimmis, even though its historical authenticity is highly questionable.

Throughout history, whenever Islamic law was strictly enforced, non-Muslims were generally treated according to the tenets attributed to the Pact of Umar—a pact which, Ibn Kathir says, "ensured [the Christians'] continued humiliation, degradation and disgrace." In return for "safety for ourselves, children, property and followers of our religion," the Christians agreed in this pact not to:

1. Build "a monastery, church, or a sanctuary for a monk."
2. "Restore any place of worship that needs restoration."
3. Use such places "for the purpose of enmity against Muslims."

4. "Allow a spy against Muslims into our churches and homes or hide deceit [or betrayal] against Muslims."

5. Imitate the Muslims' "clothing, caps, turbans, sandals, hairstyles, speech, nicknames and title names."

6. "Ride on saddles, hang swords on the shoulders, collect weapons of any kind or carry these weapons."

7. "Encrypt our stamps in Arabic."

8. "Sell liquor"—Christians in Iraq in the last few years ran afoul of Muslims reasserting this rule.

9. "Teach our children the Qur'an."

10. "Publicize practices of Shirk"—that is, associating partners with Allah, such as regarding Jesus as the Son of God. In other words, Christian and other non-Muslim religious practice will be private, if not downright furtive.

11. Build "crosses on the outside of our churches and demonstrating them and our books in public in Muslim fairways and markets"—again, Christian worship must not be public, where Muslims can see it and become annoyed.

12. "Sound the bells in our churches, except discreetly, or raise our voices while reciting our holy books inside our churches in the presence of Muslims, nor raise our voices [with prayer] at our funerals, or light torches in funeral processions in the fairways of Muslims, or their markets."

13. "Bury our dead next to Muslim dead."

14. "Buy servants who were captured by Muslims."

15. "Invite anyone to Shirk"—that is, proselytize.

16. "Prevent any of our fellows from embracing Islam, if they choose to do so"—thus the Christians can be the objects of proselytizing, but must not engage in it themselves.

17. "Beat any Muslim."

Meanwhile, the Christians will:

1. Allow Muslims to rest "in our churches whether they come by day or night."
2. "Open the doors [of our houses of worship] for the wayfarer and passerby."
3. Provide board and food for "those Muslims who come as guests" for three days.
4. "Respect Muslims, move from the places we sit in if they choose to sit in them"—shades of Jim Crow.
5. "Have the front of our hair cut, wear our customary clothes wherever we are, wear belts around our waist"—these are so that a Muslim recognizes a non-Muslim as such and doesn't make the mistake of greeting him with "As-salaamu aleikum," or "Peace be upon you," which is the Muslim greeting for a fellow Muslim.
6. "Be guides for Muslims and refrain from breaching their privacy in their homes."

The Christians swore, "If we break any of these promises that we set for your benefit against ourselves, then our Dhimmah (promise of protection) is broken and you are allowed to do with us what you are allowed of people of defiance and rebellion."[29]

Of course, the Pact of Umar is a dubious seventh-century document. But there is no doubt that the imperative to subjugate non-Muslims as mandated by verse 9:29 and elaborated by this pact became and remained part of Islamic law. In Baghdad in the early nineteenth century, Sheikh Syed Mahmud Allusi, author of the noted commentary on the Koran *Ruhul Ma'ani*, complained that the Muslims have grown so weak that the dhimmis pay the jizya through agents, rather than delivering it themselves on foot. In our own age, Bulandshahri laments the abolition of the dhimma, saying that

> in today's times, the system of Atonement (*Jizya*) is not prac-
> tised at all by the Muslims. It is indeed unfortunate that not
> only are the Muslim States afraid to impose Atonement (*Jizya*)
> on the disbelievers (*kuffar*) living in their countries, but they
> grant them more rights than they grant the Muslims and respect
> them more. They fail to understand that Allah desires that the
> Muslims show no respect to any disbeliever (*kafir*) and that
> they should not accord any special rights to them.

Qutb emphasizes that these rules should be revived, for "these verses are given as a general statement, and the order to fight the people of the ear-lier revelations until they pay the submission tax with a willing hand and are subdued is also of general import."[30]

For his part, Maududi states that "the simple fact is that according to Islam, non-Muslims have been granted the freedom to stay outside the Islamic fold and to cling to their false, man-made, ways if they so wish." That heads off any potential contradiction between his understanding of 9:29 and 2:256, a verse asserting that "there is no compulsion in religion." Maududi then clarifies that the unbelievers

> have, however, absolutely no right to seize the reins of power in
> any part of God's earth nor to direct the collective affairs of
> human beings according to their own misconceived doctrines.
> For if they are given such an opportunity, corruption and mis-
> chief will ensue. In such a situation the believers would be
> under an obligation to do their utmost to dislodge them from

political power and to make them live in subservience to the Islamic way of life.[31]

Islamic apologists in the West today commonly assert that verse 9:29 commands warfare only against the Jews and Christians who fought against Muhammad. It would be comforting if every Muslim believed that, but unfortunately that has never been the mainstream Islamic understanding of this verse. Indeed, if it had been, the regulations delineated in the Pact of Umar would never have been formulated—and Islamic tradition even specifies that they were formulated after Muhammad's death with Christians against whom he did not fight. That in itself, as well as the teachings of all the schools of Islamic law, illustrates that this verse was always understood to have a universal application.

The rewards of fighting

Those who fight please Allah more than those who do not, according to the Koran, and this clearly refers to war fighting, not engaging in an interior spiritual struggle:

> Not equal are those believers who sit (at home) and receive no hurt, and those who strive and fight in the cause of Allah with their goods and their persons. Allah hath granted a grade higher to those who strive and fight with their goods and persons than to those who sit (at home). Unto all (in Faith) Hath Allah promised good: But those who strive and fight hath He distinguished above those who sit (at home) by a special reward (4:95).

It is hard to see how fighting spiritual battles could involve one's "goods" and "person."

The martial nature of the fighting to which Muslims are called is underscored also by Allah's calling upon his people to fearlessly face death in view of the rewards he offers afterward: "And if ye are slain, or die, in the way of Allah, forgiveness and mercy from Allah are far better than all they could amass. And if ye die, or are slain, lo! It is unto Allah that ye are brought together" (3:157–58).

Allah guarantees Paradise to those who sacrifice their lives for him: "He who forsakes his home in the cause of Allah, finds in the earth many a refuge, wide and spacious: should he die as a refugee from home for Allah and His Messenger, His reward becomes due and sure with Allah: and Allah is Oft-forgiving, Most Merciful" (4:100). Others, however, may enter Paradise even if they are unable to fight: "No blame is there on the blind, nor is there blame on the lame, nor on one ill (if he joins not the war): but he that obeys Allah and his Messenger, (Allah) will admit him to Gardens beneath which rivers flow; and he who turns back, (Allah) will punish him with a grievous Penalty" (48:17). The obedience in question here

THE HADITH ILLUMINATES THE KORAN

More mercy and compassion

"Anas said, 'Some people of 'Ukl or 'Uraina tribe came to Al-Madina and its climate did not suit them. So the Prophet ordered them to go to the herd of (milch) camels and to drink their milk and urine (as a medicine). So they went as directed and after they became healthy, they killed the shepherd of the Prophet and drove away all the camels.

The news reached the Prophet early in the morning and he sent (men) in their pursuit and they were captured and brought at noon. He then ordered to cut their hands and feet (and it was done), and their eyes were branded with heated pieces of iron. They were put in Al-Harra and when they asked for water, no water was given to them.' Abu Qilaba said, 'Those people committed theft and murder, became infidels after embracing Islam and fought against Allah and His Messenger.'"[32]

is not general religious obedience, but obeying the specific call to go to war for the sake of Allah.

Indeed, those who wage jihad rank highest among the believers:

> Do ye make the giving of drink to pilgrims, or the maintenance of the Sacred Mosque, equal to (the pious service of) those who believe in Allah and the Last Day, and strive with might and main in the cause of Allah [*jihad fi sabil Allah*]? They are not comparable in the sight of Allah: and Allah guides not those who do wrong. Those who believe, and suffer exile and strive with might and main, in Allah's cause [*jihad fi sabil Allah*], with their goods and their persons, have the highest rank in the sight of Allah: they are the people who will achieve (salvation). (9:19–20)

Jihad fi sabil Allah refers in Islamic theology to taking up arms for the Muslim cause.

Tolerance or war...or both?

From the looks of all this, then, it seems that the *Detroit Free Press* was right: the Koran does, in certain places, teach nonviolence. But that isn't the whole story. The Koran also teaches violence. And peace. And war. And tolerance. And the subjugation of unbelievers.

How are Infidels to understand how all these disparate teachings fit together? How do Muslims themselves understand it?

Generally, Islamic theologians have held that the Koran's teaching about warfare against unbelievers unfolded in stages. Originally, explained Ibn Ishaq, "the apostle had not been given permission to fight or allowed to shed blood....He had simply been ordered to call men to God and to endure insult and forgive the ignorant." And this remained true even in the face of persecution: "The Quraysh had persecuted his followers, seducing some from their religion, and exiling others from their country. They had to choose whether to give up their religion, be maltreated at home, or to flee the country, some to Abyssinia, others to Medina."

Did Muhammad endure this mistreatment as a matter of principle, or simply because he lacked the resources to retaliate? In any case, at some point the divine commands began to change. The Infidels "became insolent towards" Allah—although Ibn Ishaq doesn't explain how this was different from their earlier persecution of the Muslims. "When Quraysh became insolent towards God," Ibn Ishaq explained, "and rejected His gracious purpose, accused His prophet of lying, and ill treated and exiled those who served Him and proclaimed His unity, believed in His prophet, and held fast to His religion, He gave permission to His apostle to fight and to protect himself against those who wronged them and treated them badly."[33]

Then Ibn Ishaq explains the progression of Koranic teaching on warfare. After the period of tolerance, Allah allowed Muslims to wage defensive warfare. Explaining verse 22:39, which grants "permission to fight" to Muslims whom Infidels have treated unjustly, Ibn Ishaq says that Allah allows the Muslims to fight "only because they have been unjustly treated while their sole offence against men has been that they worship God. When they are in the ascendant they will establish prayer, pay the poor-tax, enjoin kindness, and forbid iniquity, i.e. the Prophet and his companions all of them."[34]

"When they are in the ascendant"—in other words, they will establish an Islamic state, in which Muslims will pray regularly, pay the poor-tax (*zakat*), and institute Islamic laws ("forbid iniquity").

But there was more. "Then God sent down to him: 'Fight them so that there be no more seduction,' i.e. until no believer is seduced from his religion. 'And the religion is God's,' i.e. Until God alone is worshipped."[35] This is Koran 2:193, commanding, as we have seen, much more than defensive warfare: Muslims must fight until "the religion is God's"—that is, until Allah alone is worshipped and the Infidels are either converted to Islam or subjugated under the rule of Islamic law.

No compassion, no mercy

One of the principal sources of exhortations to Muslims to wage jihad against unbelievers is the Koran's ninth chapter, "Repentance." Significantly, this is the only one of the Koran's 114 chapters that does not begin with *Bismillah ar-Rahman ar-Rahim*—"In the name of Allah, the compassionate, the merciful." Explanations for this vary. Some say it is simply because suras eight and nine were originally a single chapter, while Ibn Kathir says that the omission is simply "because the Companions did not write it in the complete copy of the Qur'an (*Mushaf*) they collected."[36] Maududi asserts that the *Bismillah* was left off because Muhammad himself didn't recite it at the beginning of this sura.[37] Another commentator counters that Muhammad not only didn't recite the *Bismillah*, but commanded that it not be recited at the beginning of this sura.[38]

Why not? The *Tafsir al-Jalalayn* notes that while this sura is commonly called "Repentance," it is "in fact, the Sura of Punishment." It explains Muhammad's command by saying that the *Bismillah* "is security, and this *sura* was revealed to remove security by the sword."[39] Ali, one of Muhammad's foremost followers and stoutest warriors, agreed, saying that the *Bismillah* "conveys security while this sura was sent down with the sword. That is why it does not begin with security."[40]

That may be because this chapter contains the much-discussed Verse of the Sword, which includes the notorious injunction to "slay the idolaters wherever you find them" (9:5). Unsurprisingly, present-day jihadists love to cite this verse. In a 2003 sermon, Osama bin Laden rejoiced, "Praise be to Allah who revealed the verse of the Sword to his servant and messenger [the Prophet Muhammad], in order to establish truth and abolish falsehood."[41]

One Koranic scholar, Ibn Juzayy, notes that 9:5 abrogates "every peace treaty in the Qur'an," and specifically abrogates the directive in 47:4 to "set free or ransom" captive unbelievers. According to as-Suyuti, this verse "abrogates pardon, truce and overlooking"—that is, the overlooking of the pagans' offenses.[42] The *Tafsir al-Jalalayn* is particularly belligerent, saying that the Muslims must "kill the idolaters wherever you find them—whether they be in the Haram [the sacred precincts of Mecca] or outside it—and seize them by capture and besiege them in citadels and fortresses until they either fight or become Muslim and lie in wait for them on every road on which they travel. If they repent of their unbelief and establish the prayer and pay zakat, let them go on their way and do not interfere with them."[43]

Ibn Kathir echoes this, directing that Muslims should "not wait until you find them. Rather, seek and besiege them in their areas and forts, gather intelligence about them in the various roads and fairways so that what is made wide looks ever smaller to them. This way, they will have no choice, but to die or embrace Islam."

He also doesn't seem to subscribe to the view commonly put forward by Muslim spokesmen in the West today that this verse applies only to the pagans of Arabia in Muhammad's time, and has no further application. He asserts, on the contrary, that "slay the idolaters wherever you find them" means unbelievers must be killed "on the earth in general, except for the Sacred Area"—that is, the sacred mosque in Mecca.[44]

But . . . but . . . my Muslim friends tell me Islam is peaceful!

Your Muslim friends may indeed be peaceful and reject these teachings. Or they may not know about them, because their teachers did not emphasize them.

Or, they may be lying.

It's unfortunate, but true: Islam is the only major religion with a developed doctrine of deception. Many believe this doctrine, called *taqiyya*, is exclusively Shi'ite, but actually it is founded upon Koranic passages. Chief among these is this one: "Let not the believers take for friends or helpers unbelievers rather than believers. If any do that, in nothing will there be help from Allah; except by way of precaution, that ye may guard yourselves from them" (3:28).

Ibn Kathir explains that in this verse, "Allah prohibited His believing servants from becoming supporters of the disbelievers, or to take them as comrades with whom they develop friendships, rather than the believers." However, exempted from this rule were

> those believers who in some areas or times fear for their safety from the disbelievers. In this case, such believers are allowed to show friendship to the disbelievers outwardly, but never inwardly. For instance, Al-Bukhari recorded that Abu Ad-Darda' said, "We smile in the face of some people although our hearts curse them." Al-Bukhari said that Al-Hasan said, "The *Tuqyah* [*taqiyyah*] is allowed until the Day of Resurrection."[45]

Another influential and authoritative early Koranic scholar, Al-Tabari, explained this verse: "If you [Muslims] are under their [infidels'] authority, fearing for yourselves, behave loyally to them, with your tongue, while harboring inner animosity for them.... Allah has forbidden believers from being friendly or on intimate terms with the infidels in place of believers—except when infidels are above them [in authority]. In such a scenario, let them act friendly towards them."[46]

This practice is also sanctioned by the Koran's warning to Muslims that those who forsake Islam will be consigned to Hell—except those forced to do so, but who remain true Muslims inwardly: "Any one who, after accepting faith in Allah, utters unbelief—except under compulsion, his heart remaining firm in faith—but such as open their breast to unbelief, on them is wrath from Allah, and theirs will be a dreadful penalty" (16:106). Ibn Kathir explains that "the scholars agreed that if a person is forced into disbelief, it is permissible for him to either go along with them in the interests of self-preservation, or to refuse."[47]

But what about "there is no compulsion in religion"?

It is one of the most famous and celebrated verses in the Koran—the one that above all others proves that no matter what bin Laden or Zawahiri or Ahmadinejad or Hamas or Hizballah may do, Islam is tolerant and peaceful: "Let there be no compulsion in religion: Truth stands out clear from Error: whoever rejects evil and believes in Allah hath grasped the most trustworthy hand-hold, that never breaks. And Allah heareth and knoweth all things" (2:256). Following this renowned and generous verse, interestingly enough, comes another threat of damnation: "Allah is the Protector of those who have faith: from the depths of darkness He will lead them forth into light. Of those who reject faith the patrons are the evil ones: from light they will lead them forth into the depths of darkness. They will be companions of the fire, to dwell therein (for ever)" (2:257).

Islamic spokesmen in the West frequently quote this verse to claim that Islam is a religion of peace. And while an early Muslim, Mujahid ibn Jabr, argued that this verse was abrogated by 9:29, in which the Muslims are commanded to fight against the People of the Book, others say this verse was never abrogated, but was revealed precisely in reference to the People of the Book: they are not to be forced or compelled to accept Islam, but may practice their religions freely as long as they pay the jizya (poll-tax) and "feel themselves subdued"—as per 9:29.[48]

Many see the assertion that "there is no compulsion in religion" as contradicting the Islamic imperative to wage jihad against unbelievers. But there is really no contradiction at all. This is because the aim of jihad is not the forced conversion of non-Muslims, but their subjugation within the Islamic social order. Says Asad, "All Islamic jurists (*fuqahd'*), without any exception, hold that forcible conversion is under all circumstances null and void, and that any attempt at coercing a non-believer to accept the faith of Islam is a grievous sin: a verdict which disposes of the widespread fallacy that Islam places before the unbelievers the alternative of 'conversion or the sword.'"

Quite so: the choice, as laid out by Muhammad himself, is conversion, subjugation as dhimmis, or the sword.[49] Qutb accordingly denies any contradiction between the injunction that "there is no compulsion in religion" and the imperative to fight until "religion is for Allah" (2:193). He says that "Islam has not used force to impose its beliefs." Rather, jihad's "main objective has been the establishment of a stable society in which all citizens, including followers of other religious creeds, may live in peace and security"—although not with legal equity, as 9:29 emphasizes. For Qutb, that "stable society" is the "Islamic social order," the establishment of which is a chief objective of jihad.[50]

In this light, the verse saying there is no compulsion in religion and the one ordering Muslims to fight until religion is for Allah go together without any trouble. Muslims must fight until "religion is for Allah," but refrain from forcing anyone to accept Allah's religion. They enforce subservience upon those who refuse to convert, such that many of them subsequently convert to Islam so as to escape the humiliating and discriminatory regulations of dhimmitude—but when they convert, they do so freely.

Only at the end of the world, Islamic tradition informs us, will Jesus, the Prophet of Islam, return and Islamize the world, abolishing Christianity and thus the need for the jizya that is paid by the dhimmis: "He will fight

MIRACLES OF THE KORAN

SAYING THE EARTH IS ROUND— 900 YEARS BEFORE MAGELLAN!

"And after that He spread the earth," says Koran 79:30. The maverick Islamic theologian Rashad Khalifa, who was murdered in Arizona in 1990 by jihadists angered by his heterodoxy, translated this verse as, "He made the earth egg-shaped."[51] Thus, the Koran is made to assert that the Earth was round nearly nine hundred years before it was proven with the circumnavigation of the globe by Ferdinand Magellan's expedition.

Even if Khalifa's translation is correct, however, it does not quite add up to the Koran beating Magellan to the punch. In sura 18, after all, we read that the mysterious Dhul-Qarnayn "reached the setting-place of the sun," where "he found it setting in a muddy spring" (18:16). Not quite a foreshadowing of modern cosmology![52]

the people for the cause of Islam. He will break the cross, kill swine, and abolish jizyah. Allah will perish all religions except Islam. He will destroy the Antichrist and will live on the earth for forty years and then he will die. The Muslims will pray over him."[53]

Then religion will be "for Allah," as the Koran directs that it should be (2:193), and there will be no further need for jihad.

Chapter Eleven

"LOVE YOUR ENEMIES" AND OTHER THINGS THE KORAN *DOESN'T* SAY

False assumptions

Now that we have seen what is in the Koran, let's consider what is *not* in the Muslim holy book.

Islam, being one of the "world's great religions," as well as one of the "three great Abrahamic faiths," enjoys the benefit of certain assumptions on the part of uninformed Americans and Europeans. Many people believe that since Islam is a religion, it must teach universal love and brotherhood—because that is what religions do, isn't it? It must teach that one ought to be kind to the poor and downtrodden, generous, charitable, and peaceful. It must teach that we are all children of a loving God whose love for all human beings should be imitated by those whom he has created.

Certainly Judaism and Christianity teach these things, and they are found in nearly equivalent forms in Eastern religions. But when it comes to Islam, the assumptions are wrong. Islam makes a distinction between believers and unbelievers that overrides any obligation to general benevolence.

A moral code from the Koran

As we have seen, the Koran recounts how Moses went up on the mountain and encountered Allah, who gave him tablets—but says nothing about what was written on them (7:145). Although the Ten Commandments do not appear in the Koran, the book is not bereft of specific moral guidelines: its seventeenth chapter enunciates a moral code (17:22–39). Accordingly, Muslims should:

1. Worship Allah alone.
2. Be kind to their parents.
3. Provide for their relatives, the needy, and travelers, and not be wasteful.
4. Not kill their children for fear of poverty.
5. Not commit adultery.
6. Not "take life—which Allah has made sacred—except for just cause." Also, "whoso is slain wrongfully, We have given power unto his heir, but let him not commit excess in slaying"—that is, one should make restitution for wrongful death.
7. Not seize the wealth of orphans.
8. "Give full measure when ye measure, and weigh with a balance that is straight"—that is, conduct business honestly.
9. "Pursue not that of which thou hast no knowledge."
10. Not "walk on the earth with insolence."

Noble ideals, to be sure, but when it comes to particulars, these are not quite equivalent to the Ten Commandments. The provision about not taking life "except for just cause" is, of course, in the same book as the thrice-repeated command to "slay the idolaters wherever you find them" (9:5; 4:89; 2:191)—thus Infidels must understand that their infidelity, their non-acceptance of Islam, is "just cause" for Muslims to make war against them. In the same vein, one is to be kind to one's parents—unless they are Infidels: "O ye who believe! Choose not your fathers nor your brethren for friends if they take pleasure in disbelief rather than faith. Whoso of you taketh them for friends, such are wrong-doers" (9:23).

You killed a Christian? Fine.
But if the victim had been a Muslim...

The rules for restitution for wrongful death are also illuminating for Infidels. The Koran (2:178) establishes a law of retaliation (*qisas*) for murder: equal recompense must be given for the life of the victim, which can take the form of blood money (*diyah*): a payment to compensate for the loss suffered. In Islamic law (Sharia), the amount of compensation varies depending on the identity of the victim. *'Umdat al-Salik* (*Reliance of the Traveller*), a Sharia manual that Cairo's prestigious Al-Azhar University certifies as conforming to the "practice and faith of the orthodox Sunni community," says that the payment for killing a woman is half that to be paid for killing a man. Likewise, the penalty for killing a Jew or Christian is one-third that paid for killing a male Muslim.[1]

The Iranian Sufi Sheikh Sultanhussein Tabandeh, one of the architects of the legal codes of the Islamic Republic of Iran, explains that punishments in Iran for other crimes differ as well, depending on whether the perpetrator is a Muslim. If a Muslim "commits adultery," Tabandeh explains, "his punishment is 100 lashes, the shaving of his head, and one year of banishment." (He is referring, of course, to a Muslim male; a Muslim female would in all likelihood be sentenced to be stoned to death.) "But if the man is not a Muslim," Tabandeh continues, "and commits adultery with a Muslim woman his penalty is execution."

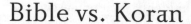

Bible vs. Koran

"Muhammad is the messenger of Allah. And those with him are hard against the disbelievers and merciful among themselves."

—Koran 48:29

"So whatever you wish that men would do to you, do so to them."

—Matthew 7:12

Furthermore, if a Muslim kills a Muslim, he is to be executed, but if he kills a non-Muslim, he incurs a lesser penalty: "If a Muslim deliberately murders another Muslim he falls under the law of retaliation and must by law be put to death by the next of kin. But if a non-Muslim who dies at the hand of a Muslim has by lifelong habit been a non-Muslim, the penalty of death is not valid. Instead the Muslim murderer must pay a fine and be punished with the lash."

Tabandeh explains this disparity as arising from basic Islamic principles:

Since Islam regards non-Muslims as on a lower level of belief and conviction, if a Muslim kills a non-Muslim...then his punishment must not be the retaliatory death, since the faith and conviction he possesses is loftier than that of the man slain.... Again, the penalties of a non-Muslim guilty of fornication with a Muslim woman are augmented because, in addition to the crime against morality, social duty and religion, he has committed sacrilege, in that he has disgraced a Muslim and thereby cast scorn upon the Muslims in general, and so must be executed.

Tabandeh's conclusion follows naturally from all this: "Islam and its peoples must be above the infidels, and never permit non-Muslims to acquire lordship over them."[2]

Do unto others as you would have them do unto you—if they're Muslims

The disparity in the treatment of Muslims and non-Muslims—and in the value placed upon the lives of each—runs through the entire Koran and all of Islamic tradition and law. It has also left its mark on Islamic societies; even today, although Islamic law is not fully enforced in most majority-Muslim countries, nonetheless non-Muslims do not enjoy full legal equality with Muslims in any of those countries—not even secular Turkey.

This is logical, since the Koran contains nothing comparable to the Golden Rule. Jesus enunciates a universal ethic when he says in the New Testament, "So whatever you wish that men would do to you, do so to them" (Matthew 7:12). And the twentieth-century Christian apologist C. S. Lewis showed in his book *The Abolition of Man* that the same principle, which he calls the Law of General Beneficence, prevailed among people in a wide

How's that again?

The Koran tells Muslim men, "Do not marry unbelieving women (idolaters), until they believe. A slave woman who believes is better than an unbelieving woman, even though she allures you" (2:221). And Christians are unbelievers, since they believe in the divinity of Christ: "They indeed have disbelieved who say: Lo! Allah is the Messiah, son of Mary" (5:17), calling Christ the Son of God, by which saying they "imitate what the unbelievers of old used to say" (9:30).

Then it would stand to reason that Muslim men are forbidden to marry Christian women, right? Wrong. The Koran says, "(Lawful unto you in marriage) are (not only) chaste women who are believers, but chaste women among the People of the Book, revealed before your time..." (5:5).

So Muslim men are not to marry unbelieving women, and Christians are unbelievers, but somehow Muslim men are permitted to marry Christian women.

variety of cultures and civilizations. To illustrate this commonality, he quotes material from the ancient Babylonians, Confucius' *Analects*, Roman writers, the Hebrew Scriptures, and other sources—but nothing from the Koran, Hadith, or any other Islamic text.[3]

One might assume this was an unintentional omission, or one borne of ignorance. After all, Lewis could have quoted the Koranic passages that direct Muslims to "overcome evil with good," or "repel evil with that which is better" (13:22; 23:96; 28:54; 41:34). He could have noted the passage that counseled forgiving wrongs: "The recompense for an injury is an injury equal thereto (in degree): but if a person forgives and makes reconciliation, his reward is due from Allah: for (Allah) loveth not those who do wrong" (42:40). He could even have quoted the passage that counsels Muslims to "do good" to "neighbors who are near, neighbors who are strangers, the companion by your side, the wayfarer (ye meet), and what your right hands possess" (4:36).

This is essentially the same as the Judeo-Christian "love thy neighbor as thyself"—isn't it?

That depends on how a Muslim would answer the question that the lawyer asks Jesus, eliciting from Christ the parable of the Good Samaritan: "Who is my neighbor?" (Luke 11:29). The Koran says that "Muhammad is the messenger of Allah," and that "those with him are hard against the disbelievers and merciful among themselves" (48:29). This would suggest that non-Muslims are not deemed worthy of charity and kindness. And indeed, the reader of the Koran will search in vain for even a single verse that specifically tells Muslims to be kind to Infidels or to befriend them, unless it be "by way of precaution, that ye may guard yourselves from them" (3:28)—a verse that, as we have seen, Islamic theologians explain as mandating a false solicitude toward unbelievers for self-protection and/or the protection of Islam.

The Koran also lacks any admonition that all human beings are equal in dignity before God, or the corresponding conviction that all people should have legal equality. And the absence of these principles makes itself felt all through Islamic cultures and societies.

Turn the other cheek, and get it slapped, too

Jesus says, "Do not resist one who is evil. But if any one strikes you on the right cheek, turn to him the other also" (Matthew 5:39). This has seldom been interpreted in the Christian tradition as utter passivity in the face of evil; rather, it has more frequently been understood as an exhortation to mercy and kindness toward one's enemies, while not ruling out self-defense when necessary. One may wonder whether something like the post-World War II reconstruction of Japan and Germany could ever have been conceived in anything but a Judeo-Christian civilization; certainly the phenomenon of the victor extending a helping hand to the vanquished is not rich in precedent in other cultures.

A Muslim counterpart to this principle may be, oddly enough, in the Koran's celebrated "Verse of the Sword" (9:5), right after Allah tells the Muslims to "slay the idolaters wherever ye find them, and take them (captive), and besiege them, and prepare for them each ambush." The passage that immediately follows

---

THE HADITH ILLUMINATES THE KORAN

. . . .

It's witchcraft! Wicked witchcraft!

"Narrated Aishah: Magic was worked on Allah's Messenger so that he used to think that he had sexual relations with his wives while he actually had not. (Sufyan said: 'That is the hardest kind of magic as it has such an effect).'"[4]

this enjoins mercy: "But if they repent and establish worship and pay the poor-due, then leave their way free. Lo! Allah is Forgiving, Merciful."

This, however, only enjoins mercy on those Infidels who convert to Islam: the Arabic word used for "establish worship" is a form of *salat*, and for "pay the poor-due" a form of *zakat*—the Islamic "pillars" of prayer and almsgiving. So the Koran is saying that once these non-Muslims convert to Islam and begin to observe Islamic laws for prayer and charitable giving, Muslims should not fight them. And this widens the scope of justifiable Islamic warfare even further: the renowned Islamic jurist Al-Shafi'i, according to the influential Islamic scholar as-Suyuti, "took this as a proof for killing anyone who abandons the prayer and fighting anyone who refuses to pay zakat [alms]. Some use it as a proof that they are kafirun [unbelievers]."[6] Ibn Kathir notes, "Abu Bakr As-Siddiq [the first caliph] used this and other honorable Ayat [verses] as proof for fighting those who refrained from paying the Zakah."[7]

Thus, Muslims are obligated to fight even other Muslims who do not adequately fulfill Islamic obligations. This is a principle that latter-day Salafist movements apply broadly in branding governments that do not rule according to strict Islamic law as unbelievers who must be fought by true Muslims. This is playing out today in the Taliban's conflict against the government of Pakistan, and to a lesser degree in Egypt and elsewhere.

So much for turning the other cheek.

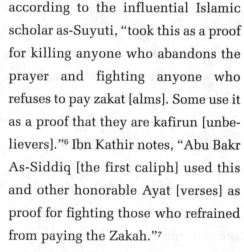

THE HADITH ILLUMINATES THE KORAN

Pawn to swine's bishop 3

"Buraida reported on the authority of his father that Allah's Apostle (may peace be upon him) said: He who played chess is like one who dyed his hand with the flesh and blood of swine."[5]

Chapter Twelve

"BAN THIS FASCIST BOOK?"

The Calcutta Quran Petition

They tried to ban it in India.

In March 1985, two Hindus, Chandmal Chopra and Sital Singh, entered a Writ Petition at the Calcutta High Court alleging that the Koran violated Indian law because it "incites violence, disturbs public tranquility, promotes, on ground of religion, feelings of enmity, hatred and ill-will between different religious communities and insults other religions or religious beliefs of other communities in India."[1] Quoting numerous belligerent Koranic verses, Chopra explained why these were hardly irrelevant sayings from a dusty, unread book:

> While the Koran abounds with sayings which incite violence,
> insult the religious beliefs of other communities and even

exhort the Muslims to kill and murder non-Muslims, the problem is aggravated by yet another fact which has been true in the
past and is universally true in our own times, that unlike other
communities Muslims are, and even fresh converts tend to
become, highly orthodox people and follow the sayings of the
book with a fanatical zeal with the result that whichever country has their sizable number amongst its population can never
have peace on its soil.[2]

The Writ mocked Muslim convert Mohammed Marmaduke Pickthall's
assertion that the Arabic Koran is an "inimitable symphony, the very
sounds of which move men to tears and ecstasy:"[3]

The offending expressions contained in the Koran . . . are not so
offensive in their translation in which they are so quoted as they
are in the original verses in Arabic or in Urdu, the very sound of
whose inimitable symphony not only sends the Muslims to tears
and ecstasy but arouses in them the worst communal passions
and religious fanaticism which have manifested themselves in
murder, slaughter, loot, arson, rape and destruction or desecra-
tion of holy places in historical times as also in contemporary
period not only in India but almost all over the world.[4]

Quickly dismissing the petition, Judge Bimal Chandra Basak played the
ever-popular "out of context" card, explaining that "some passages containing interpretation of some chapters of the Koran quoted out of context cannot be allowed to dominate or influence the main aim and object
of this book. It is dangerous for any court to pass its judgement on such a
book by merely looking at certain passages out of context."[5]

Basak then purported to explain the genuine context of the verses quoted in the petition: "In my opinion it cannot be said that [the] Koran offers any insult to any other religion. It does not reflect any deliberate or malicious intention of outraging the religious feelings of non-Muslims. Isolated passages picked out from here and there and read out of context cannot change the position."[6]

And that was that. Unfortunately, however, Muslims in India who apparently do not know the true context of the Koran's denunciations of unbelievers continue to this day to victimize Hindus and other non-Muslims, and to point to those verses as their inspiration. In the city of Mumbai alone, Islamic jihadists murdered over 250 people in bombings on March 12, 1993, over two hundred in bombings on the city's commuter trains in 2006, and 164 in a series of attacks in November 2008.[7]

Whatever the wisdom of the Calcutta petition, it was a sincere attempt to address a problem that has existed since the first days of Muhammad's prophecy, and that will undoubtedly continue to exist as long as there are people who believe

How's that again?

Muslims should not seek peace when they have the upper hand against the Infidels: "Be not weary and faint-hearted, crying for peace, when ye should be uppermost: for Allah is with you, and will never put you in loss for your (good) deeds" (47:35).

Yet if the Infidels ask for peace, which obviously they would be more likely to do if the Muslims have the upper hand, the Muslims should grant it: "But if the enemy incline towards peace, do thou (also) incline towards peace, and trust in Allah: for He is One that heareth and knoweth (all things)" (8:61).

Faced with the patent contradiction, the great early authority on the Koran, Muhammad's cousin Ibn Abbas, stated—not surprisingly—that the verse about inclining toward peace had been abrogated by the Verse of the Sword (9:5).[8]

the Koran contains the unadulterated words of the one, true God: Muslims will commit violence against non-Muslims, believing that they have been ordered to do so by Allah in the Koran.

Few wish to admit this, or to acknowledge that the problem is immensely larger than that posed by Jews or Christians incited to violence by the Bible. Even fewer have grappled with what precisely can be done about it. Besides Chandmal Chopra and Sital Singh, Geert Wilders is one of the few people who has done so.

Geert Wilders' call to ban the Koran

Dutch Parliamentarian Geert Wilders is the producer of the film *Fitna*, which touched off worldwide Islamic rage as well as ongoing attempts by the Muslim world to compel Western nations to limit free speech about Islam.

He has also sparked controversy for calling upon the Netherlands to ban the Koran, explaining, "The book incites hatred and killing and therefore has no place in our legal order."[9] Since Wilders has called for an "International First Amendment" and the repeal of "hate speech" laws, which he denounces as tools used by the politically powerful to silence dissent, many have charged him with inconsistency in urging a ban on the Koran. Ian Buruma commented in the *New York Times*, "Whether Mr. Wilders has deliberately insulted Muslim people is for the judges to decide. But for a man who calls for a ban on the Koran to act as the champion of free speech is a bit rich."[10]

Is supporting Wilders as a champion of free speech really "a bit rich?" Is he at heart just a totalitarian book-banner?

In fact, no. Wilders made a speech in the Dutch Parliament about banning the Koran in September 2007. "The Koran's core theme," he said, "is about the duty of all Muslims to fight non-Muslims; an Islamic *Mein Kampf*, in which fight means war, jihad. The Koran is above all a book of war—a call to butcher non-Muslims (2:191; 3:141; 4:91; 5:3), to roast them (4:56;

69:30–32), and to cause bloodbaths amongst them (47:4). Jews are compared to monkeys and pigs (2:65; 5:60; 7:166), while people who believe in Jesus Christ as the Son of God must according to the Koran be fought (9:30)."[11]

Wilders then noted that Dutch laws restricting violent incitement are applied inconsistently—namely, books like *Mein Kampf* are banned, but hate-filled imams who preach Koran-inspired jihad and Islamic supremacism are left alone:

> Madam Speaker, the Koran is a book that incites to violence. I remind the House that the distribution of such texts is unlawful according to Article 132 of our Penal Code. In addition, the Koran incites to hatred and calls for murder and mayhem. The distribution of such texts is made punishable by Article 137(e). The Koran is therefore a highly dangerous book; a book which is completely against our legal order and our democratic institutions. In this light, it is an absolute necessity that the Koran be banned for the defence and reinforcement of our civilisation and our constitutional state.[12]

As a matter of Dutch law, Wilders' statements are absolutely correct and should not even be controversial—it is inconsistent to apply hate speech laws to fascist incitement, but not to Islamic incitement. In the United States, of course, the picture is different. I myself believe hate speech laws as well as the banning of any book are both unconstitutional. While there is no justification for genuinely hateful speech such as racial slurs, hate speech laws are indeed weapons in the hands of those who are empowered to decide what constitutes "hate speech:" these laws can all too easily be used to silence politically incorrect speech simply by calling it "hateful."

But the Netherlands has no First Amendment right to free speech, and if the Dutch are going to pass hate speech laws, it's quite reasonable to expect their consistent enforcement, without carving out politically correct exceptions. In reality, of course, although countless jihadists point to the Koran every day as the inspiration for their violent acts, there is about as much chance that the Koran will be banned in the Netherlands or any Western country as there is that the Saudis will replace the Black Stone in the Ka'aba with a Bible.

So what can be done?

Can the Koran be reinterpreted?

Most Western analysts assume—generally without ever having opened a Koran—that the primary interpretation of its martial and hateful verses is benign. Thus, verses enjoining warfare against unbelievers are described as applying only to ancient historical situations that are never to recur, or to precise conditions for warfare that are unlikely to be met today.

Many of these benign interpretations are deceptive and untenable. For example, Muslim theologians and scholars in the West commonly assert that the Koran sanctions only defensive warfare, and to equate this with Catholic just war theory. As we have seen, however, what constitutes a "defensive" conflict is quite different in an Islamic context from what is generally understood in the West. A few years ago, at the popular website "Islam Q & A Online," the South African mufti Ebrahim Desai was asked a question of critical concern to Infidels: "I have a question about offensive jihad. Does it mean that we are to attack even those non-Muslims which [sic] don't do anything against Islam just because we have to propagate Islam?"

Desai's response was telling: "You should understand that we as Muslims firmly believe that the person who doesn't believe in Allah as he is required to, is a disbeliever who would be doomed to Hell eternally. Thus one of the primary responsibilities of the Muslim ruler is to spread Islam throughout the world, thus saving people from eternal damnation." Referring to a commentary on the Koran, he explained that "if a country doesn't allow the propagation of Islam to its inhabitants in a suitable manner or creates hindrances to this, then the Muslim ruler would be justifying [sic] in waging Jihad against this country, so that the message of Islam can reach its inhabitants, thus saving them from the Fire of Jahannum [Hell]. If the Kuffaar [unbelievers] allow us to spread Islam peacefully, then we would not wage Jihad against them."[13]

In other words, a country is left alone as long it passively acquiesces to its Islamization. But if it is perceived to be hindering the spread of Islam, then Muslims are obliged to wage jihad against it. And such a jihad would be considered defensive—against the aggression of unbelief.

This doesn't mean, of course, that every benign interpretation of the Koran is deceptive. Some Islamic reformers undoubtedly consider "defensive" warfare to mean "defensive" in the Western sense of responding to a military attack.

But there is a fundamental obstacle facing all attempts to reinterpret the Koran, whether by spiritualizing its bellicose passages or by restricting their application: such reinterpretations would take a great deal of time to

---

Bible vs. Koran

"Therefore, when ye meet the unbelievers in fight, smite at their necks; at length, when ye have thoroughly subdued them, bind a bond firmly on them: thereafter is the time for either generosity or ransom, until the war lays down its burdens. . . . But those who are slain in the Way of Allah, He will never let their deeds be lost."
—Koran 47:4

"And he sent messengers ahead of him, who went and entered a village of the Samaritans, to make ready for him; but the people would not receive him, because his face was set toward Jerusalem. And when his disciples James and John saw it, they said, 'Lord, do you want us to bid fire come down from heaven and consume them?' But he turned and rebuked them. And they went on to another village."
—Luke 9:52–56

gain general acceptance—and Islamic culture has never been a hospitable environment for new approaches and understandings. The Koran itself discourages innovation that would allow non-literal interpretations, as Wilders pointed out in his speech to the Dutch Parliament:

> Madam Speaker, I acknowledge that there are people who call themselves Muslims and who respect our laws. My party, the Freedom Party, has nothing against such people, of course. However, the Koran does have something against them. For it is stated in the Koran in Sura 2, verse 85, that those believers who do not believe in everything the Koran states will be humiliated and receive the severest punishment; which means that they will roast in Hell. In other words, people who call themselves Muslims but who do not believe, for example, in Sura 9, verse 30, which states that Jews and Christians must be fought, or, for example, in Sura 5, verse 38, which states that the hand of a thief must be cut off, such people will be humiliated and roast in Hell. Note that it is not me who is making this up. All this can be found in the Koran. The Koran also states that Muslims who believe in only part of the Koran are in fact apostates, and we know what has to happen to apostates. They have to be killed.[14]

This is not to say that reinterpretation or reform of the Koran and Islam cannot happen. But they will inevitably face extraordinary obstacles. A case in point is the twentieth-century Sudanese Muslim theologian Mahmud Muhammad Taha. According to Islamic scholar Daniel Pipes, "Taha built his interpretation on the conventional division of the Koran into two. The initial verses came down when Muhammad was a powerless prophet living in Mecca, and tend to be cosmological. Later verses came down when Muhammad was the ruler of Medina, and include many specific rulings. These commands eventually served as the basis for the Shari'a, or Islamic law."

Generally Muslim theologians follow the practice of Ibn Ishaq: they regard Medinan suras—which constitute the bulk of Koranic teaching on warfare against unbelievers—as taking precedence over the earlier Meccan ones. This effectively enshrines the validity of the Koran's most bellicose and supremacist injunctions. On the other hand, Pipes notes, Taha was different. He "argued that specific Koranic rulings applied only to Medina, not to other times and places. He hoped modern-day Muslims would set these aside and live by the general principles delivered at Mecca."

Pipes delineates the startling implications of such a reinterpretation: "Were Taha's ideas accepted, most of the Shari'a would disappear, including outdated provisions concerning warfare, theft, and women. Muslims could then more readily modernize."[15]

Taha himself, however, was tried for apostasy and executed by the Sudanese government in January 1985.

And any new Taha who challenges settled understandings in the Islamic world will likely face similarly virulent outrage and resistance. Does this mean that a large-scale reevaluation of the Koran is impossible? That cannot be said, for circumstances may change in the future, opening the door for a widespread rejection of Koranic literalism. For now, however, any such reform will be branded heresy and will struggle to gain any significant acceptance among Muslims.

In the meantime, Infidels will need to protect themselves and defend their free societies.

But how?

What *not* to do

It is futile to pretend the problem doesn't exist and hope that it will go away. Yet, absurdly, this has been American policy since the September 11 attacks. U.S. officials seem to believe that if they act as if Islam is a religion of peace and the Koran a book of peace, Muslims will feel themselves compelled to behave accordingly.

An extreme example of this bizarre assumption came in President Obama's heralded speech to the Islamic world in Cairo on June 4, 2009.[16] Obama was extremely anxious to appear sympathetic and accommodating to Muslim grievances—so much so that he not only quoted the Koran (and did so ham-handedly and out of context, as we have seen), but also signaled in several ways, whether by ignorance or by design, that he was Muslim himself.

For example, Obama extended "a greeting of peace from Muslim communities in my country: assalaamu alaykum"—that is, peace be upon you. According to Islamic law, however, this is the greeting that a Muslim extends to a fellow Muslim. To a non-Muslim he is to say, "Peace be upon those who are rightly guided"—in other words, "Peace be upon the Muslims." Islamic law is silent about what Muslims must do when naïve, non-Muslim, Islamophilic presidents offer the greeting to Muslims. Obama also said the words that Muslims traditionally utter after mentioning the names of prophets—"peace upon them"—after mentioning Moses, Jesus, and Muhammad. Does he, then, accept Muhammad as a prophet? No reporter has asked him, but that was decidedly the impression he gave, intentionally or not, to the Islamic world.

Obama spoke of a "relationship between Islam and the West" marked by "centuries of coexistence and cooperation, but also conflict and religious wars." He then named three sources of present-day tensions between Muslim countries and the United States: the legacy of Western colonialism; "a Cold War in which Muslim-majority countries were too often treated as proxies without regard to their own aspirations;" and "the sweeping change brought by modernity and globalization," which "led many Muslims to view the West as hostile to the traditions of Islam."

Significantly, Obama only listed ways in which the West has allegedly mistreated the Islamic world. He said not a word about the Koran's doctrines of jihad and religious supremacism. Nothing at all about the Koranic imperative to make war against and subjugate non-Muslims as dhimmis. Not a word about the culture of hatred and contempt for non-Muslims that arises from Koranic teachings and which existed long before the ostensibly harmful spread of American culture ("modernity and globalization") around the world.

Obama did refer to "violent extremists" who have "exploited these tensions in a small but potent minority of Muslims." The idea that Islamic jihadists are a "small but potent minority of Muslims" is universally accepted dogma, born of ignorance of the Koran's contents. The jihadists may indeed be a minority of Muslims, but there is no solid evidence that the vast majority of Muslims reject in principle what the jihadists do—and indeed, how could they, given the Koran's explicit mandates for warfare against Infidels?

With a similar blindness to Islamic religious imperatives to fight Infidels, Obama declared that "the attacks of September 11, 2001 and the continued efforts of these extremists to engage in violence against civilians" have "led some in my country to view Islam as inevitably hostile not only to America and Western countries, but also to human rights." Of course, this perception was also fueled by the Koranic teachings that inspired those attacks. But in his refusal to acknowledge such teachings, Obama was

THE HADITH ILLUMINATES THE KORAN

Snake in the parlor? Learn to live with it.

"[After] Abu Lubaba informed him (Ibn 'Umar) that the Prophet had forbidden the killing of snakes living in houses, he gave up killing them."[17]

simply following the policy of former President George W. Bush and echoing the views of most influential U.S. politicians, diplomats, and analysts.

America clearly needs a dramatic change of policy. But what measures would most effectively protect us from the jihadist threat?

Some first steps

Rejecting Obama's naïveté and appeasement, informed Infidels can and should take a few specific steps.

First, we must recognize that the contents of the Koran have implications for public policy. The fact that significant numbers of Muslims worldwide consider the book to be a mandate for violence should concern government and law enforcement authorities, who should act to prevent Koran-inspired violence. Officials should refuse to accept the deceptions and half-truths that U.S.-based Islamic groups routinely offer regarding the Koran's violent teachings. They should also dismiss the spurious claims of moral equivalency between the Koran and the Bible; ultimately, if the Koran is being used to recruit terrorists and to justify terrorism and Islamic supremacism, then it makes no difference if Christians have historically engaged in violence, or if the Bible also has violent passages, or even if the terrorists are misunderstanding the Koranic passages that inspire them.

U.S. officials should also monitor mosques and Islamic schools in America, demanding that they institute large-scale, transparent programs, open to full and comprehensive inspection, that teach against the doctrines of violence, subjugation, and hatred that we have examined in this book.

Such programs should unambiguously tell Muslims that any and all passages in the Koran that mandate contempt for, violence against, and the subjugation of Infidels are not to be regarded as having any literal application—not now and not at any time in the future. They should teach that Muslims should live with non-Muslims as equals on an indefinite basis, without ever acting to make non-Muslims "feel themselves subdued" (9:29).

These programs should be conducted in an atmosphere of full cooperation with law enforcement and a readiness to alert relevant authorities to the activities of any Muslims who appear inclined toward applying the traditional, mainstream understanding of jihad.

Anything short of this would be inadequate, and even these programs would not guarantee, of course, that no Muslim would ever act upon the Koran's violent and supremacist imperatives. In any case, authorities should thoroughly investigate the reasons why any Muslim institution would refuse to implement such programs.

Would such a demand infringe upon Muslims' religious freedom? No more than the proscription of polygamy infringed upon the Mormons' free exercise of their religion in the late nineteenth century. Islam has always been not just a religion in the Western sense, but a political and social system that acknowledges no legitimate distinction between the sacred and secular realms, and mandates religious law as the only legitimate system of law and governance. American jurists can and should distinguish between the political and the religious aspects of Islam, restricting the former as incompatible with the Constitution, and allowing for the free exercise of the latter.

A historical precedent for this comes from post-World War II Japan. Historian John Lewis explains that "the basic principles of a rational policy toward Islamic Totalitarianism—with clear strategic implications—were revealed in a striking telegram sent by the U.S. Secretary of State James Byrnes to General Douglas MacArthur, the American commander in Japan, in October, 1945." The telegram made a clear distinction between Shintoism as an individual religious faith and Shintoism as an engine of Japanese militarism:

> Shintoism, insofar as it is a religion of individual Japanese, is
> not to be interfered with. Shintoism, however, insofar as it is

directed by the Japanese government, and as a measure enforced from above by the government, is to be done away with. People would not be taxed to support National Shinto and there will be no place for Shintoism in the schools. Shintoism as a state religion—National Shinto, that is—will go.... Our policy on this goes beyond Shinto.... The dissemination of Japanese militaristic and ultra-nationalistic ideology in any

THE HADITH ILLUMINATES THE KORAN

Turn off that radio

"The Prophet (Allah bless him and give him peace) said:

1   'Allah Mighty and Majestic sent me as a guidance and mercy to believers and commanded me to do away with musical instruments, flutes, strings, crucifixes, and the affair of the pre-Islamic period of ignorance.'

2   'On the Day of Resurrection, Allah will pour molten lead into the ears of whoever sits listening to a songstress.'

3   'Song makes hypocrisy grow in the heart as water does herbage.'

4   'This Community will experience the swallowing up of some people by the earth, metamorphosis of some into animals, and being rained upon with stones.' Someone asked, 'When will this be, O messenger of Allah?' and he said, 'When songstresses and musical instruments appear and wine is held to be lawful.'

5   'There will be peoples of my Community who will hold fornication, silk, wine, and musical instruments to be lawful....'"[18]

form will be completely suppressed. And the Japanese Government will be required to cease financial and other support of Shinto establishments.

"The telegram is clear," observes Lewis,

> about the need for separation between religion and state—between an individual's right to follow Shinto and the government's power to enforce it. This requirement applies to Islam today (and to Christianity and Judaism) as strongly as it did to Shinto. In regard to Japan, the job involved breaking the link between Shinto and state; in regard to Islamic Totalitarianism the task involves breaking the link between Islam and state. This is the central political issue we face: the complete lack of any conceptual or institutional separation between church and state in Islam, both historically and in the totalitarian movement today.[19]

Indeed. And at the heart of this is a fundamental conceptual failure: the failure to acknowledge that the contents of the Koran pose any difficulty or challenge for free societies in the first place.

In search of foreign policy coherence

Meanwhile, U.S. policymakers need to recognize that millions of people around the world are reading the Koran, believing that it is the perfect word of Allah that reveals a plan of action for our own day—one that is relentlessly hostile toward Infidels. And this hostility has not arisen because the Infidels have pursued unpopular foreign policies, or because we spread a morally rotten popular culture, or because we support Israel—the front-line state against the global jihad in our age—but simply because we are Infidels, whom the Koran generally portrays as objects of contempt, hatred, and incitement to violence.

Infidel policymakers, take note. A foreign policy based on a realistic appraisal of the contents of the Koran and how they have always been understood in mainstream, authoritative Islam will reevaluate standing U.S. policies in numerous areas, notably these two:

- *Immigration.* Since there is no completely reliable way to tell if any given Muslim believer takes the Koran's dictates about warfare against Infidels literally, immigration of Muslims into the United States should be halted. This is not a racial or even a religious issue, contrary to the claims of Islamic advocacy groups. In reality, this measure is a simple matter of national security aimed at curbing the threat posed by a violent political ideology.

  But since America is so easily mau-maued on any issue where race is invoked, however illegitimately, Muslim immigration into the United States has about as much chance of being restricted—much less halted altogether—as Prohibition has of being reinstated. (Of course, once enough believing Muslims are here, we might see a return to Prohibition along with the adoption of other provisions of Islamic law, but that's another story.) Consequently, immigration officials should at the very least adopt procedures to screen prospective immigrants for jihadist sentiments. As mentioned above, there's no completely reliable way to do this, especially due to the Islamic doctrines of deception. But if law enforcement officials were trained in these doctrines, and if giving deceptive answers were made grounds for deportation, we may be able to stymie a good deal of jihadist and Islamic supremacist activity before it begins.

- *Foreign aid.* "For years," the *New York Times* reported in September 2008, "the survival of Pakistan's military and civilian leaders has depended on a double game: assuring the United States that they were vigorously repressing Islamic militants—and in some cases actually doing so—while simultaneously tolerating and assisting the same militants. From the anti-Soviet fighters of the 1980s and the Taliban of the 1990s to the homegrown militants of today, Pakistan's leaders have been both public enemies and private friends."[20]

  Generally mystified as to why Pakistani leaders would behave this way, foreign policy analysts continue to recommend that the United States shower yet more billions in aid upon Pakistan. But to those who know the Koran's teachings on Infidels, especially the permissibility of deceiving them when necessary (3:28), Pakistan's behavior comes as no surprise. What is instead surprising is America's willingness, even eagerness, to continue bankrolling this double game, without calling the Pakistanis on their deception and challenging them to show their authenticity as allies before receiving any more American largesse.

  Analysts, of course, warn that such actions will "drive our allies into the arms of our enemies." But what's the difference? If Pakistan is aiding the Islamic jihadists it is pledging to fight, how do its pledges to fight them aid the United States? Why should the United States continue to finance the cutting of our own throat?

Ideas have consequences

Many commentators have opined that Islam, like all religions, amounts to nothing more or less than what its adherents make of it. Nothing could be farther from the truth. Ideas matter; they are not always interchangeable, and they lead to human action. It is no accident that monasticism, representational art, and philosophy thrive in a Christian context but not in a Muslim one: Islam forbids monasticism, representational art, and zealous inquiry into divine truths, while Christianity encourages all three—is it any wonder, then, that serious and pious believers in both religions would end up behaving quite differently from each other?

Despite the inclusion of some verses that ostensibly counsel tolerance, the Koran's overall message is that Infidels should be converted to Islam, subjugated as legal inferiors to Muslims, or killed. Consequently, for Infidels, the Koran is a dangerous book. Whatever policy prescriptions Infidel lawmakers choose to adopt in the face of that fact will determine whether or not their Infidel polity survives as such, or becomes an Islamic Sharia polity.

THE HADITH ILLUMINATES THE KORAN

Keep your head bowed— or else

"Abu Huraira reported: People should avoid lifting their eyes towards the sky while supplicating in prayer, otherwise their eyes would be snatched away."[21]

We should not, and indeed must not, abandon our principles of legal equality and freedom of speech in order to defend ourselves against the jihadist threat. Nor should we allow ourselves to be cowed into silence by the manipulative and deceptive intimidation tactics practiced by U.S.-based Islamic groups and their allies.

The situation today is grave for Infidels. The willful blindness of Western leaders threatens us all, and the very survival of free societies. We can only hope that, before it is altogether too late and the principles of our societies are irretrievably compromised, they will *open the Koran and begin to read.*

ACKNOWLEDGMENTS

Once again I must express my gratitude to Jack Langer, an editor of enormous tact and skill, whose patient and discerning hand has given this book whatever merit it may have. Harry Crocker and the entire Regnery team are, as always, a joy to work with, and the Jihad Watch team of Hugh Fitzgerald, Marisol Seibold, and Raymond Ibrahim did extraordinary work in providing daily news and commentary at *www.jihadwatch.org* while much of my attention was occupied by this book. Special thanks are due also to the superb website Answering Islam (*www.answering-islam.org*), a huge storehouse of reliable information on the Koran and related issues. Thanks also to the many whom I am, as always, not at liberty to name publicly, but they know who they are. And no acknowledgments page in any of my books would be complete without a tip of the hat to Jeff Rubin, without whom none of this would have been possible.

NOTES

Chapter One

1. The name of the Islamic holy book has various spellings in English. The most common are "Koran," which is used throughout this book except in quotations, and "Qur'an."

2. Ahmed ibn Naqib al-Misri, *Reliance of the Traveller ('Umdat al-Salik): A Classic Manual of Islamic Sacred Law*, trans. Nuh Ha Mim Keller (Beltsville, MD: Amana Publications, 1999), e8.1, e8.3.

3. Howard Kurtz, "Newsweek apologizes," *Washington Post*, May 16, 2005; available online at: http://www.washingtonpost.com/wp-dyn/content/article/2005/05/15/AR2005051500605.html.

4. Michael Potemra, "The Flames of Religious Hatred: The pope, the Koran & Andrew Sullivan," *National Review*, September 18, 2006; available online at: http://article.nationalreview.com/?q=NTAzMTFjYzVmNTMzNjJmMzcwYmJkZWQ3ZmFhNWY1N2Q=.

5. Department of Defense memorandum, http://www.defenselink.mil/news/Jun2005/d20050601KoranSOP.pdf.

6. "Explore the Quran," http://www.cair.com/explorethequran/.

7. Adil Salahi, "Baseless Campaign Against Islam," *Arab News*, June 19, 2006; available online at: http://www.arabnews.com/?page=5&section=0&article=84036&d=21&m=6&y=2006.

8. Staff Sgt. Russell Bassett, "Respect the faith, not the fanatics," Army News Service, May 14, 2004.

9. Ruth Gledhill, "Tony Blair calls on world to wage war on militant Islam," *Times Online*, April 23, 2009; available online at: http://www.timesonline.co.uk/tol/comment/faith/article6153607.ece.

10. George W. Bush, Second Inaugural Address, January 20, 2005.

11. Bruno Waterfield, "Ban Koran like Mein Kampf, says Dutch MP," *Telegraph*, August 9, 2007; available online at: http://www.telegraph.co.uk/news/worldnews/1559877/Ban-Koran-like-Mein-Kampf-says-Dutch-MP.html.

12. Oriana Fallaci, *The Force of Reason* (New York: Rizzoli International, 2004), 305.

13. Winston Churchill, *The Gathering Storm* (Boston: Houghton Mifflin Harcourt, 1986), 50.

14. Sita Ram Goel, *The Calcutta Quran Petition* (New Dehli, India: Voice of India, 1999), 276–77.

15. Bruno Waterfield, "Ban Koran like Mein Kampf."

16. Oriana Fallaci, *The Force of Reason*, 305.

17. "Italian author to be tried for defaming Islam," Associated Press, June 12, 2006.

18. Khalid Sheikh Mohammed, Walid bin 'Attash, Ramzi bin As-Shibh, 'Ali 'Abd al-'Aziz 'Ali, and Mustafa Ahmed al-Hawsawi, "The Islamic Response to the Government's Nine Accusations," March 9, 2009.

19. Osama Bin Laden, "Declaration of War against the Americans Occupying the Land of the Two Holy Places," 1996; available online at: http://www.mideast-web.org/osamabinladen1.htm.

20. The parenthetical glosses here appear to be Osama's own. See "Full text: bin Laden's 'letter to America,'" *Observer*, November 24, 2002.

21. "Bin Laden's Sermon for the Feast of the Sacrifice," Middle East Media Research Institute (MEMRI), Special Dispatch No. 476, March 6, 2003.

22. "Arab Mother Cried For Mercy, They Responded - And She Murdered Them," *Israel National News*, January 15, 2004; available online at: http://www.israel-nationalnews.com/News/News.aspx/56237.

23. "Paris: Gang suspected of killing Jew nabbed," *Ynet News*, February 19, 2006; available online at: http://www.ynetnews.com/articles/0,7340,L-3218190,00.html.

24. "Mohammed Taheri-Azar's letter to police," *The Herald-Sun*, March 29, 2006; available online at: http://www.investigativeproject.org/documents/case_docs/248.pdf.

25. Robert Spencer, "Letters from a mujahid," Jihad Watch, May 12, 2006; available online at: http://www.jihadwatch.org/archives/011397.php.

26. "Focus: Undercover in the academy of hatred," *The Sunday Times*, August 7, 2005; available online at: http://www.timesonline.co.uk/tol/news/uk/article552649.ece.

27. "Pakistan Taleban vow more violence," BBC News, January 29, 2007; available online at: http://news.bbc.co.uk/2/hi/south_asia/6292061.stm.

28. "Jihad in the Koran and Ahadeeth," www.waaqiah.com, 2002. (Website no longer operative.)

29. Amir Taheri, *Holy Terror: Inside the World of Islamic Terrorism* (Chevy Chase, MD: Adler & Adler, 1987), 241–43.

30. John Lofton, "Timothy McVeigh was not a 'Christian' terrorist," *Human Events*, May 6, 2002.

31. Barack Obama, Remarks By The President On A New Beginning, June 4, 2009.

32. Ibid.

33. "From the Fatwa Department: 'the Kuffaar can never be trusted,'" Jihad Watch, January 8, 2005; available online at: http://www.jihadwatch.org/archives/004582.php.

34. John Derbyshire, "June Diary," National Review Online, July 2, 2007; available online at: http://article.nationalreview.com/?q=YTMxZmVkYjhkNzgzMzY2NzAyYzI3NTUxMjY3ZWQ3OWQ=.

35. "The Bible v the Koran," *The Economist*, December 19, 2007.

36. Abu Abdir Rahmaan, "The Sunnah: The Second Form of Revelation," *Al-Haramain Online Newsletter*, July 2000; available online at: http://alharamain.org/english/newsletter/issue38/sunnah.htm.

37. Mohammed Nasir-ul-Deen Al-Albani, "The Status of Sunnah in Islam," translated by A. R. M. Zerruque; available online at: http://www.orst.edu/groups/msa/books/sunnah1.html.

38. Waed B. Hallaq, *A History of Islamic Legal Theories* (New York: Cambridge University Press, 1997), 60. Hallaq refers to Muhammad ibn Idris al-Shafi'i (767–819), founder of the school of Islamic jurisprudence that bears his name and an enormously important figure in Islamic jurisprudence as a whole.

39. These are *Sahih Bukhari*, that is, the collection of hadiths made by the imam Muhammad Ibn Ismail al-Bukhari (810–870); and *Sahih Muslim*, a similar

collection compiled by Muslim ibn al-Hajjaj al-Qushayri (821–875). The other four of the six trustworthy collections are the *Sunan* of Abu Dawud as-Sijistani (d. 888); *Sunan Ibn Majah* by Muhammad ibn Majah (d. 896); *Sunan At-Tirmidhi* by Abi 'Eesaa Muhammad At-Tirmidhi (824–893); and *Sunan An-Nasai* by Ahmad ibn Shu'ayb an-Nasai (d. 915).

40. The word *hadith*'s Arabic plural is *ahadith*, and this is found in much English-language material on Islam. However, to avoid confusion I have used the English plural form.

41. Denis MacEoin with Dominic Whiteman, *Music, Chess, and Other Sins: Segregation, Integration, and Muslim Schools in Britain* (Civitas, 2009).

42. Paloma Esquivel, "Some influential Muslim groups question FBI's actions," *Los Angeles Times*, April 20, 2009; available online at: http://articles.latimes.com/2009/apr/20/local/me-muslims-fbi20.

Chapter Two

1. Tilman Nagel, *The History of Islamic Theology from Muhammad to the Present*, trans. Thomas Thornton (Princeton, NJ: Markus Wiener Publishers, 2000), 1.

2. Seyyed Hossein Nasr, *A Young Muslim's Guide to the Modern World* (Chicago: Kazi Publications, 1994), 15.

3. Caesar E. Farah, *Islam*, 6th ed. (Hauppauge, NY: Barrons, 2000), 77.

4. V. S. Naipaul, *Among the Believers: An Islamic Journey* (London: Vintage Books, 1982), 103.

5. Council on American-Islamic Relations, "About Islam and American Muslims," Cair.com; full text available online at: http://www.cair.com/AboutIslam/IslamBasics.aspx.

6. "Full text: bin Laden's 'letter to America,'" *Observer*, November 24, 2002.

7. Muhammad Ibn Ismail al-Bukhari, *Sahih Bukhari*, vol. 4, book 61, no. 3624.

8. Ibid., vol. 5, book 63, no. 3806.

9. Ibn Abi Dawud, *Kitab al-Masahif*, p. 23, in John Gilchrist, *Jam' Al-Qur'an, The Codification of the Qur'an Text: A Comprehensive Study of the Original Collection of the Qur'an Text and the Early Surviving Qur'an Manuscripts*, MERCSA, 1989; available online at: http://www.answering-islam.org/Gilchrist/Jam/index.html.

10. Bukhari, *Sahih Bukhari*, vol. 6, book 65, no. 4679.

11. Ibn Abi Dawud, *Kitab al-Masahif*, in John Gilchrist, *Jam' Al-Qur'an*, 11.

12. As-Suyuti, *Al-Itqan fii Ulum al-Qur'an*, in John Gilchrist, *Jam' Al-Qur'an*, 524.

13. Ibid., 525.

14. ibn al-Hajjaj al-Qushayri, *Sahih Muslim*, book 5, no. 2296. The surahs of Musabbihat are chapters 57, 59, 61, 62, and 64 of the Koran, each of which begin with "All that is in the heavens and the earth glorifieth [*sabbaha*] Allah; and He is the Mighty, the Wise." That this man would remember as passages of a lost chapter verses that are actually in the Koran does not necessarily mean that his memory was faulty; since the Koran is highly repetitive, it is by no means impossible that there once existed, but is now lost, a Koranic chapter containing these two verses.

15. Bukhari, *Sahih Bukhari*, vol. 8, book 82, no. 816. Online version available at: http://www.usc.edu/schools/college/crcc/engagement/resources/texts/muslim/hadith/bukhari/082.sbt.html#008.082.816

16. As-Suyuti, *Al-Itqan fii Ulum al-Qur'an*, in John Gilchrist, *Jam' Al-Qu'ran*, 524.

17. Bukhari, *Sahih Bukhari*, vol. 6, book 66, no. 4987.

18. Ibid.

19. Ibid., no. 3295.

20. Ibn Abi Dawud, *Kitab al-Masahif*, in John Gilchrist, *Jam' Al-Qu'ran*, 15.

21. Ibid.

22. S. Moinul Haq and H. K. Ghazanfar, Introduction to Ibn Sa'd, *Kitab Al-Tabaqat Al-Kabir*, vol. I, S. Moinul Haq and H. K. Ghazanfar, trans. Kitab Bhavan, n.d., vol. 2, p.441.

23. Harun Yahya, "Signs of the Last Day"; available online: http://www.harunyahya.com/signs03.php;http://www.answering-islam.org/Emails/moon_prophecy.htm.

24. 'A'isha 'Abdarahman at-Tarjumana and Ya'qub Johnson, trans., *Malik's Muwatta,* vol. 8, book 8, no. 26. http://www.usc.edu/schools/college/crcc/engagement/resources/texts/muslim/hadith/muwatta/008.mmt.html#008.8.8.26

Chapter Three

1. Ibn Kathir, *Tafsir Ibn Kathir* (Abridged), vol. 4 (Houston, TX: Darussalam, 2000), 29.

2. Jalalu'd-Din Al-Mahalli and Jalalu'd-Din As-Suyuti, *Tafsir Al-Jalalayn*, trans. Aisha Bewley (London: Dar Al Taqwa, Ltd., 2007), 328.

3. Muhammad Asad, *The Message of the Qur'an* (Watsonville, CA: The Book Foundation, 2003), 1135.

4. Zakir Naik, *Most Common Questions asked by Non-Muslims who have some knowledge of Islam*, quoted in Sam Shamoun, "Is Satan an Angel or a Jinn?

Analyzing the Quran's Confusing Statements," *Answering Islam*; available online at: http://www.answering-islam.org/Quran/Contra/iblis.html.

5. William St. Clair-Tisdall, *Sources of the Quran*, chapter three; available online at: http://www.truthnet.org/islam/src-chp3.htm.

6. Ibn Kathir, *Tafsir Ibn Kathir*, vol. 7, p. 320.

7. Ibid.

8. Ibid., 321.

9. Ibid., 327.

10. Jalalu'd-Din Al-Mahalli and Jalalu'd-Din As-Suyuti, *Tafsir Al-Jalalayn*, trans. Aisha Bewley (London: Dar Al Taqwa Ltd., 2007), 818.

11. William St. Clair-Tisdall, *Sources of the Quran*, chapter three.

12. Ibid.

13. Ibn Kathir, *Tafsir Ibn Kathir*, vol. 6, p. 120.

14. Bukhari, *Sahih al-Bukhari*, vol. 4, book 59, no. 3289.

15. Ibn Kathir, *Tafsir Ibn Kathir*, vol. 6, 129.

16. Ibid., p. 121.

17. Muhammad Aashiq Ilahi Bulandshahri, *Illuminating Discourses on the Noble Qur'an* (*Tafsir Anwarul Bayan*), trans. Afzal Hussain Elias and Muhammad Arshad Fakhri (Darul Ishaat, 2005), vol. I, p. 386.

18. "Gospel of Thomas Greek Text A," from *The Apocryphal New Testament*, trans. M. R. James (Gloucestershire: Clarendon Press, 1924); available online at: http://wesley.nnu.edu/biblical_studies/noncanon/gospels/inftoma.htm.

19. Bukhari, *Sahih al-Bukhari*, vol. 4, book 59, no. 3303.

20. Ibid., book 60, no. 3402.

21. Sayyid Abul Ala Maududi, *The Meaning of the Qur'an* (*Tafhim al-Qur'an*), "Al-Kahf"; available online at: http://www.usc.edu/schools/college/crcc/engagement/resources/texts/muslim/maududi/mau18.html#S18.

22. Abdullah Yusuf Ali, *The Meaning of the Holy Qur'an* (Beltsville, MD: Amana Publications, 1999), 725.

23. Irfan Omar, "Khidr in the Islamic Tradition," *The Muslim World*, vol. LXXXIII, no. 3-4, July-October, 1993.

24. Ibn Saad, "Ibn Taymiyya says Khidr is Alive," *Seeking Ilm*, September 20, 2007.

25. Bukhari, *Sahih al-Bukhari*, vol. 6, book 66, no. 5011.

26. Abdul Hamid Siddiqi, trans. *Sahih Muslim* (New Dehli, India: Kitab Bhavan, revised edition 2000), Book 19, no. 4457.

27. Ibn Kathir, *Tafsir Ibn Kathir*, vol. 6, p. 113.

28. Ibid., 203.

29. Ibid., 203–4.

30. Jalalu'd-Din Al-Mahalli and Jalalu'd-Din As-Suyuti, *Tafsir Al-Jalalayn*, 639.

31. Sayyid Abul Ala Mawdudi, *Towards Understanding the Qur'an* (*Tafhim al-Qur'an*), trans. Zafar Ishaq Ansari (Markfield, Leicestershire: The Islamic Foundation, 1995), 127.

32. Muhammad al-Ghazali, *Journey Through the Qur'an: The Content and Context of the Suras* (London: Dar Al-Taqwa, Ltd., 1998), 207.

33. Bukhari, *Sahih al-Bukhari*, vol. 4, book 59, no. 3270.

34. Khalid Jan, "Why Zul-Qarnain of the Qur'an is not Alexander the Great," IslamAwareness.net; http://www.islamawareness.net/FAQ/zulqarnain.html.

35. Muhammad Asad, *The Message of the Qur'an* (Watsonville, CA: The Book Foundation, 2003), 503.

Chapter Four

1. Gary Stern, "N.Y. Muslims denounce terror in response," LoHud.com, May 22, 2009.

2. Bukhari, *Sahih al-Bukhari*, vol. 4, book 59, no. 3322.

3. Mohammed Marmaduke Pickthall, *The Meaning of the Glorious Koran* (New York: New American Library, 1991).

4. Ahmed ibn 'Abdullah al-Baatilee, "Arabic: The Language of the Qur'an," *Al Haramain*, www.alharamain.org; http://63.104.232.198/issue35/quraan.htm

5. Ibn Kathir, *Tafsir Ibn Kathir*, vol. 5, 134–35.

6. Ibn Ishaq, *The Life of Muhammad: A Translation of Ibn Ishaq's Sirat Rasul Allah*, trans. A. Guillaume (New York: Oxford University Press, 1955), 287–88.

7. Sayyid Qutb, *In the Shade of the Qur'an* (*Fi Zilal al-Qur'an*), vol. 1, trans. M. A. Salahi and A. A. Shamis (Markfield, Leicestershire: The Islamic Foundation, 1999), 259–60.

8. Muhammad Aashiq Ilahi Bulandshahri, *Illuminating Discourses on the Noble Qur'an* (*Tafsir Anwarul Bayan*), vol. 1, trans. Afzal Hussain Elias and Muhammad Arshad Fakhri (Darul Ishaat, 2005), 501.

9. Aashiq Ilahi Bulandshahri, *Illuminating Discourses on the Noble Qur'an*, vol. I, p. 502.

10. Bernard Lewis, *Race and Slavery in the Middle East* (New York: Oxford University Press, 1994); reprinted at: http://www.fordham.edu/halsall/med/lewis1.html.

11. David G. Littman, "'Traditional concept of Jihad does allow Slavery as a by-product.' Sudan: UN affirmation by former prime minister Sadiq al-Mahdi,"

Jihad Watch, June 12, 2009; available online at: http://www.jihadwatch.org/archives/026553.php.

12. "'Thousands made slaves' in Darfur," BBC News, December 17, 2008; available online at: http://news.bbc.co.uk/2/hi/africa/7786612.stm.

13. Pascale Harter, "Slavery: Mauritania's best kept secret," BBC News, December 13, 2004; available online at: http://news.bbc.co.uk/2/hi/africa/4091579.stm.

14. Pascal Fletcher, "Slavery still exists in Mauritania," Reuters, March 21, 2007; available online at: http://www.reuters.com/article/latestCrisis/idUSL18334379.

15. Liesl Louw, "Slavery lives on," Media24 Africa, September 2, 2004; available online at: http://www.news24.com/News24/Africa/Features/0,,2-11-37_1582738,00.html.

16. Barbara Ferguson, "Saudi Gets 27 Years to Life for Enslaving Maid," *Arab News*, September 1, 2006; available online at: http://www.arabnews.com/?page=4&section=0&article=80144&d=1&m=9&y=2006.

17. George W. Bush, Message on the observance of Eid al-Adha, January 8, 2007.

18. Karen Hughes, Celebration of Eid al-Adha at the Islamic Society of Frederick, Maryland, January 10, 2006.

19. Günter Lüling, *A Challenge to Islam for Reformation. The Rediscovery and Reliable Reconstruction of a Comprehensive Pre-Islamic Christian Hymnal Hidden in the Koran under the Earliest Islamic Reinterpretation* (New Dehli, India: Motilal Banarsidass Publishers, 2003).

20. Bukhari, *Sahih al-Bukhari* vol. 4, book 60, no. 3329.

21. Ibn Kathir, *Tafsir Ibn Kathir*, vol. 10, p. 253.

Chapter Five

1. Ibn Kathir, *Tafsir Ibn Kathir*, vol. 5, p. 68.

2. Jalalu'd-Din Al-Mahalli and Jalalu'd-Din As-Suyuti, *Tafsir Al-Jalalayn*, 134.

3. Ibn Kathir, *Tafsir Ibn Kathir*, vol. 2, p. 185.

4. Jalalu'd-Din Al-Mahalli and Jalalu'd-Din As-Suyuti, *Tafsir Al-Jalalayn*, 461.

5. Sayyid Abul Ala Maududi, "Yusuf," *The Meaning of the Qur'an* (Tafhim al Qur'an), http://www.usc.edu/schools/college/crcc/engagement/resources/texts/muslim/maududi/mau12.html#S12.

6. Ibn Kathir, *Rafsir Ibn Kathir*, vol. 5, p. 136.

7. Bukhari, *Sahih al-Bukhari*, vol. 7, book 76, no. 5747.

8. *Tanwîr al-Miqbâs min Tafsîr Ibn 'Abbâs* for Koran 12:18, trans. Mokrane Guezzou; available online at: http://www.altafsir.com/tafasir.asp?tmadhno=0&ttafsirno=73&tsorano=12&tayahno=18&tdisplay=yes&userprofile=0&languageid=2.

9. Sayyid Abul Ala Maududi, "Yusuf," *The Meaning of the Qur'an*.

10. Ibn Kathir, *Tafsir Ibn Kathir*, vol. 5, pp. 161–62.

11. Muhammad Asad, *The Message of the Qur'an*, 391.

12. Muhammad al-Ghazali, *Journey Through the Qur'an*, 217.

13. Sayyid Abul Ala Maududi, "Al-Mu'min," *The Meaning of the Koran*, http://www.usc.edu/schools/college/crcc/engagement/resources/texts/muslim/maududi/mau40.html#S40.

14. Masud Masihiyyen, "Noah's Ark or Noah's Steamboat?" *Answering Islam*; available online at: http://www.answering-islam.org/authors/masihiyyen/noahs_ark.html.

15. Ibn Kathir, *Tafsir Ibn Kathir*, vol. 4, p. 178.

16. Bukhari, *Sahih al-Bukhari*, vol. 4, book 59, no. 3320.

17. Ibid., vol. 6, book 61, no. 3579.

18. Jalalu'd-Din Al-Mahalli and Jalalu'd-Din As-Suyuti, *Tafsir al-Jalalayn*, p. 904.

19. Abu Ja'far Muhammad bin Jarir al-Tabari, *The History of al-Tabari*, Volume VIII, *The Victory of Islam*, trans. Michael Fishbein (Albany, NY: State University of New York Press, 1997), 2.

20. Maxime Rodinson, *Muhammad*, trans. Anne Carter (New York: Pantheon Books, 1980), 279–83.

21. Bukhari, *Sahih al-Bukhari*, vol. 7, book 68, no. 5267.

22. Ibid., vol. 4, book 61, no. 3583.

Chapter Six

1. Muhammad Aashiq Ilahi Bulandshahri, *Illuminating Discourses on the Noble Qur'an*, vol. 1, p. 363.

2. Ibn Kathir, *Tafsir Ibn Kathir*, vol. 3, p. 326.

3. Jalalu'd-Din Al-Mahalli and Jalalu'd-Din As-Suyuti, *Tafsir Al-Jalalayn*, 285.

4, "Shirk: the ultimate crime," *Invitation to Islam Newsletter*, Issue 2, July 1997; available online at: http://www.geocities.com/askress2009/articles/shirk_the_ultimate_crime.html.

5. Abdul Hamid Siddiqi, trans. *Sahih Muslim*, book 23, no. 5113.

6. Muhammad Asad, *The Message of the Qur'an*, 21.

7. Ibn Kathir, *Tafsir Ibn Kathir*, vol. 1, pp. 248–49.

8. Sayyid Qutb, *In the Shade of the Qur'an* (*Fi Zilal al-Qur'an*), trans. M. A. Salahi and A. A. Shamis, vol. I (Markfield, Leicestershire: The Islamic Foundation, 1999), 73.

9. 'A'isha 'Abdarahman at-Tarjumana and Ya'qub Johnson, trans. *Malik's Muwatta*, book 3, no. 3.9.39.

10. Robert Spencer, "Islamic Supremacy at the DNC," *FrontPageMagazine.com*, February 6, 2007; available online at: http://frontpagemagazine.com/readArticle.aspx?ARTID=278.

11. Robert Spencer, "Prayers for the Enemy," *FrontPageMagazine.com*, April 9, 2007; available online at: http://www.frontpagemag.com/readArticle.aspx?ARTID=25990.

12. See, for example, the book by Islamic apologist John Esposito, *Islam: The Straight Path* (New York: Oxford University Press, 2005).

13. Ibn Kathir, *Tafsir Ibn Kathir*, vol. 1, p. 87.

14. This is the view of Tabari, Zamakhshari, the *Tafsir al-Jalalayn*, the *Tanwir al-Miqbas min Tafsir Ibn Abbas*, and Ibn Arabi, as well as Ibn Kathir.

15. Mahmoud M. Ayoub, *The Qur'an and its Interpreters*, vol. 1 (Albany, New York: State University of New York Press, 1984), 49.

16. The quoted verse is Koran 3:110; bracketed and parenthetical material added by the translator. See Bukhari, *Sahih al-Bukhari*, vol. 6, book 65, no. 4557.

17. Bukhari, *Sahih al-Bukhari*, vol. 5, book 63, no. 3827.

18. Jalalu'd-Din Al-Mahalli and Jalalu'd-Din As-Suyuti, *Tafsir al-Jalalayn*, 941.

19. *Tanwir al-Miqbas min Tafsir ibn Abbas*, trans., 36:9, http://www.altafsir.com/Ibn-Abbas.asp; available online at: http://www.altafsir.com/Tafasir.asp?tMadhNo=2&tTafsirNo=73&tSoraNo=36&tAyahNo=9&tDisplay=yes&UserProfile=0&LanguageId=2.

20. Ibn Kathir, *Tafsir Ibn Kathir*, vol. 8, p. 171.

21. Ibid.

22. Jalalu'd-Din Al-Mahalli and Jalalu'd-Din As-Suyuti, *Tafsir al-Jalalayn*, 524.

23. Ibn Kathir, *Tafsir Ibn Kathir*, vol. 8, p. 172.

24. Ibid., vol. 1, p. 120.

25. G. F. Haddad, "The Qadariyya, Mu'tazila, and Shî'a," *Living Islam*; available online at: http://www.livingislam.org/n/qms_e.html.

Chapter Seven

1. Ibn Ishaq, *The Life of Muhammad*, 259.

2. Harun Yahya, "'People Of The Book' & The Muslims: The Natural Alliance Between Christianity, Judaism and Islam," IslamDenouncesTerrorism.com.

3. Yvonne Ridley, "Beware The Happy Clappies," *Bismika Allahuma*, December 1, 2006.

4. "Are today's Christians and Jews considered from the people of the book?" *Jihad Watch*, July 5, 2004.

5.   Abdul Hamid Siddiqi, trans. *Sahih Muslim,* book 19, no. 4294.

6.   Andrew Bostom, *The Legacy of Islamic Antisemitism* (Amherst, NY: Prometheus, 2008), 35.

7.   Jalalu'd-Din Al-Mahalli and Jalalu'd-Din As-Suyuti, *Tafsir Al-Jalalayn*, 259.

8.   Muhammad Aashiq Ilahi Bulandshahri, *Illuminating Discourses on the Noble Qur'an*, vol. 2, pp. 98–99.

9.   Ibn Kathir, *Tafsir Ibn Kathir*, vol. 3, p. 221.

10.   "The Covenant of the Islamic Resistance Movement (Hamas)," August 18, 1988; available online at: http://www.mideastweb.org/hamas.htm.

11.   Simon Rocker, "What the Koran says about the land of Israel," *The Jewish Chronicle*, March 19, 2009.

12.   Ibn Kathir, *Tafsir Ibn Kathir*, vol. 3, p. 142.

13.   Ibid., 142–43.

14.   Andrew Bostom, *The Legacy of Islamic Antisemitism* (Amherst, NY: Prometheus, 2008), 33.

15.   John Esposito, "Practice and Theory: A response to 'Islam and the Challenge of Democracy,'" *Boston Review*, April/May 2003; "Al-Qaradawi full transcript," BBC News, July 8, 2004.

16.   'Atiyyah Saqr, "Jews as Depicted in the Qur'an," Islam Online, March 23, 2004; available at *Jihad Watch*, http://www.jihadwatch.org/dhimmiwatch/archives/006908.php.

17.   Jalalu'd-Din Al-Mahalli and Jalalu'd-Din As-Suyuti, *Tafsir Al-Jalalayn*, 1218.

18.   Tanwir al-Miqbas min Tafsir ibn Abbas, 65:12.

19.   Jochen Katz, "The Seven Earths: Their Existence and their Location," *Answering Islam*, n.d.; available online at: *http://www.answering-islam.org/Quran/Science/seven_earths.html*.

20.   'Atiyyah Saqr, "Jews as Depicted in the Qur'an."

21.   Ibid.

22.   Ibid.

23.   Ibid.

24.   Ibid.

25.   Bukhari, *Sahih al-Bukhari*, vol. 4, book 60, no. 3330.

26.   'Atiyyah Saqr, "Jews as Depicted in the Qur'an."

27.   Harry de Quetteville, "Christians still 'swine' and Jews 'apes' in Saudi schools," *Telegraph*, June 25, 2006.

28.   Alexandra Frean, "Teacher accuses Islamic school of racism," *The Times*, April 15, 2008.

29.   "PA Supervised Sermon: Jews the sons of apes and pigs," IMRA, March 15, 2004.

30. "Egyptian Religious Endowments Ministry Official: The Pigs Living Today Are Descended from Jews—And Must Be Slaughtered," Middle East Media Research Institute, Special Dispatch No. 2359, May 15, 2009.

31. "Egyptian Cleric Muhammad Hussein Ya'qoub: The Jews Are the Enemies of Muslims Regardless of the Occupation of Palestine," MEMRITV Clip No. 2042, January 17, 2009.

32. Sayyid Abul Ala Mawdudi, *Towards Understanding the Qur'an*, vol. 1, p. 70.

33. Ibn Kathir, *Tafsir Ibn Kathir*, vol. 1, p. 211.

34. Sayyid Qutb, *In the Shade of the Qur'an*, vol. 1, p. 62.

35. Sayyid Abul Ala Mawdudi, *Towards Understanding the Qur'an*, vol. 1, p. 73.

36. Abdul Hamid Siddiqi, trans. *Sahih Muslim*, book 41, no. 6985.

37. Ibn Kathir, *Tafsir Ibn Kathir*, vol. 1, p. 245.

38. Ibn Ishaq, *The Life of Muhammad*, 182.

39. Bukhari, *Sahih al-Bukhari*, vol. 5, book 63, no. 3887.

40. Abdul Hamid Siddiqi, trans. *Sahih Muslim*, book 1, no. 309.

41. Ibn Ishaq, *The Life of Muhammad*, 182.

42. Bukhari, *Sahih al-Bukhari*, vol. 4, book 59, no. 3305.

43. Ibid., vol. 5, book 63, no. 3887.

44. Ibn Ishaq, *The Life of Muhammad*, 183.

45. Ibn Kathir, *Tafsir Ibn Kathir*, vol. 8, pp. 271–72.

Chapter Eight

1. Ibn Ishaq, *The Life of Muhammad*, 402–3.

2. Abdul Hamid Siddiqi, trans. *Sahih Muslim*, book 25, no. 5326.

3. Muhammad Aashiq Ilahi Bulandshahri, *Illuminating Discourses on the Noble Qur'an*, vol. 1, p. 375.

4. *The Protoevangelium of James*, NewAdvent.org; available online at: http://www.newadvent.org/fathers/0847.htm.

5. Ibn Kathir, *Tafsir Ibn Kathir*, vol. 6, p. 237.

6. Ibid., vol. 2, p. 158.

7. Ibid., vol. 6, p. 244.

8. Ibid., 249.

9. Muhammad Aashiq Ilahi Bulandshahri, *Illuminating Discourses on the Noble Qur'an*, vol. 1, p. 386.

10. Ibn Kathir, *Tafsir Ibn Kathir*, vol. 3, pp. 26–27.

11. Muhammad Aashiq Ilahi Bulandshahri, *Illuminating Discourses on the Noble Qur'an*, vol. 2, p. 8.

12. Bukhari, *Sahih al-Bukhari*, vol. 3, book 34, no. 2222.

13. Ibn Kathir, *Tafsir Ibn Kathir*, vol. 3, p. 32.
14. Bukhari, *Sahih al-Bukhari*, vol. 4, book 60, no. 3448.
15. Ibn Ishaq, *The Life of Muhammad*, 409.
16. Ibid., 410.
17. Abdullah Yusuf Ali, "On the *Injil*," *The Meaning of the Holy Qur'an* (Beltsville, MD: Amana Publications, 1999), 291.
18. "Friday Sermons in Saudi Mosques: Review and Analysis," *Middle East Media Research Institute*, Special Report No. 10, September 26, 2002.
19. Bukhari, *Sahih al-Bukhari*, vol. 1, book 10, no. 696.

Chapter Nine

1. Amatul Rathman Omar and Abdul Mannan Omar, "Introduction to the Study of the Holy Qur'an," in *The Holy Qur'an: Arabic Text-English Translation* (New York: Noor Foundation International, 1990), 43-A.
2. "Islam protects rights of women: UK judge," *Dawn*, December 2, 2005.
3. Muslim Women's League, "Gender Equality in Islam," September 1995; available online at: http://www.mwlusa.org/topics/equality/gender.html.
4. Tony Blair, "A Battle for Global Values," *Foreign Affairs*, January/February 2007.
5. Murtaza Mutahheri, *Woman and Her Rights*, trans. M. A. Ansari, Al-Islam.org; available online at: http://www.al-islam.org/Womanrights/.
6. Abdul Hamid Siddiqi, trans. *Sahih Muslim*, book 8, no. 3467.
7. "Bangladesh retreats on women's rights after clerics protest," Agence France Presse, March 12, 2008.
8. Ashiq Ilahi Bulandshahri, *Illuminating Discourses on the Noble Quran* (*Tafsir Anwarul Bayan*), translation edited by Afzal Hussain Elias (Darul Ishaat, 2005), Vol. I, p. 503.
9. Ibn Kathir, *Tafsir Ibn Kathir*, vol. 2, pp. 376–77.
10. Moni Basu, "Women in Iran march against discrimination," CNN, June 19, 2009.
11. Bukhari, *Sahih al-Bukhari*, vol. 1, book 6, no. 304.
12. Ahmed ibn Naqib al-Misri, *Reliance of the Traveller ['Umdat al-Salik]: A Classic Manual of Islamic Sacred Law*, trans. Nuh Ha Mim Keller (Beltsville, MD: Amana Publications, 1999), m11.10 (1).
13. Bukhari, *Sahih al-Bukhari*, vol. 3, book 52, no. 2639.
14. "Wife Must Take Temporary Husband If She Wants To Keep Her Old One," AHN Media Corp., August 21, 2006.
15. Ahmed Abdullah and Ismail Naseer, "Temporary marriage breaks a troubled knot, and brings a woman new happiness," *Huvaas*, July 10, 2001.

16. Bukhari, *Sahih al-Bukhari*, vol. 7, book 67, no. 5119.

17. Baqer Moin, *Khomeini: Life of the Ayatollah* (New York: St. Martin's Press, 1999), 30.

18. Abdul Hamid Siddiqi, trans. *Sahih Muslim*, book 8, no. 3363.

19. Sayyid Qutb, *In the Shade of the Qur'an*, vol. 1, p. 273; Sayyid Abul Ala Mawdudi, *Towards Understanding the Qur'an*, vol. 1, p. 173.

20. Bukhari, *Sahih al-Bukhari*, vol. 5, book 63, no. 3896; vol. 7, book 67, no. 5158.

21. Ramita Navai, "Broken lives: Nigeria's child brides who end up on the streets," *Times Online*, November 28, 2008; available online at: http://www.timesonline.co.uk/tol/news/world/africa/article5248224.ece.

22. Ibid.

23. "Morocco shuts schools advocating child marriage," Agence France Presse, September 26, 2008.

24. Lisa Beyer, "The Women of Islam," *Time*, November 25, 2001.

25. Robert F. Worth, "Tiny Voices Defy Child Marriage in Yemen," *New York Times*, June 29, 2008.

26. "Images of Extremes - German First Lady Eva Luise Köhler honors winning photographer in UNICEF Photo of the Year 2007 competition," UNICEF; available online at: http://www.unicef.org/ceecis/media_8117.html.

27. Ibid.

28. Muhammad Aashiq Ilahi Bulandshahri, *Illuminating Discourses on the Noble Qur'an*, vol. 1, p. 500.

29. Ibn Kathir, *Tafsir Ibn Kathir*, vol. 2, p. 375.

30. Muhammad Asad, *The Message of the Qur'an*, 118.

31. "Two wives," *Jerusalem Post*, July 12, 2005.

32. "Islam: Moderate Muslims To Report Polygamy In Italy, Sbai," ANSAmed, February 4, 2008.

33. Tom Godfrey, "Harems pay off for Muslims," *Toronto Sun*, February 8, 2008.

34. "Oslo Muslims recommend polygamy," *Norway Post*, January 12, 2004.

35. Jonathan Wynne-Jones, "Multiple wives will mean multiple benefits," *Telegraph*, February 3, 2008.

36. Bukhari, *Sahih al-Bukhari*, vol. 1, book 4, no. 230.

37. Tom Godfrey, "Harems pay off for Muslims," *Toronto Sun*, February 8, 2008.

38. "Polygamy in Sharon, MA!" *Miss Kelly*, November 9, 2007; available online at: http://misskelly.typepad.com/miss_kelly_/2007/11/polygamy-in-sha.html.

39. David J. Rusin, "Take My Wives, Please: Polygamy Heads West," Pajamas Media, March 1, 2008.

40. Barbara Bradley Hagerty, "Some Muslims in U.S. Quietly Engage in Polygamy," National Public Radio, May 27, 2008.

41. Maryclaire Dale, "Pa. bigamist slain hours before trip," Associated Press, August 8, 2007.

42. Noor Javed, "GTA's secret world of polygamy," *Toronto Star*, May 24, 2008.

43. Qanta A. Ahmed, "Commentary: Wife-slapping not OK in Islam," CNN, May 12, 2009.

44. Muhammad Asad, *The Message of the Qur'an*, 127.

45. Muhammad Aashiq Ilahi Bulandshahri, *Illuminating Discourses on the Noble Qur'an*, vol. 1, pp. 550–51.

46. Abu Dawud, *Sunan Abu Dawud, English Translation with Explanatory Notes*, trans. Ahmad Hasan (New Dehli, India: Kitab Bhavan, 1990), Book 11, no. 2141.

47. Abdul Hamid Siddiqi, trans. *Sahih Muslim*, book 4, no. 2127.

48. "Chad Struggles to Pass New Family Law," *VOA News*, April 15, 2005.

49. "Turkish health workers condone wife beating," Physorg.com, December 13, 2007.

50. "Tunisia: Home Violence, 1 of 5 Married Women Abused," ANSAmed, August 12, 2008.

51. "Saudi Marriage 'Expert' Advises Men in 'Right Way' to Beat Their Wives," FoxNews, November 2, 2007.

52. Mark Dunn, "It's OK to hit your wife, says Melbourne Islamic cleric Samir Abu Hamza," *Herald Sun*, January 22, 2009.

53. Steven Stalinsky and Y. Yehoshua, "Muslim Clerics on the Religious Rulings Regarding Wife-Beating," *Middle East Media Research Institute*, Special Report No. 27, March 22, 2004.

54. Keith Moore, "A scientist's interpretation of references to embryology in the Qur'an," reprinted in "Dr Keith Moore confirms embryology in Quran," Quran & Science, nd; available online at: http://www.quranandscience.com/index.php?option=com_content&view=article&id=135:dr-keith-moore-confirms-embryology-in-quran&catid=51:human&Itemid=63.

55. Bukhari, *Sahih al-Bukhari*, vol. 8, book 82, no. 816. Online version available at: http://www.usc.edu/schools/college/crcc/engagement/resources/texts/muslim/hadith/bukhari/082.sbt.html#008.082.816.

56. Jalalu'd-Din Al-Mahalli and Jalalu'd-Din As-Suyuti, *Tafsir Al-Jalalayn*, 180.

57. Barack Obama, Remarks By The President On A New Beginning, June 4, 2009.

58. Phyllis Chesler, "What is Justice for a Rape Victim?" *On The Issues*, Winter 1995.

59. Devika Bhat and Zahid Hussain, "Female Pakistani minister shot dead for 'breaking Islamic dress code,'" *Times Online*, February 20, 2007; available online at: http://www.timesonline.co.uk/tol/news/world/ asia/article1414137.ece.

60. Ibn Kathir, *Tafsir Ibn Kathir*, vol. 7, p. 67.

61. Jalalu'd-Din Al-Mahalli and Jalalu'd-Din As-Suyuti, *Tafsir Al-Jalalayn*, 756.

62. *Sunan Abu Dawud, English Translation with Explanatory Notes*, trans. Ahmad Hasan (New Dehli, India: Kitab Bhavan, 1990), Book 14, no. 2482.

63. Ibn Kathir, *Tafsir Ibn Kathir*, vol. 7, p. 73.

Chapter Ten

1. Detroit Free Press, *100 Questions and Answers About Arab Americans*; available online at: http://www.freep.com/legacy/jobspage/arabs/.

2. Fedwa Wazwaz, "Does the Qur'an promote Violence?" Islamic Resource Group; available online at: http://www.islamicresourceonline.org/files/qv.html.

3. Ali ibn Ahmad al-Wahidi, *Asbab al-Nuzul*, trans. Mokrane Guezzou, Sura 109, altafsir.com.

4. Jalalu'd-Din Al-Mahalli and Jalalu'd-Din As-Suyuti, *Tafsir Al-Jalalayn*, 1359.

5. Muhammad al-Ghazali, *Journey Through the Qur'an*, 547.

6. Ibn Kathir, *Tafsir Ibn Kathir*, vol. 8, p. 331.

7. "Al Baqara (The Cow)," University of California, Center for Muslim–Jewish Engagement; available online at: http://www.usc.edu/schools/college/crcc/engagement/resources/texts/muslim/quran/002.qmt.html.

8. Muhammad Asad, *The Message of the Qur'an*, 51.

9. Jalalu'd-Din Al-Mahalli and Jalalu'd-Din As-Suyuti, *Tafsir Al-Jalalayn*, 69.

10. Ibn Kathir, *Tafsir Ibn Kathir*, vol. 1, p. 527.

11. Ibn Ishaq, Ibn Ishaq, *The Life of Muhammad*, 314.

12. Ibn Kathir, *Tafsir Ibn Kathir*, vol. 1, p. 531.

13. Muhammad Aashiq Ilahi Bulandshahri, *Illuminating Discourses on the Noble Qur'an*, vol. 1, p. 235.

14. These include Ibn Abbas, Abu Al-`Aliyah, Mujahid, Al-Hasan, Qatadah, Ar-Rabi` bin Anas, As-Suddi, Muqatil bin Hayyan, and Zayd bin Aslam.

15. Jalalu'd-Din Al-Mahalli and Jalalu'd-Din As-Suyuti, *Tafsir Al-Jalalayn*, 385.

16. Abdul Hamid Siddiqi, trans. *Sahih Muslim*, book 10, no. 31.

17. "Surat at-Tawba: Repentance, Tafsir"; available online at: http://www.islamicity.com/forum/forum_posts.asp?TID=4106.

18. Ibn Kathir, *Tafsir Ibn Kathir*, vol. 4, p. 405.

19. "Surat at-Tawba: Repentance, Tafsir."

20. Bat Ye'or, *The Decline of Eastern Christianity Under Islam: From Jihad to Dhimmitude* (Madison, NJ: Fairleigh Dickinson University Press, 1996), 78–79.

21. Ibid., 271–72.
22. "Surat at-Tawba: Repentance, Tafsir."
23. Bukhari, *Sahih al-Bukhari*, vol. 4, book 56, no. 3044.
24. Ibn Kathir, *Tafsir Ibn Kathir*, vol. 4, p. 406.
25. "Surat at-Tawba: Repentance, Tafsir."
26. Ibn Kathir, *Tafsir Ibn Kathir*, vol. 4, p. 405.
27. Muhammad Asad, *The Message of the Qur'an*, 295.
28. Ibn Kathir, *Tafsir Ibn Kathir*, vol. 4, p. 406.
29. Ibid., 406–7.
30. Sayyid Qutb, *In the Shade of the Qur'an*, vol. 8, p. 126.
31. Sayyid Abul Ala Mawdudi, *Towards Understanding the Qur'an*, vol. 3, p. 202.
32. Bukhari, *Sahih al-Bukhari*, vol. 1, book 4, no. 233.
33. Ibn Ishaq, *The Life of Muhammad*, 212–13.
34. Ibid.
35. Ibid.
36. Ibn Kathir, *Tafsir Ibn Kathir*, vol. 4, p. 370.
37. Sayyid Abul Ala Maududi, 'At-Taubah," *The Meaning of the Qur'an*.
38. "Surat at-Tawba: Repentance, Tafsir."
39. Jalalu'd-Din Al-Mahalli and Jalalu'd-Din As-Suyuti, *Tafsir al-Jalalayn*, 397.
40. "Surat at-Tawba: Repentance, Tafsir," http://www.islamicity.com/forum/forum_posts.asp?TID=4106.
41. "Bin Laden's Sermon for the Feast of the Sacrifice," Middle East Media Research Institute, Special Dispatch No. 476, March 6, 2003.
42. "Surat at-Tawba: Repentance, Tafsir," http://www.islamicity.com/forum/forum_posts.asp?TID=4106.
43. Jalalu'd-Din Al-Mahalli and Jalalu'd-Din As-Suyuti, *Tafsir Al-Jalalayn*, 398.
44. Ibn Kathir, *Tafsir Ibn Kathir*, vol. 4, p. 376.
45. Ibid., vol. 2, p. 142.
46. Raymond Ibrahim, "Islam, War, and Deceit: A Synthesis (Part I)," Jihad Watch, February 14, 2009.
47. Ibn Kathir, *Tafsir Ibn Kathir*, vol. 5, p. 530.
48. Mahmoud M. Ayoub, *The Qur'an and its Interpreters*, 253.
49. Abdul Hamid Siddiqi, trans. *Sahih Muslim*, book 19, no. 4294.
50. Sayyid Qutb, *In the Shade of the Qur'an*, vol. 1, pp. 327–30.
51. Eric Anderson, "Slain Islamic leader was outspoken," *Denver Post*, October 21, 1993.
52. Sayyid Qutb, *In the Shade of the Qur'an*, vol. 1, pp. 327–30.
53. Ibn Abu Dawud, *Kitab al-Masahif*, book 37, no. 4310.

Chapter Eleven

1. Ahmed ibn Naqib al-Misri, *Reliance of the Traveller ('Umdat al-Salik): A Classic Manual of Islamic Sacred Law*, p. xx, section o4.9.
2. Sultanhussein Tabandeh, *A Muslim Commentary on the Universal Declaration of Human Rights*, trans. F. J. Goulding (Guilford, England: F. J. Goulding, 1970).
3. C. S. Lewis, *The Abolition Of Man* (San Francisco: Harper, 2001), 84–87.
4. Bukhari, *Sahih al-Bukhari*, vol. 7, book 76, no. 5765.
5. ibn al-Hajjaj al-Qushayri, *Sahih Muslim*, book 28, no. 5612.
6. "Surat at-Tawba: Repentance, Tafsir"; article formerly available online at: http://ourworld.compuserve.com/homepages/ABewley/tawba1.html.
7. Ibn Kathir, *Tafsir Ibn Kathir*, vol. 4, p. 377.

Chapter Twelve

1. Sita Ram Goel, *The Calcutta Quran Petition* (New Dehli, India: Voice of India, 1999), 276–77.
2. Ibid., 285.
3. Mohammed Marmaduke Pickthall, *The Meaning of the Glorious Koran* (New York: New American Library, 1991).
4. Sita Ram Goel, *The Calcutta Quran Petition*, 286.
5. Ibid., 302.
6. Ibid., 303.
7. "1993: Bombay hit by devastating bombs," BBC News, March 12, 1993; "Special Report: Mumbai Train Attacks," BBC News, September 30, 2006; "Pakistan admits Mumbai terror attack partly planned on its soil," Associated Press, February 12, 2009.
8. Jalalu'd-Din Al-Mahalli and Jalalu'd-Din As-Suyuti, *Tafsir Al-Jalalayn*, 392.
9. Nicoline den Boer, "Dutch MP Wilders strikes again: calls for ban on Quran," Radio Netherlands, August 8, 2007.
10. Ian Buruma, "Totally Tolerant, Up to a Point," *New York Times*, January 29, 2009; available online at: http://www.nytimes.com/2009/01/30/opinion/30buruma.html.
11. "Mr Wilderss [sic] contribution to the parliamentary debate on Islamic activism," Party for Freedom, http://www.groepwilders.com/website/details.aspx?ID=44.
12. Ibid.
13. "I have a question about offensive Jihad," Islam Q & A Online with Mufti Ebrahim Desai, Question 12128 from Canada; previously available online at: http://www.islam.tc/ask-imam/view.php?q=12128; article available online at Stealth Jihad: http://www.jihadwatch.org/archives/002530.php.

14. "Mr Wilderss [sic] contribution to the parliamentary debate on Islamic activism."

15. Daniel Pipes, "The Pope and the Koran," *New York Sun*, January 17, 2006.

16. Barack Obama, Remarks By The President On A New Beginning, June 4, 2009.

17. Bukhari, *Sahih al-Bukhari*, vol. 4, book 59, no. 3313.

18. Ahmed ibn Naqib al-Misri, *Reliance of the Traveller ('Umdat al-Salik): A Classic Manual of Islamic Sacred Law*, Section r40.1.

19. John David Lewis, "'No Substitute for Victory': The Defeat of Islamic Totalitarianism," *The Objective Standard*, vol. 1, no. 4, Winter 2006–2007.

20. Dexter Filkins, "Right at the Edge," *New York Times Magazine*, September 7, 2008.

21. Abdul Hamid Siddiqi, trans. *Sahih Muslim*, book 4, no. 863.

INDEX